The
Jazz Word

300.-

DEDICATIONS

For Paula . . . .
Burt Korall

For Dee . . . .
Dom Cerulli

For Valerie . . . . *ipse dixit*
Mort L. Nasatir

The

Jazz Word

Edited by

- **Dom Cerulli**

- **Burt Korall**

- **Mort Nasatir**

New introduction by **Nat Hentoff**
New foreword by the editors

A DA CAPO PAPERBACK

Library of Congress Cataloging in Publication Data

Cerulli, Dom.
    The jazz word.

    (A Da Capo paperback)
    Reprint. Originally published: New York: Ballantine
Books, 1960. With new introd.
    1. Jazz music. I. Korall, Burt. II. Nasatir, Mort.
III. Title.
ML3507.C47   1987   785.42   87-519
    ISBN 0-306-80288-0 (pbk.)

ACKNOWLEDGMENTS

For time and effort beyond the bounds of reason . . .
    Pat Smith
    Myrna Greenfield

For time and effort beyond the call of duty . . .
    Nat Hentoff
    John Hammond
    Deborah Ishlon of Columbia Records
    Orrin Keepnews of Riverside Records
    Vic Lownes III and Don Gold of Playboy Magazine
    Bob Thiele of Hanover-Signature Records
    Bob Altshuler of United Artists Records
    Martin P. Salkin of Decca Records
    Lou Didier of Down Beat Magazine
    Ira Gitler
    Paul Ackerman of The Billboard
    Dick Bock of World Pacific Records
    Nesuhi Ertegun of Atlantic Records
    Bill Simon
    Bill Coss
    Gil Millstein

For time and effort beyond the call of devotion . . .
    Mercer Ellington
    George Russell
    Tony Scott
    Jon Hendricks

This Da Capo Press paperback edition of *The Jazz Word*
is an unabridged republication of the edition published
in New York in 1960, here supplemented with a new introduction
by Nat Hentoff. It is reprinted by arrangement
with the editors.

Published by Da Capo Press, Inc.
A Subsidiary of Plenum Publishing Corporation
233 Spring Street, New York, N.Y. 10013

Manufactured in the United States of America

FOREWORD TO THE DA CAPO EDITION

The Jazz Word is a document of its time.

The 1950s, some say, was just a bland interval. This book says differently. The period was turbulent, and in many ways a time when things were changing in the music.

Historians may remember the 1950s as the years of Eisenhower and Nixon. But in jazz, the image was different. Miles, Coltrane, Mingus, Sonny Rollins and Ornette helped set the tone. Art Blakey moved through a fruitful period. On the West Coast there were Shorty Rogers, Jimmy Giuffre, Chico Hamilton and the ubiquitous Gerry Mulligan.

Talk about excitement.... there were still the big bands: the omnipotent Duke Ellington, the ever-swinging Count Basie, Stan Kenton with his walls of sound, Woody Herman working on his fifth or sixth Herd...

BG was around. So was Lionel Hampton, Maynard "The Fox" Ferguson and Harry James. And how about Johnny Richards?

Giants like Lester Young and Coleman Hawkins still walked the earth. "Little Jazz" Roy Eldridge was cooking. So were Diz and Thelonious Monk. Bird carried on until mid-decade, then succumbed.

And at the very center was Satchmo, Louis Armstrong, playing, singing and laying it out for all who would listen. It was jazz at its natural best.

We lost Art Tatum, but we still had Bud Powell and Ben Webster and Jack Teagarden and Gene Krupa.

Erroll Garner romped. And the Modern Jazz Quartet arrived, bringing new tone and elegance to jazz. In so many ways it was a memorable time.

Jazz remained a popular music. Records were released frequently and in large numbers. The music began to be an international phenomenon.

During this period, George Wein introduced the concept of the jazz festival, now accepted on a world-wide level. Those of us who were there warmly remember that very special ambiance at Newport. At last jazz had more than a modicum of respect. Those first festivals had a little of everything — a variety of styles and musicians. One year there was an international band, comprised of musicians from all over Europe.

Charlie Parker, Lester Young, and so many other jazz creators. With few exceptions, the schools do not teach this heritage of what Max Roach has called "America's classical music." Little of it is seen on television and, in many cities, little is heard on the radio.

Accordingly, millions of Americans are culturally deprived — deprived of their own culture. Musicians have told me of playing in Japan or in certain European cities where they're stopped on the street by people who know their work very well. And the crowds at some of their concerts abroad rival in numbers and enthusiasm the crowds at rock concerts in the United States. But once these jazz musicians come home, they are largely anonymous again.

Wynton Marsalis has written compellingly in *Ebony* of the need to keep alive and strengthen the heritage of this music. Billy Taylor, who is in this book, works for the same goal in myriad ways, including a superb series of essay-interviews on CBS-TV's *Sunday Morning*. The Jazzmobile harvests young musicians from the schools, and there are other attempts throughout the country to bring the jazz word home. But there are not nearly enough.

An integral part of this movement is to keep alive key books on jazz. If a principal or more likely, a teacher, decides to bring the music and its history into the classroom, he or she needs a booklist. Too many of the most vital books on jazz were out-of-print until Da Capo started to reissue them, thereby producing the most valuable list of jazz titles in the country.

With *The Jazz Word* now added to that list, I would propose a kind of citizen action. Bring *The Jazz Word* to the attention of teachers, department heads, or school board members. Suggest a unit on jazz history, musical and social, and point out that the students' understanding of this singularly American art will be further enhanced by hearing it — by bringing local jazz musicians into the schools. Again, this does happen in a few places, but in not nearly enough places.

There is also another role for musicians in schools. Consider the impact on students if some of the players from the big leagues were to visit classes in music, in American history, in social studies: Roy Eldridge, Max Roach, David Murray, Doc Cheatham, Henry Threadgill, Cecil Taylor, Mel Lewis, Benny Carter.

Jazz is so multi-dimensional, let alone multi-pleasurable, that it's sad to realize how many Americans hardly know it exists. For those who do, *The Jazz Word* is a valuable companion restored to life. For those who don't, *The Jazz Word* -accompanied by listening to the music it talks bout - can be a most satisfying discovery.

And if some of the readers of this book actually do try to use it as a way to bring jazz time and soul into schoolrooms, why, this could be an historic revitalization of more than a book.

— NAT HENTOFF
New York City
November, 1986

INTRODUCTION TO THE DA CAPO EDITION

My copy of the first edition of *The Jazz Word* is secured by several rubber bands to keep the loose pages from disappearing. The pages are loose because I have used the book so often since its 1960 appearance. It's a rare anthology in that practically all of it has remained as illuminating as when it was put together by the indefatigable Cerulli-Korall-Nasatir trio.

Actually, this wide-ranging exploration of the jazz experience is even more pertinent now than it was at the start. In recent years, there has been a significant change in new jazz audiences, particularly among younger aficionados. By contrast with the bitter factionalism that was rife a quarter-century ago and more, these new listeners are much more ecumenical. They want to know more about *all* of the music — traditional jazz and swing and bop and cool. They want to know where it all came from. And that's what this book is about.

Charles Mingus and Eddie Condon are back-to-back, as are Lester Young and Charlie Parker. Coleman Hawkins is heard in his own booming voice, while Miles Davis whispers fiercely. There are probes into the past and into the future. The book is a microcosm which was so well put together that it will be a clear window into a significant cross-section of the jazz microcosm as the music is heard.

Now that *The Jazz Word* is available again, I have a few probes of my own into the future. There will come a time, as it has already in a few schools, when this book and others will be on required reading lists in courses on American civilization or social studies. The history of the men and women who made jazz can reveal much about the American experience — its powerful persevering thrust, its legacy of bigotry, and the high art that transcended bigotry.

At a jazz festival on the south lawn of the White House in June, 1978, President Jimmy Carter told of his own long-term love for jazz and added that racism had a good deal to do with the fact that it has yet to receive anywhere its full measure of honor and understanding in its own country.

Racism has been one factor. Ignorance is another. Most American youngsters, for example — black, white, Hispanic, Asian-American, et al — have no idea of the strikingly, durable original contributions to American culture of Duke Ellington,

Many of them couldn't speak to each other. But they could communicate; they had the music in common.

Contrary to that bland image we mentioned earlier, the music spoke in bold and far-reaching terms. It inspired us because there was so much being said and there was such a diversity of styles and language.

Contrary to what was being written by some commentators away from the arts, the 1950s was a highly musical decade, and a bridge to the future was built.

Because of this, we were motivated to put together *The Jazz Word* as a document of the period. Looking back, the excitement of those days returns, and bits of the music linger in the mind.

We envisioned *The Jazz Word* as reflective of all the diversity of those years. It wasn't a text book. It wasn't a history book. It wasn't a collection of biographies. It wasn't a critical treatise. It didn't try to prove anything to anyone. It was just about jazz the way jazz was then.

We wanted a book that people could dip into, enjoy, put down and pick up later with a sense of anticipation. We tried to make the book as unpretentious and accessible as possible. We hoped people who cared about the music would gain a deeper pleasure by reading an assemblage of work that makes its point in a most direct manner.

Yes, historians may remember the 1950s as the Eisenhower and Nixon years. But for us, it was the best of times, it was the worst of times...

...and you could see Louis Armstrong *live*.

BURT KORALL,
DOM CERULLI,
MORT L. NASATIR
January 1987
New York City

CONTENTS

CONTENTS (cont'd)

CONTENTS (cont'd)

8. NEW YORK: It's a Soul Town

9. CRITICS: The Sound and the Furious

10. DIRECTIONS: Routes and Detours

THE OUT CHORUS: The End

"I have always thought that art is not a category, not a realm covering innumerable concepts and derivative phenomena, but that, on the contrary, it is something concentrated, strictly limited. It is a principle that is present in every work of art, a force applied to it and a truth worked out in it. And I have never seen art as form but rather as a hidden, secret part of content. All this is as clear to me as daylight. I feel it in every bone of my body, but it's terribly difficult to express or to define this idea.

". . . It is all, I think, one and the same art through thousands of years. You can call it an idea, a statement about life, so all-embracing that it can't be split up into separate words; and if there is so much as a particle of it in any work that includes other things as well, it outweighs all the other ingredients in significance and turns out to be the essence, the heart and soul of the work."

—Boris Pasternak, *Doctor Zhivago*

(Published by Pantheon Books Inc., N.Y., N.Y. Reprinted by permission.)

SETTING UP: An Introduction

As LONG as jazz is played, words will be written about it. The music itself resists easy definition. Jazz writing, like the playing of the music, can be heated, complex, simple, imaginative, stolid, narrow, ungrammatical, even dull. It is almost invariably writing of the moment. For in jazz, the music is here-and-now; the performance is one-time-only. The writer constantly strives to record the personality of the men, the essence of their music.

Every writer in every field has the problems of deadlines and space limitations. The jazz writer has a few special pressures peculiar to his craft. Sources for information and research are limited. The writer has to turn to the musicians themselves; and they are often forgetful, sometimes diffident, usually preoccupied. Interviews are frequently limited to what can be gathered on the fly between sets at a night club or in a hurried telephone call. Musicians, too, are constantly on the move, physically, intellectually, and most certainly musically. Naturally, the writing reflects this restless motion.

Not all jazz writing is enthusiastic or impressionistic. Much of it is documented, serious work, drawn from a background of years of study. The fan has given way to the student, and the student is likely to give way to the critic. Despite the limited anarchy in which he functions, the jazz writer can, and does, produce work that captures the essence of his world.

It was our aim in this book to gather as many of these successful attempts as possible, bounded not so much by what was *best,* as by what was most provocative, authentic, and trail-breaking.

For the most part, material we drew on has appeared previously in print—in magazines, record-album liner notes, press releases, books, documentary recordings, newspapers, and trade journals. We discovered early in compiling the book that there were some important areas as yet unexplored. For example, despite all the hue and cry about narcotics, apparently no one had taken the time and the trouble to write something of lasting value about the problem. Accordingly, we commissioned Gary

9

Kramer, who has been interested in the subject for some time, to do a well-documented analysis of the problem in all its aspects. He called it *Skyhook*; it appears for the first time in *The Jazz Word*.

We have attempted to bring some of the men of jazz into perspective through the eyes of interested, if not unbiased, viewers. We owe a debt of gratitude to Nat Shapiro of Columbia Records, through whose efforts the devastating article on Charlie Mingus—containing, in his own words, his personal and particular *moment of truth* —was obtained. Much has appeared in print about Ella Fitzgerald, but here you see her in four aspects as captured by four perceptive jazz chroniclers.

Ellington, like Ella, has been extensively covered in all media of communication. We asked Mercer Ellington, Duke's talented son, to cast back over the years. In telling the story of his childhood and youth, much emerges about his father and is documented here for the first time.

When we assembled the chapter on fiction, we thought we had included the only two noteworthy pieces available. Then one day clarinetist Tony Scott produced a short story he had been moved to write after the death of Charlie Parker. Although Tony usually tells his jazz stories through his clarinet, *Destination K.C.* deserves to appear with the work of the professional writers.

Self-styled "actionist" William Morris doesn't know the meaning of the word "polish." His piece, *Beat and Jazzbeat,* appears exactly as it emerged from his beer-stained typewriter, which apparently has no capital letters. In the area of painting and poetry, however, Mr. Morris is an artist to be reckoned with.

The fact that Jack Kerouac's poetry appears in this volume does not necessarily constitute endorsement of his jazz philosophy by the editors. Thank you.

The chapter, five. *Blues: They Died of Everything,* sort of sums up our tribute to four late and great jazz personalities.

It is partly because jazz today is in and of Our Time that it serves as a catalyst to the fine arts. For some time, jazz has been a muse of potent symbolism, useful, but very special, to art and artists. Many not-so-struggling artists and photographers of note not only identify themselves with jazz, but actually make their livings from it. Just as the music itself has invaded the main titles of

Hollywood and TV, so too has the artistic influence of jazz invaded Sunday supplements, national magazines, album cover design, and other outlets, through the utilization of jazz art and photography. Our pictorial section presents representative selections in two areas: photography and album-cover design. Here, again, we have not concerned ourselves with selecting "the best," but have sought the new, the interesting, the provocative.

Readers who are venturing for the first time into the choppy but exhilarating waters of conversational jazz are invited to wet their toes with Elliott Horne's *Argot of Jazz*. Reading Horne's brief but idiomatic dictionary first may illuminate other selections in the book and make the shock of recognition more invigorating.

The critics. The story of our encounter with the critics is presented in a chapter called *Critics: The Sound and the Furious*. We emerged bruised and battered, but triumphant. The answers to our question took some getting, but were well worth it.

Jazz constantly draws upon its past to refresh its present and enrich its future. In charting a course for modern jazz, the authors of the selections in *Directions: Routes and Detours,* move backward and forward freely in time. The result is an examination of the roots and an indication of the buds and flowers yet to come.

Briefly, this sums up the design of *The Jazz Word*. We are deeply indebted to many people for making this book possible. More than that, we are thankful that these pieces *exist* to be chronicled and perpetuated in this form. For these writings, more than most, seem to capture the quintessence of fire and ice that is jazz.

DOM CERULLI, BURT KORALL, MORT NASATIR
Oct. 6, 1959   New York City

"The Pre-Raphaelite Brotherhood of young Americans is more likely to be found in hot and cool jazz than in the elite arts of poetry, painting or the novel. In the 1940's Harry James meant more to most young Americans than Henry James or William James. Negro and white trumpet players, saxophonists and pianists were heard and appraised by the young American elite with a critical fierceness that few of them applied to poetry or philosophy. The whole structure was in some ways reminiscent of the Christian Church in its earlier phases. There were raging rivalries as to which style is orthodoxy or heresy, but there was agreement that salvation can only be found inside the musical church of jazz. There was the basic religious nostalgia for the lost Eden, the Golden Age when the church was founded amidst the apathy of surrounding heathendom. There was the rivalry between the adherents of St. Louis and the adherents of New Orleans, of Beale Street and Basin Street, for the nativity of the cult. There was the mythology growing up around the Early Fathers.

. . . . .

"One should be wary of using the analogy of the Early Church, since there is little of the Orphic element in jazz, and therefore far less of the Christian than of the Dionysian. Yet the lives, exploits and sufferings of these men are discussed by young Americans in the same terms as those of the saints were discussed in other centuries: there is the same discovery of vocation, the same dedication to the new work, the same revelation of a special gift, the same entrance into the mystery, the same epiphanies, the same final state of grace."—Max Lerner

(From *America As A Civilization* by Max Lerner; quoted by permission of the publishers, Simon and Schuster, Inc., New York City.)

12

I. JAZZMEN: Theme and Variations

THE OPENER

RECENTLY Birdland played host to one of the top modernists in jazz. After a long, loud, highly personal, viciously blown set, the leader of the group stepped off the bandstand for his break. As he walked toward the bar, a member of the audience rose and grabbed his arm.

"The hell with you, too!" he said to the musician.

The feelings of jazzmen, like their music, fit into no pigeonhole. This very fact may distress, antagonize, or elate the listener. But the listener is exposed to the personality of the jazzman as expressed through his music. However, his music is not a totally reliable index to the jazzman's personality.

What are jazzmen really like?

Perhaps no one has answered this question as ably as Reverend Norman O'Connor:

"Musicians, as most artists, are the subjects of much talk, rumor, prejudice, and wonderment.

"Musicians get married, have children, buy homes, take part in community affairs when they can . . . they are of all nationalities and faiths, and they donate huge hunks of time and talent to Protestant churches, Catholic charities, and Jewish appeals.

"They are short, tall, fat, skinny, good-looking, mediocre-looking, well-educated, not so well-educated, financially comfortable, and not so financially comfortable.

"They worry about dental bills for their children, sons who drive too fast, daughters growing up whom they can't quite understand, and wives who sometimes nag too much.

"They hope that automation won't put them out of work because a machine is now being developed which can make sounds that rival a full orchestra in quality and

13

brilliance, and all you have to do to make it work is push a button.

"Musicians, as newspaper men and doctors and lawyers and salesmen, hang together and they develop a language that includes words and expressions an outsider can't understand.

"The real problem is that most of us can't appreciate and accept the person who just wants to make music. There are men in the world who enjoy melody and harmony, all day long, and they think about it as they walk the streets, ride the subway, and as they eat, and they want to put this into the form of music.

"Musicians, as artists, are sometimes petulant and petty or become snobbish and high-toned. When this happens, they are not being true to their art, and they aren't being true to their own human nature." *

* Quoted from Rev. Norman O'Connor's jazz column in the *Boston Sunday Globe*, May 26, 1957. *Reprinted by permission.*

As Nat Hentoff wrote in his liner notes to Charlie Mingus' album, The Clown,* *"Mingus tries harder than anyone I know to walk naked. He is unsparing of phoniness and pomposity, and is hardest of all on himself when he feels he has conned himself in any respect. In his dealings with people he is unpredictable because people are." Bassist Charlie Mingus' unpredictability and essential honesty are perfectly illustrated in this account of his recent explosion in a New York jazz club related by Miss Diane Dorr-Dorynek, writer and close friend of the musician.*

* The Clown: *The Charles Mingus Jazz Workshop, Atlantic 1260.*

MINGUS ...

by Diane Dorr-Dorynek

I

LET'S talk about the problems of Mingus, or of jazz in 1959, which are one and the same. The problem, or question, seems twofold: How is a musician to gain the financial security he must have to remain creative (and

14

without giving in to the robot-grind of studio work)? And who will listen to him?

First, where is there to perform?

There's a club on the lower west side of New York. About two years ago the owners signed Mingus to a lifetime contract and promised to make it a home for his group. Last February this contract was broken, ostensibly over another issue, but the real reason had to do with the police, who told the owners they didn't want colored bands in the club because they brought mixed audiences and too many colored people into the vicinity. The owners are nice folks with no quarrel with anyone, but the police have a way of making their wishes felt when it comes to night-club owners: they can fine them repeatedly on minor violations, or even revoke their license, for any one of a number of reasons on the books that may serve their momentary purpose. For instance, one night a lieutenant fined them for having no soap in the men's room; but Mingus had washed his hands one minute earlier with that very soap-that-wasn't-there.

At the present, although Mingus had consistently drawn record-breaking crowds to the club, one white band follows another with very little interruption, and there aren't that many first-rate ones, so they frequently have to dig into the second-rate pile.

Mingus took his group to Harlem. But there the police complained to the owner that this brought too many white people to 118th street. There are the east side clubs, but they seem to be sewn up by cocktail-jazz. There's Birdland, but Mingus hadn't played there for several years until this spring, and then only for two one-nighters. And the Five Spot. The Five Spot brings up the question, who listens in clubs anyway?

II

Last December John Handy joined Mingus, and Mingus was anxiously looking for a gig to keep the new group working and (therefore) together. He landed one at the Five Spot, but on one of those hellish, noise-filled nights, he almost gave up—and how many other musicians *have* given up trying to reach an audience at the level of honesty and love? Mingus intoned into the mike the following, which I have condensed, and to which was later added the Mother's Conversation, just to give you a more concrete idea of The Bandstand View:

15

"You, my audience, are all a bunch of poppaloppers. A bunch of tumbling weeds tumbling 'round, running from your subconscious, running from your subconscious unconscious . . . minds. Minds? Minds that won't let you stop to listen to a word of artistic or meaningful truth. You think it all has to be in beauteous colors. Beautiful, like your 'lovely' selves. You don't want to see your ugly selves, the untruths, the lies you give to life.

"So you come to me, you sit in the front row, as noisy as can be. I listen to your millions of conversations, sometimes pulling them all up and putting them together and writing a symphony. But you never hear that symphony —that I might dedicate to the mother who brought along a neighbor and talked three sets and two intermissions about the old man across the hall making it with Mrs. Jones' son in the apartment below where the school teacher lives with Cadillac Bill. And how she's thinking of taking up teaching if Mary gets any more minks like that white one she just gave her sister Sal who's in and out on week days and leaves town on week ends with her Rolls Royce full of pretty teachers. And how it's difficult to keep the facts of life from her daughter Chi-Chi. The insurance man got fresh with me too . . . giggle giggle. Just a little kiss . . . and oh! how cute he got he musta thought . . . ?

"I finally asked her to change to a table where she could talk better and let some people sit there who wanted to listen, and the jazzy mother answered me for the rest of the set about how she has to listen to jazz all day long, and don't accuse her of not liking the stuff, she lives on it . . .

". . . So *I* profit, not her, or most of you, who will leave here tonight and say I've heard Charlie Mingus. You haven't even heard the conversation across the table, and that's the loudest! Have you heard the announcement of a single song title during the night? Or a pause in between tunes, hoping you'd hear yourselves, then quiet down and listen? Joe says he has two very loud bands and he's going for a walk. Maybe the other band has no dynamics, but if my band is loud in spots, ugly in spots, it's also beautiful in spots, soft in spots. There are even moments of silence. But the moments of beautiful silence are hidden by your clanking glasses and your too wonderful conversations.

"Joe tells me: This club is mainly taken over by the artists of the village. Would you like to show your paintings to blind men? Should I like to play my music for blind ears that are clogged up with the noises and frustrations of their own daily problems and egos, carrying on conversations just to be noticed that they are there?

"You haven't been told before that you're phonies. You're here because jazz has publicity, jazz is popular, the word jazz, and you like to associate yourself with this sort of thing. But it doesn't make you a connoisseur of the art because you follow it around. You're dilettantes of style. A blind man can go to an exhibition of Picasso and Kline and not even see their works. And comment behind dark glasses, Wow! They're the swingingest painters ever, crazy! Well so can you. You've got your dark glasses and clogged-up ears.

"You sit there in front of me and talk about your crude love affairs. You sit there in front of me and push your junky-style glasses up on your noses. You sit there and swing your undulating legs. You bare your loosely covered bosoms in front of me and your boyfriends give an embarrassed look up at the bandstand, so you pretend you don't want us to look down into your unveilings. You stuff in your hankie if you have one, or an old white glove or a dirty dollar bill, or just press your hand to yourself every time you bend forward. All of you sit there, digging yourselves and each other, looking around hoping to be seen and observed as hip. *You* become the object you came to see, and you think you're important and digging jazz when all the time all you're doing is digging a blind, deaf scene that has nothing to do with any kind of music at all . . .

"And the pitiful thing is that there are a few that do want to listen. And some of the musicians . . . we want to hear each other, what we have to say tonight, because we've learned the language. Some of us know it too well. Some of us know it only mechanically. But by listening to others who play it spiritually, soulfully, we can learn *to speak* a little less technically. But imagine an artist of rhetoric, with thinking faculties, performing for an audience devoid of concern for communication . . . imagine his attempting a sensible communicating association even in plain verbal language. Then open your eyes, look around at yourselves posing as listeners to music, which is *another* language, so much more wide in range and vivid, and warm and full and expressive of thoughts you are seldom able to convey. . . ."

Someone taped this that night, and the tape breaks off here. Add to this scene most of the audience yelling, "Bravo!" "Tell 'em Charlie!" "Someone has been needed to say that for years!" "Most of us want to listen." "Tell 'em Charlie. . . ."

Eddie Condon, guitarist, sometime banjoist, raconteur, entrepreneur, newspaper columnist, author, impresario, friend of the great and the near-great, is, above all, a wry and pungent philosopher. This sketch of Condon was written under duress: attempting to capture him on paper is like trying to scoop up spilled milk with a fork.

(Reprinted by permission of Maher Publications, Inc., from Down Beat, *Dec. 12, 1956.)*

EDDIE CONDON—JAZZ' EVELYN WAUGH
by Dom Cerulli

EDDIE Condon, the Evelyn Waugh of the banjo, surveyed the scene from his living-room window. Rain pounded into huge puddles gleaming across the street in Washington Square Park.

"Let's call up a hotel . . . any hotel," he said. "Ask if there are any dry towels."

One of the plankowners of the Chicago School of Jazz, Condon was recovering from a second bout with a virus. He prowled his spacious apartment restlessly, pausing to look from time to time at some of the mementos of his long career in jazz on his mantel or gracing end tables and walls.

"That's a Wettling abstract," he said pointing to a colorful painting hanging over his living-room mantel. "You know, I've got the first thing George ever painted.

"It's a picture of my oldest girl . . . she's 13 now. She hates it."

He displayed a painting of a chubby-faced infant with black hair and blue eyes. "She's wearing a robe here that Joe Bushkin brought back from Tokyo or somewhere.

"I call it 'No Neck McGraw.' Wouldn't part with it for anything."

He returned the picture to its hanging place in his bedroom, a chamber highlighted by an enormous tie rack running virtually the length of one wall and giving the side a look of wall-to-wall bow ties.

As identified with Condon as the bow ties is his dedication to the promotion of jazz.

Born in Goodland, Ind., on Nov. 16, just 52 years ago, Condon grew up physically and musically in Chicago, where he picked up the banjo and ukulele. During the '20s he became associated with Gene Krupa, Bud Freeman, Frank Teschemacher, Jimmy McPartland, and Joe Sullivan.

Later, he became associated with Red McKenzie and assisted in the siring of the McKenzie-Condon Chicagoans. He was also an intimate friend and co-worker musically with the legendary Bix Beiderbecke.

Reminiscing about the budding days three decades ago, Condon remarked, "They were the ones who were careless . . . but careless with an understanding.

"Brubeck, for instance, is not careless. He's a studied guy. And even if his picture ends up on the back cover of *Life,* he's still a studious guy.

"That alto player with him . . . Desmond? Paul Desmond, is he a big guy or what?" Eddie was assured that Desmond is among the mildest and gentlest of God's creatures.

"He sounds like a female alcoholic," Condon smiled.

Eddie's writing career includes volumes entitled *We Called It Music* and *A Treasury of Jazz.* Now and again he pops into print with a magazine article on jazz and the music scene.

"We've got one coming up, I think, in the December *Cosmopolitan.* The title is *What Is Elvis Presley?*

"Right off we switch to Johnnie Ray. After hearing both those sending crooners, I said to somebody . . . I don't recall just now who it was . . . 'Let's go down to either the mountains or the Mississippi River and hear some group stuff.' "

Along the way, Eddie announced he also had written a piece for *Holiday* magazine, "about when Benny Goodman and I were kids."

"Benny's not a bad guy," Condon said. "I enjoyed
19

those meals at his house. Even if I did live on the north side. Benny lived on the west side."

From time to time, the phone rang and Condon shuffled to answer it. From his telephone table at the end of a long, red-carpeted and red-walled hall, Eddie pointed around and shook his head:

"People come in here the first time, and they think they're in the Russian embassy."

Eddie began to emerge as a promoter of jazz sessions and concerts in the late '30s. In addition to a series of Town Hall concerts in the '40s and the operation of his own night club in New York City's Greenwich Village, he and a group of kindred musicians have appeared at two of the three Newport Jazz Festivals.

"This last one was like today," he grimaced, indicating the window and the still-pouring rain.

Eddie conducted his session at the festival in a downpour. He lugged his guitar case onstage and put it down on the sodden piano, where it remained through the set. At the outset, with water pouring down his face and running into his upturned coat collar, he announced to the audience huddled in ponchos and other plastic wrappings, "We're mixing it with water tonight."

He quoted Columbia's jazz Artists and Repertoire man as having told him that Columbia was recording the proceedings, adding, "And George Avakian tells me this is the first time a jazz concert was recorded under water."

At times through the set Condon peered into the falling sheets of water to announce, "We're moving into the inner pool now . . . If the weather clears, we're flying in Elvis Presley . . ."

His ability to express himself concisely, often brilliantly and always with wit, has won him friends and admirers from the literary and art worlds. They find that he's not merely a funnyman but a stimulating conversationalist with a rich and varied background from which to draw for illustration, color, and information.

Behind the wry turn of a witty phrase is the musician who has been around, observed, and remembered.

In 1948, he conducted an hour-long network television program called *Floor Show,* which featured Cutty Cutshall, Bobby Hackett, Billy Butterfield, Peanuts Hucko, a dozen or so more musicians, and the Condon personality.

The show eventually died, but Eddie still remembers it sourly.

"I don't know why I feel so rotten about it," he said, "but I do.

"We had a basic band, and the Butterfields, the Mc-Garitys, the Wileys . . . no blood relatives understand . . . would come in and out, and I'd call out who would play what. They said it was too informal . . . too reckless . . .

"I created more ulcers over there. Vice presidents were firing vice presidents . . . but we were doing what we always do. We just set the boys up and let them go.

"Now everybody is doing informal shows. What more can I say?"

He noted that Mr. and Mrs. Louis Lorillard, mainstays of the Newport Jazz Festival, had moved to New York.

"I think they are very pleasant people," he said. "I'm glad they're abandoning Newport to rough it on Sutton Place. And I'm delighted neither plays a musical instrument."

He also noted that of George Wein, Newport impresario, it had been said, "He should play piano, but not in public."

Condon added, "Okay—at a fire sale, though."

He paced some more and then picked up a newspaper which carried a full page of pictures of jazz artists. Under the headline "Go, men, go!" was a large picture of Eddie.

"See what I mean?" he asked. "See why I put on this jazz talk? Go, men, go!" He shook his head, and unfolded the page. In one corner was a large photo of Louis Armstrong.

"There is the absolute champ," he said. "When he plays, when he sings . . . just the absolute champ."

He crossed to a large glass bell under which rested a pair of Stetson patent-leather and gray suede button shoes and a plastic banjo.

"This all came of a conversation I had with [John] Steinbeck once when we were standing in a men's room somewhere," he said.

"Steinbeck asked me why I didn't play the banjo any more, and I told him that went out with high-button shoes.

"Jerry Shattuck, who not only looks like Boris Karloff

21

but is Boris Karloff, and Art Lynch got my shoe size and came up with this. That Lynch, one thing you've got to remember about him, he's a golfer, and the toughest thing is, don't try to whip him."

Condon started recording in 1927, but never has had a hit record.

"I've tried every way in the world to make records that do not sell," he laughed. "Look, we even used the Gershwin songbook thing as a handle, and they didn't sell."

The records, however, do hold a valid place in recorded jazz, although they cannot compare with the offerings of the pop stars as far as the millions sold is concerned. Condon's informal Columbia LP albums have sold well and steadily, largely because the musicians were relaxed and comfortable physically and musically.

"In some cases I pick the tunes for a date," Eddie said. "In others we leave it up to the guys. The whole point is to be as completely happy as possible."

On the current scene, Condon admitted he was impressed with the work of clarinetist Bob Wilber.

"He plays like Peanuts, and Peanuts plays like Goodman. God knows who Goodman plays like." He also praised trumpeter Johnny Windhurst, but said, "Emphasize that Wilber. He's good."

Condon smiled. "Then there's another young fellow. A comer. Wild Bull Davison. He's extra young.

"And don't forget Cutty Cutshall. There's one thing I'd like to say about Cutty: he's all male."

Among other Condon observations was one from Joseph Conrad. "Don't ever attempt writing before you're 40. Hooray for Joe. What can you say before you're 40, anyway?"

Of Johnny Mercer, sometime ad lib-topper, Eddie urged: "Condon thinks Johnny Mercer is a champ of stupidity and charm. Plus due bills."

Of Mezz Mezzrow: "Mezz taught me some hot chords on the tenor banjo."

On the most important feature of a recording session: "Be there."

He glanced out the window again, at the still-falling rain.

"There's no end to it," he mused. "Just like Presley."

When one hears the phrase, "The first lady of song," it can only refer to Ella Fitzgerald. In our time, there are no exceptions to this rule. Ella wears this phrase as strikingly and exclusively as a Dior original. While much has been written about her from many points of view, the following four articles, appearing in a single context,* place her in full perspective.

* The Best of Ella Fitzgerald, *Decca Records DXB-156. Reprinted by permission.*

ELLA: THEME

by Burt Korall

AT A COCKTAIL party not too long ago, a barrage of positive commentary concerning a then popular singer filled the room. The singer had a hit record, and her press agent, obviously feeling his oats, made a rather startling comparison: "Such phrasing, and that sound, she's another Ella Fitzgerald!"

The singer in question, like many fads of the music business, did not measure up. She was no Ella Fitzgerald or anyone of importance. She lingered briefly under the revealing light cast by the public and soon disappeared from the scene. The mass audience initially was attracted to this artist and shrugged her off when it realized its mistake.

Unlike Don Juan, the legendary libertine, who had little interest in the good and the lasting, the public *does* have an eye and ear for that which is substantial. Ultimately it gives support to deserving artists. Always a favorite of musicians, Ella has been around for over twenty years. But only recently have fans banded together to provide her with the wide-ranging success she so richly deserves.

A slim, gawky, musically precocious teenager at the outset, she now is an imposing figure of a woman with a talent to match. Her story began with a win in an amateur contest at Harlem's Apollo Theater in 1934. The next step was onto the Chick Webb band-stand. Fame followed.

23

After Chick's death in 1939, she led the band for a while. Then she went out as a single. She has been a solo performer ever since.

The years have been kind to the wide-eyed innocent of *A-Tisket, A-Tasket*, bringing a significant share of musical understanding to her work, and a progressive widening of scope. Identified as a jazz singer, familiar to the habitué of jazz clubs, certain theaters, and the buyer of jazz records, Ella now has a more diversified repertoire and audience, plays the best supper clubs and theaters, and has appeared in several movies. Indeed, she is recognized on all musical strata, for hers is the nearly perfect vocal instrument for pop-jazz singing.

In the process of developing musically, Ella has emphasized her jazz roots. Undoubtedly she realizes that they are essential to her artistic strength and individuality. The close relationship with jazz continues as she moves into the future.

ELLA, THE WOMAN
by Bill Coss

ON HER seventeenth anniversary as a professional singer, Ella Fitzgerald attended a party celebrating her twentieth anniversary as a professional singer. The only thing that bothered Ella about this confusing matter of addition, which is part and parcel of the made world of show business and press-agentry, was that so many hundreds of people had gathered to wish her well, to cheer her past and to hope that she had twenty times twenty (or, perhaps, seventeen times twenty) more years of warm-throated success.

For the lady who has received spontaneous acclaim from everyone finds it difficult to imagine that she is that good or that people are being other than generous when they praise her. The dean of jazz critics, George Simon, spoke for most jazz writers when he noted that Ella's modesty was her prime virtue, that she was "unspoiled, unselfish, unaffected and understanding."

I am sure that all those things are so. But such a high degree of self-effacing modesty as she possesses is, it seems to me, much ado about something: that something

24

has to do with a tremendous lack of sureness about herself and her talents.

It may seem strange to write about these things in an album devoted to that talent, but it is precisely because we are interested in Ella the superb singer that we should be interested in Ella as a human being. Because out of that human comes that special sweetness of sound and soul. And that human has apparently found much to be unsure of in life.

Perhaps it all began with her appearance at an Apollo amateur contest. She came to perform as a dancer and became so frightened that she sang instead. Contrary to the many stories, bandleader Chick Webb was not in the audience when she won. But Bardu Ali, who fronted the Webb band, heard Ella and tried to convince Chick of her worth. The little bandleader would have nothing of it. Finally, Bardu smuggled Ella into Chick's dressing room, locked the door and practically sat in his lap until Ella had a chance to sing.

Chick liked what he heard but when he asked her to join his band it was with something less than complete enthusiasm. Ella repaid his gesture many times though, and has since repaid that memory by giving dozens of others a first chance or a big break whenever it was possible for her to do so.

Perhaps she's never forgotten those early days, for she still shows signs of unsureness at the strangest times. She accounts for her enormous popularity during recent European tours thus: "I suppose it's because they don't see us very often." Or, again, she will be seemingly at a loss at an all-star session, imagining complete inability, or be completely bewildered by an arranger who complimented her after a session which was one of her best.

When bop arrived on the scene, she felt a sudden sense of loss. "I felt that I was being left behind, and I was." In an effort to catch up to the musical progress, she started singing wordless vocals again. "All I did was sing *How High the Moon*. It seemed like the only song I ever sang." Now, in the most recent years, since she has begun to sing in supper clubs and to sing the very best of songs, she has the same feeling about her inability. Listeners would request *Flying Home* and Ella, with many a nervous look toward her mentor Norman Granz, would sing Cole Porter, and Rodgers and Hart songs.

25

Out of this unsureness comes an occasional flight into saltiness. At Newport in 1957 she showed obvious signs of displeasure about some of the musicians accompanying her. Although it was true that the drummer was having time-trouble, the real reason for her actions was a microphone that squealed once or twice throwing her into a nonprofessional panic. But these occasions are not the real Ella, as her friends will tell you, but lapses from the norm and all caused by her lack of self-confidence.

Or, again, she will betray by an awkward gesture or word her uneasiness during an interview. She has little to say about herself. She owns few of her own records. She sometimes suspects the enthusiasm of others. She speaks with enthusiasm about the picture of herself which is on the wall of a Danish nightclub, but she has not really been filled with the significance of that fact.

All of this is a strange and compelling part of the total portrait. It is the inconsistent part of her life, considering the charity which she brings to her judgments, the catholicity of her taste for others' music and the particular delicacy of the taste which she brings to her own work. She says, for example, that she likes "all kinds of music, as long as it's played well. Like hillbilly music, it tells a story, and that's good."

Yet she would never have this much charity for her own rendition of a folk song which would probably be infinitely better than the average rachitic tune from the hills.

Instead, most of her enthusiasm is for others. And I wonder and am sad about so much timidity amidst so much grandeur, and, perhaps, you do too, whether you are being made cognizant of it for the first time or reminded of it for the seventh. I sit enraptured, listening to a voice that is at once bright and hauntingly beautiful, hearing and watching a grace which transcends a sometimes awkward gesture. I sit and hear good tunes, fair tunes and bad tunes, all given new warmth and beauty because of her. But most of all, more than any song, I hear Ella.

ELLA FITZGERALD: THE CRITERION
OF INNOCENCE FOR POPULAR SINGERS
by Nat Hentoff

"Hey nonny no!
Men are fools that wish to die!
Is't not fine to dance and sing
When the bells of death do ring?
Is't not fine to swim in wine,
And turn upon the toe
And sing hey nonny no,
When the winds blow and the seas flow?
Hey nonny no!"

—An Anonymous Elizabethan

THERE are fewer and fewer certainties in our civilization of quicksand; but among the predictabilities
that remain (aside from mortality and deficit spending)
is that when a singer of popular songs is asked his or her
favorite vocalist, the IBM answer is: "Ella Fitzgerald."

Such suzerains of the field as Bing Crosby and Frank
Sinatra have been proclaiming Miss Fitzgerald's position
as a criterion of pop singing for many years, long before
that opinion was the fashion. In the past few years, however, everyone has joined in the chorus of hosannas to
Ella, and I suspect that there have been some new singers
confronted with their first interview who have given Ella's
name mainly because they dimly realized that choosing
her was a bridge to musical respectability, sometimes a
stronger bridge than their own voices.

In any case, the accolades for Ella in this context are
exactly deserved. By my own nonconformist criteria, in
fact, Ella is more consistently entertaining as a pop
singer than in jazz, a field in which she also sweeps
most polls, official and conversational. I do not mean to
minimize her supple skill as one of the rare jazz singers
who *do* fit naturally into an instrumental jazz setting,
but I have suspected for many years that Ella became a
jazz singer less through fierce personal conviction than
through the gradual force of circumstances. As it happened, she did and does possess an instrumentalized
approach to singing, a jazzman's concept of phrasing, and

27

a wholly flowing beat. But in general, the most inflamma-ble and irreparably convincing jazz—instrumental or vocal—has been the self-expression of souls that some-where within them have had more of the tiger than the lamb. I mean Louis Armstrong (his dressing-room per-sonality is somewhat at variance with his euphoric grin on TV), Billie Holiday, Miles Davis, John Lewis (no lamb he), Ivie Anderson, and many other jazz players and singers.

It is not that Ella does not sing jazz; but she is happier, I feel, in the less naturalistic pop world where she can sing popular songs and standards in a jazz-influenced style and never meet anything more forbidding than the Wizard of Oz. The conditions of the two worlds—jazz and pop—are different, although there have been viable enough singers, like Ella, to wander in both. Essentially, however, the pop singer does not have to expose her own feelings as nakedly and urgently as the jazz singer; nor in fact, does she have to draw on the depth of aware-ness of her own experiences that a jazz singer requires. She can be an innocent at home because, except for the work of a few writers of standards, pop music concerns paper moons more than it realistically examines empty beds. And even in those more urbane standards that are used as often in the jazz as in the pop world, the pop singer doesn't have to reveal the inside of herself as much as she has to be reasonably musical and reasonably faithful to the intentions of the writers.

Ella is a gentle, ingenuous woman. She is still startled that movie stars are among her fans; still nervous at each concert as if she can't quite believe yet that she has an established position in show business; still trust-ing beyond most others' capacities to imagine trust; and above and underneath all, a romantic. She loves to sing ballads, and her normally intense admiration for Frank Sinatra was even more fired when the first ques-tion he asked her at rehearsals for her guest appearance on one of his TV shows was: "Which ballads do you want to sing?" Most often on television, she has been typed as a "rhythm" singer, but it's the ballads she feels most lingeringly. And she is more likely to believe in a ballad that speaks in the idiom of Edgar Guest than she is to comprehend Billy Strayhorn's *Lush Life,* though she has sung the latter.

28

Left to herself, I think you would find that Ella would pick many more of the pop hits of the day to record than she would material better suited to jazz. Ella has never denied wanting a "hit," but unlike other singers who have deliberately "condescended" to sing "hit" material, Ella likes most pop ballads—if they're gentle and innocent enough. It's partly because she is so honestly a resident of the pop world that she can sing most pop songs so much better than her contemporaries. And she not only has the necessary belief in the material to project to her audience, but she also has such superior musicianship. She is an innocent with the musical capacity of a sweet wizard.

Ella, by being herself, has become the best of all pop singers; and by being so accurate a musician in the process, she has set a standard for skill in the field that has given even the most insensitive apprentices a firm idea of what excellence actually is. Meanwhile, her personality has remained about as unspoiled as in the time of *A-Tisket A-Tasket,* and it is another Elizabethan poet, Nashe, who for me conveys the characteristic unaffected quality of Ella in this salute:

"Spring, the Sweet Spring, is the year's pleasant king;
Then blooms each thing, then maids dance in a ring,
Cold doth not sting, the pretty birds do sing,
Cuckoo, jug-jug, pu-we, to-witta-woo!"

ELLA THE JAZZ HORN
by Dom Cerulli

ELLA knows her way around her voice as very few singers today.

But there are times when she seems to be unaware there are things a human voice just doesn't do.

She does them.

Lately, Ella has included a scat up-tempo tune in her night club and concert repertoire. Most generally it's *Air Mail Special,* although at times she sings *How High the Moon* or *Flyin' Home.*

She gets into a rhythmic groove and fires a breath-taking barrage of scat words, syllables, snatches of other tunes, interpolations to the audience, asides to her rhythm section; and then brings the piece to a dazzling con-

29

clusion by swooping on an open tone up some three octaves to the very top of her range.

It's an electrifying experience to see and hear. And it must be an exhilarating experience to do.

Ella apparently does it without thinking. She, like any competent jazz musician, works easily within the bounds of her range, saving that climactic extra for the out chorus.

Ella has always had a little of the tenor sax in her voice. Other singers have had touches of other instruments to color their way of singing: Jo Stafford and Sarah Vaughan, to me, have always phrased with a trombone-like clarity, saving a bit of vibrato for the end of a line or phrase for that polish which fully rounds it out; Anita O'Day has a bit of muted trumpet in her voice, and in the way she builds a solo with apparent disregard for bar lines and straight 4/4; and Dinah Washington certainly has the brassiness and brashness of an open-horn trumpet in her forthright singing.

But Ella's voice, as a vocal instrument, has always had the fluidity of a tenor, even when singing words. She somehow manages to slide around words and syllables, no matter how constricting, with the ease of a tenor in the capable hands, say, of Lester Young or Stan Getz.

There is this firm articulation and carry of tone in her sound which comes through like a tenor.

On up tunes, particularly the scat songs, she improvises in a steady flow, much as a tenor would. She jumps octaves and adds little breathy afterthoughts to phrases, much as a tenor.

And she builds vocal riffs exactly the way a tenor would.

It seems, too, in the syllables she uses for improvising, she chooses the ones most easily adaptable to the flow of a tenor sax.

And her vocal timbre is akin to the range of that horn. She has the depth (sometimes, to the delight of everyone listening, she can and does toss in an appropriate honk of the instrument).

She adopts many of the phrasing devices of the tenor. There are many times when she will take a word like *in* and sing it *i-hin;* or *and* will emerge *a-ha-ha-ha-hand;* and she will have improvised within the word or a vowel, in the chord, and with the mannerisms of a tenor.

Perhaps it is this facility of voice coupled with a conciousness of the aspirate device in phrasing, and climaxed with an amazing ability to create supple, intricate cadenzas that sustain this image of Ella as a tenor.

The early instrumental uses of her voice which started with her Decca recordings of *Lady Be Good* and *Flyin' Home* in the mid-40s have carried into her ballad work and today's instrumental uses of her voice.

One thing for sure: as a singer, Ella is also a great instrumentalist.

Bill Simon is a veteran jazz writer while still in his thirties. He knows jazz from virtually every angle: he has produced jazz records for National, Gotham, and Brunswick Records; written extensively in the field; been on intimate terms with many top jazz performers; and is himself a performing jazzman. He is superbly qualified to discuss the responsibility of the jazz artist in our time.

(Responsibility of the Artist, *Accompanying brochure for American Recording Society Album,* Anita Sings For Oscar, *ARS G-426. Reprinted by permission of the author.*)

THE RESPONSIBILITY OF THE ARTIST
by Bill Simon

ONE thing strikes us about jazz—it is almost unique in that it is, at the same time, a creative art and a performing art.

This is assuming, as this writer does, that jazz is jazz essentially when it is being improvised. The notes and rhythms used by jazzmen can be written down, but they don't *sound* like jazz unless played by musicians who themselves know how to shape a jazz phrase and to become one with the jazz beat.

Now, we have had plenty of jazz people who could create, who have been capable of using harmonic and melodic materials, and rhythmic materials, in highly original combinations and variations. Creation in any of the arts, in our free society, demands that the artist isolate himself at least part of the time. The artist's responsibility is mainly to himself. He seeks to find himself and fulfill himself; then, if he opens new areas—advances his art—society stands to gain from his perhaps "selfish" pursuits.

The performing artist, on the other hand, has his prime obligation to his audience. His job is to *communicate* ideas to an audience; ideas created in the abstract, or in one dimension, which he must make into a living experience—musical, literary, dramatic. Perhaps the ideas were created by artists who only create, or perhaps they were created by him, who also is the performer. Jazz people and dancers or mimists have this dual responsibility as creators and performers, but dancers still rely on somebody else's music, and mimists generally build on somebody else's story or character. Only in jazz do the performers have so demanding a role of complete on-the-spot creation in the course of actual performance.

If jazz has failed to find the mass audience, the fault has been mostly with the jazz musicians who have been unaware of, or have refused to accept their dual responsibility.

Jazz, after all, is said to be a form of American folk music. It shouldn't be difficult to understand or to love. It's expressive of so much of the thoughts, feelings, moods of our everyday life. Its very sounds frequently are the scunds of our time—the dissonances we have come to accept as commonplace, the shifting, driving rhythms—accents, inflections and flavors from everywhere in the world. The blues, hymns, spirituals, work songs—from Africa and from Elizabethan England. The relentless shuffle rhythm of the trains that cross through every little town. The "smart" sequential melodies of the best Broadway show writers. The rhapsodic outbursts inspired by Brahms, Wagner and the Russian school . . . the impressionistic harmonies of Debussy and Ravel . . . the neo-primitive thumping and crying of early Stravinsky. Marches, polkas, dirges, mazurkas . . . These are just a few of the things that have gone into jazz. There's a part of all of us in jazz, some link with something we know well. Why then hasn't jazz become the popular pastime that, let's say—baseball—has become?

Baseball people long ago accepted the idea that baseball was show business. Babe Ruth established that

32

for all time. The premium was placed on the performer who had color, that extra bit of personality or flair that he was able to get across to the audience . . . the ability to come through with a climactic bit of business at the proper time. Baseball stars can draw down fabulous salaries for six months' work each year, and many of them can add considerably to the totals by cashing in on their names and personal popularity in the off-season.

There are jazz performers today who can play all types of clubs and theaters, who draw large audiences and command big salaries. But all too few. This handful knows how to put on a show and always is aware of its paying audience. Some make unnecessary compromises with good taste, but others can take a new, advanced work and stage it in a way that completely captures the audience's attention and then holds it until the full message has gotten across.

Duke Ellington can do it, and Woody Herman—even Stan Kenton, even when the "message" doesn't always merit the attention. Ella Fitzgerald can make a "square" audience digest some of her most "knocked-out" scat singing. She seems to have so much fun doing what she's doing that the listener must become infected. Anita O'Day recently discovered that she could inspire the same type of rapport and understanding. This after many years of being aware only of fellow-musicians.

Since most creative artists would seem to be naturally introspective, most jazz artists have been lacking in the extroversion that show business requires of performers. Many of them, including some of the very best, have set up defenses, have even cultivated attitudes of contempt for their audiences. Some refuse to talk to their audiences. Others will persist in playing one number interminably without even the slightest variation in dynamics en route. The musical ideas may be great, but a performance must have some sense of drama, some variety of mood, or at least exploration of the several sides of a mood. The most complex idea can be gotten across to a "square" audience if it's properly staged or spotlighted.

Refusal to go along with this could be simply a manifestation of immaturity among jazzmen, including some who, in the matter of years, might be said to be mature. But then one of the essential qualities of jazz is its eternal youthfulness, its verve and its youthful contradictions.

Young 'uns reject the authority and advice of their elders more frequently perhaps than they accept them, and most of our jazz people are young 'uns in show business.

For jazz people who "wise up"—and assuming they have the talent—there's a real future in jazz and in show business. Erroll Garner isn't starving, nor Oscar Peterson, nor Count Basie, Ellington, Herman, Ella, Sarah Vaughan, Dizzy Gillespie, Kenton, Dave Brubeck, Benny Goodman, Gene Krupa, and certainly not Louis Armstrong.

The late Charlie Parker had only himself to blame that he wasn't healthy and wealthy. This most influential jazzman of the modern era could have come close to his desserts in terms of public acceptance and financial gain if he hadn't been his own worst enemy. The same has been true of Billie Holiday, Stan Getz, and many others. Such jazz people have run through or run away from fortunes.

Aside from the personalities of so many of its performers, jazz has another problem to overcome, which it has in common with most of the contemporary arts . . . that of having the whole of the art identified with its more commonplace manifestations. How much of what is created in any art medium can be termed "inspired" or a "masterpiece"? How much of the art created in any one era survives into the next era? Granted a certain artist is a genius—is every work that he turns out a work of genius?

A person newly interested in or curious about art goes to a show of modern painting. He doesn't realize that he may be viewing a collection of contemporary mediocrities, yet he comes away with the idea that he dislikes modern art. He knows that Rembrandt painted masterpieces, so he assumes that the only good art is traditional art.

What he has failed to determine is that of thousands of paintings by Rembrandt's own contemporaries, only a handful—the best—have survived.

In jazz, the curious will spend several hours in a jazz cellar and watch a group of seemingly disinterested musicians loaf their way through a couple of "cool" sets, playing strictly for themselves, neglect to announce their numbers—and generally shy away from any behavior that might serve to build rapport. They might see young musicians aping the worst mannerisms of their own idols, playing with disregard for tone, intonation or ensemble effect. This is what must pass as an introduction to jazz, and yet that's what one gets in many of our better-known jazz clubs.

Record companies grind out jazz recordings by the dozens, most of them made without any plan or central idea, and many utilizing musicians who have little or nothing to say. Record dealers get burned with bad merchandise and blame the whole of jazz for their own inability to discriminate.

And much the same is true of night-club owners and concert promoters who consider one jazzman and one school the same as the next, and then blame all of jazz when the crowds don't develop. There are club owners who will try jazz, get stuck with one headliner who misbehaves or fails to show up on time, and then rule out jazz attractions forever after.

On the other hand, Count Basie never fails to pack Birdland, or almost any other place that he plays, and Birdland apparently is open to him any time he happens to have a week unbooked. Basie and his musicians, to a man, are friendly, intelligent, outgoing and dedicated musicians. When they play England, particularly, the press and fans regard each sideman as a major personality.

Duke Ellington is one of those who have always envisioned jazz as a part of show business. His staging and his provocative scoring have enabled him to establish some of his quite off-beat, unusual songs in the standard pop repertoire. *Sophisticated Lady* is a "far-out" tune, but it has made a fortune for Duke and his publisher. Duke always is working on projects to inject jazz into Broadway shows, into television and films. His own libretti and lyrics sometimes defeat him, but never discourage his efforts. Duke is always looking for that bigger audience, just as he is looking to advance his own musical expression.

Dizzy Gillespie's recent diplomatic triumphs in the Near East and South America owe a great deal to his own tremendous showmanship and to the outgoing qualities of the men he took with him in his fine modern jazz band. He won converts to American jazz among people who had never heard such music before in their lives and who had much less basis for understanding than our American audiences. His tours were all-out efforts to please, to put on a good show, and to sell a good product.

There need be no mystery about jazz, but each listener has a right, even a duty, to be discriminating. He has a right to expect to be entertained and edified.

2. PERSPECTIVES: In Their Own Words

THE OPENER

THE MEN who make jazz are interested in a variety of subjects, and are outspoken on virtually all of them. But they use their life in jazz as a frame of reference for most of their conceptions on their life in the "other" world.

Time was when a jazzman who had something to say about the world or his personal problems said it exclusively through his horn. As the players have become more and more articulate, they have found more and more outlets in print for their feelings.

Today, a jazzman with something to say about the music is equally as effective as his counterpart, the professional writer. And while what he says may be open to as much questioning as the music he plays, he can be sure of a place in which to say it because of the growing public interest in jazz.

Jazzmen have written in magazines and newspapers in and out of the immediate jazz field. While it would be no surprise to find an article by jazz pianist Marian McPartland in *Down Beat* or *Metronome,* it would raise some eyebrows to find a critique of Duke Ellington under her byline in the *Boston Globe*. But this has actually happened, to Marian and other jazz figures.

No one knows better than the jazzman the sociological, philosophical, and psychological tensions under which he works. When he expresses his observations on them in print, they carry weight, and perception. And like his playing, his comments are honest, original, and uninhibited.

36

By now, everyone knows how "jazz came up the river." It stopped off in Kansas City. And part of it never left. Trombonist, arranger, sometime pianist Bob Brookmeyer—a native of Kansas City—expressed, concisely and personally, in the notes for one of his jazz albums,* that you can take jazz out of Kansas City, but you can't take Kansas City out of jazz.

* Kansas City Revisited, *United Artists Records LP UA-5008. Liner notes reprinted by permission.*

KANSAS CITY REVISITED
by Bob Brookmeyer

KANSAS CITY, eh? Well, I guess everyone got some kind of bell that gets a tap from that town. It ain't no good this year and hasn't been for some time. As a twenty-year resident, I think the boppers killed it, but then I'm prejudiced so we'll leave that lie. I do know that some lovely and lasting talk come out of there—some gentleness (genteelness, if you will) that could only be found around men who so fully knew what they did and wherein they spoke that relaxation was the only way to express it. When you're not sure, it gets very nervous, but that utter confidence in swing is hard to beat. If these words ever come under the scrutiny of McShann, Oliver Todd, Orville Minor, Jimmy Keith, Gus Johnson, Gene Ramey, Ben Webster, Roy Johnson, Joe Turner and so many more, I hope they will allow for a young man to talk about what he actually was playing jacks and lead soldiers to—what he thinks he heard and felt enough of that he hopes to the Lord it's really true. I do, you know. When I was one of the youngest jazz fans in the country, my dad and I would cheat on the parson a Sunday or two and stay by the radio to wait for the 15 minutes of Basie, 10:45 over KCKN (now a country and western station, bless their souls). Then, too, Basie would be through town at the Tower Theatre five, six times a year and I got to be a real pro at forging passes from school to catch three shows and two bad westerns before there would be some salt from the home kitchen. First time I ever heard any really up close was around my thirteenth year. A kiddy band I toiled with was waiting their turn at old Garrett Hall and we came upon Oliver Todd's six-piece band—they would make anybody's jaw slacken up a bit with "Little Phil" (Edward Phillips, now hopelessly a mental patient, due to our lovely and humane local "apartheid") and some of the easiest, longest time I had ever seen. My, that was a sight that I shan't forget. When I was old enough to sneak into the night clubs and dives where the good bands played, it was always the same feeling, to my heart anyway. Smooth, deep, rich, mellow, like a fine cigarette, if you will. But with a "clean-up" local government, the end of the war and the advent of the ofay bopper, that pretty well washed up swing music in K.C. There are still a lot of my friends about who went to school with Bird, danced to Basie at the old Reno Club, loved all that the easy jive stood for, but you can't hold a wake all your life, so—nothin' shakin' back home—Wolfe was right—Home in a pine box.

Long before the ghost went elsewhere the gospel had been heard, luckily enough. Almost every musician who could play spent at least a week or two there, playing, soaking, loafing, waiting. If you like well-spoken reminiscence, take a look at the K.C. chapters in *Hear Me Talkin' To Ya'* (Hentoff and Shapiro, you find the publisher). I got surprised every year, admiring a man's playing so much, then find out he was from the home town. Even today, fellow musicians will raise an eyebrow and say—"Oh, you're from K.C., eh? What's going on there these days?" with some respect though they never heard me play a note. A city that can create that immediate warmth must have had some all-pervading atmosphere to it and it's my hope that it doesn't get lost or perverted the way so many other "localized" attitudes have. If this record we are getting to is an instance, everything should be all right for one side of the crystal anyway.

Jazz in Kansas City, like jazz in most of the other early focal spots, grew up on and amid corrupt government, prohibition (such a boon to the rackets that one would think Capone himself authored the bill), a love amongst the common people for excitement and music to match, dance halls, neighborhood taverns (that now woo their sordid trade with canned music, canned beer and canned pleasure), and of course that omnipresent and

38

ugly minority nonsense. Same things as made music grow since time began I guess, in one form or another. Haydn, Mozart and such wrote for their current royalty, one of the noble forms of racketeering, and even Bach was a slave to the Church, certainly at that time a very potent political organization, as it has sometimes been accused, which in turn, at the local level, can turn into corruption and easy money. No offense, naturally. The atmosphere on this date was one that reeked of dance-hall good times, nothing to be sneered at, you know. Our benevolent, noble and protective organization saw to it that all hands were paid in American money, of course—but nobody I know will sit down and record for twelve and one-half hours unless they really want that "It" to happen, and nowadays you've got to put a bit of effort even into your music to make it come out easy and natural.

As I listened to the first dub from the editing session, I wrote down two short phrases that don't seem to need amplification—"Slice of Life" and "Dance Hall." This is positively *not* an album to play while you do a doctorate thesis on "Bergson, Webern and Charles the Vicious; Paradox or Ambiguity?"—this might be a good one for that New Year's Eve bash (which comes every day to the knowing and the wary), or something loud and festive, for I don't think that K.C. jazz is to be taken apart and peered at as you would a bug in high-school biology. You just grab a nice glass of Dewar's Finest, one big, old and very easy chair, turn the volume up and listen. Why, by neddies, you can even dance, if it's allowed in your town on Sunday. But above all, you're supposed to have a good time with it, otherwise you missed the whole point, and you can't do that.

"Even though our race created jazz, few can discuss the subject intelligently." Those lines introduced a Duke Magazine* *article by jazz pianist Billy Taylor, in which the jazzman contended that Negroes know and care little about the music to which they helped give birth. The piece is an example of Taylor's perception and writing ability, an ability which has made him a sought-after lecturer on jazz and the unofficial spokesman of the music.*

* Duke Magazine, *Aug., 1957; reprinted by courtesy of Dan Burley, editor of* Duke Magazine.

NEGROES DON'T KNOW ANYTHING ABOUT JAZZ

by Billy Taylor

STRANGE as it sounds, American Negroes who created jazz music, today hardly know anything about it. You'll find this just as true among the musicians who play jazz in order to earn a living as you will among those who play just for kicks. Only a handful are well enough informed on the subject to discuss it intelligently with anyone except other musicians in their own narrow circles.

It is just amazing how uninformed many top performers are about the historical background of the music they use as a medium of expression.

Semantics has become a fashionable word of late. And nowhere is the word more overworked than in jazz circles, where all kinds of semantic acrobatics are being performed by self-styled experts, critics and other writers on jazz. Frankly, the semantics of jazz annoy me! Such words as "hot," "bop," "progressive," "funky," "East Coast" and "West Coast" mean one thing to one person and something else to another. Actually, these labels have done much to confuse the public about jazz. Much of the public is puzzled and is asking: "Is jazz really good music and do the musicians who play it have anything really important to say?"

Certainly, the men who created jazz had much to say. They were Negroes who found it impossible to voice their opinions verbally, so they devised their own way

40

of playing to get the freedom of expression they were otherwise denied.

Today, however, jazz is no longer the exclusive medium of expression of the Negro.

As the Negro has become more articulate and outspoken, his music has reflected his growth. And in each stage of its development, jazz has become more and more the medium of expression of all types of Americans and, to a surprising degree, musicians from other lands and other cultures.

Contrary to popular conception, most of the popular jazzmen of today are serious-minded, creative artists who are trying to contribute something worth-while to the society in which they live. Men like John Lewis, Dave Brubeck, Quincy Jones and Shorty Rogers are typical of this kind of musician. But there are countless others who are also making very significant, though less publicized, contributions to jazz and to our culture. All of these musicians deserve recognition. They should be written about and listened to. They should be presented in concerts by Negro schools and other organizations who loudly proclaim their interest in enlightening our people. They should be accorded the dignity their stature as artists calls for.

Negro newspapers and magazines could be a big help in this respect, but it seems to me that most of the ones which do offer so many pictorial and written examples of the cultural achievements of Negroes in other fields, just cannot seem to find any jazz musicians to write about except the ones who use dope, drink excessively, have been arrested or have otherwise had trouble with the society in which they live.

And it also seems to me that our periodicals sometimes deliberately go out of their way to play up the personal failings of certain jazz musicians, thus continuing the ancient stereotype that jazz is bad music because of its past association with "vice," and since it is bad, everyone associated with it must consequently be bad. Writers who become livid with rage when this kind of thinking is applied to Negroes as a race, think nothing of going along with the "they're all alike, those jazz musicians" way of thinking in their own writings.

To me, this attitude by Negro editors seems completely unreasonable. To continue blasting against the old mov-

41

ing-picture stereotype of Negroes stealing chickens, toting razors, grinning and shuffling about and acting like "Uncle Toms" is standard procedure in most Negro periodicals, and I for one would like to see the same efforts extended to the music Negroes originated. By not doing this, I think these editors are shirking their responsibility as molders of the public opinion.

Today's Negro should at least be given a clear-cut idea of the importance of jazz as a contribution to American culture. There seem to be only a very few Negroes interested enough to write seriously on jazz topics. Library shelves are almost bare of books authored by Negroes on jazz. Langston Hughes, with his *Primer of Jazz*, has made a start in this direction, but there is a world of material not yet touched. At least some of this documentation should be done by Negroes.

Classes in jazz appreciation and jazz technique have long been conducted in many major U.S. colleges and universities, but I haven't heard of any such courses being even mentioned in our Negro institutions of higher learning.

Negro high schools and colleges which could do much to make promising young jazz musicians aware of their potential aren't doing it and haven't even tried! They could show these budding players the achievements of their predecessors in the field and offer them encouragement and guidance instead of, as in too many instances, treating such students as odd characters and putting them on the defensive by frustrating their attempts to practice and perform for their fellow students.

As a jazz musician with a personal stake in the future of the music I play, I would like to see the musicians who come along after me well trained and well prepared for the life and career they expect to follow.

They could get this training and guidance if schools of the caliber of Virginia State College, Howard University, Tuskegee and Hampton Institutes, Texas Southern University, Morgan State College and Atlanta University would introduce courses on jazz into their curricula. These courses should, of course, be taught by musicians who have not only been trained to teach, but who also have had practical experience playing jazz.

This suggestion isn't as far-fetched as it may sound. There are thousands of well-trained musicians who have played with top-flight jazz units who would welcome the opportunity to work at a first-rate school training and giving these youngsters the benefit of their experiences and a clear-cut insight into their musical heritage.

Somehow, we've got to make Negroes more aware and appreciative of what jazz has meant and still means to the advancement of the race. Writers like Hugues Panassie, Robert Goffin, Alan Lomax, Leonard Feather, Rudi Blesh, Charles E. Smith, Mike Levin, Barry Ulanov and Sidney Finklestein have done much to start the ball rolling in this direction, and, of course, others too numerous to mention also have written much on the subject —but where are the Negro writers who could be writing about not only yesterday's greats but today's greats as well? Will Negro writers be content to let writers like Nat Hentoff, Bill Coss, Marshall Stearns, Whitney Balliett, Orrin Keepnews and the other interested and talented white writers tell the whole story of jazz? Don't they have anything to say as Negroes?

What needs to be done right now is to instill in more Negroes a sense of pride in the accomplishments of their own music. In many ways, jazz has done more to break down the color line between the white and colored races, I would say, than religion, and it was way ahead of sports in blazing the path to firmer friendships and understanding between the races. Where are the Negro priests and ministers who could take an active part in showing the good that jazz has done? Where are the Negro counterparts to Father Norman O'Connor and Reverend Alvin Kershaw?

The startling discovery way back in the early days of jazz that good music knows no color line has worked for the better ever since. Today in recording studios across the country, colored and white musicians put on tape for posterity the best efforts of their combined talents. Negro and white musicians tour all over the country in jazz shows and even perform side by side in the South.

But it is surprising to note that the percentage of white jazz fans is considerably higher than the percentage of Negro jazz fans. Surely a musician like Duke Ellington, with his great compositions and his great orchestras, has done enough to advance the cause of Negroes as a race to warrant the same enthusiasm and support which we give to Jackie Robinson and our other great athletes.

43

It is an accepted fact that jazz is more popular today than it has ever been. It is possible for more people to hear it, and today, more than ever before, it is being presented as an art form in concerts and in supper clubs designed for listening. Even the U.S. State Department is sending jazz groups all over the world to give concerts under its auspices and is presenting a daily jazz program on the *Voice of America.*

Jazz festivals, forums and seminars are being organized on a larger scale than ever before. Jazz is being analyzed, studied and played at such famous resorts as the Music Inn at Lenox, Mass., and at Newport, Rhode Island. Concerts are regularly scheduled at such temples of music as New York's Carnegie Hall, Philadelphia's Academy of Music, Chicago's Ravinia Park, the Hollywood Bowl in Los Angeles, the Civic Opera House in Chicago, and elsewhere. A pitifully few of those concerts are sponsored by Negroes and Negro organizations.

Most Negro school kids respond to jazz. They dance to it, listen to it, argue about it and collect it on records. But their knowledge of the music is much too incomplete. One reason for this lack of knowledge is the fact that they can't hear many of the best jazz musicians perform in person. Negro theaters, like New York's Apollo, rarely offer a show composed solidly of top jazz talent, and they say that this is because there is no demand for such a show. Negro night clubs offer the same answer when asked why they don't present jazz to their clientele.

I have lectured to groups and spoken privately to many Negroes who could learn to understand and love the music which some of their not-so-distant relatives helped bring into being. These are intelligent and mature individuals as well as excited kids who are listening for more in the music they enjoy than the frenzy of a drum beat and a twanging guitar. And because their interest has been aroused they are being given a better idea of the tremendous impact jazz has made, not only in this country, but all over the world.

It would indeed be wonderful if the American public could be made aware through every medium possible that jazz is a contribution to American culture of which we can be justly proud.

Most of us who are active in jazz circles today are sincerely trying to express through our music our emo-

44

tions, attitudes and thoughts on many varied subjects.
Some of us raise our voices in protest over problems and
situations which disturb us, while others among us are
more concerned with the age-old search for truth and
beauty. If we are to be heard, we must be supported by
people who understand and love our music. I, for one,
sincerely believe that more of this support should come
from members of my race.

---

*Perhaps the one individual who symbolizes
jazz to most of the world is Louis Armstrong.
So much has been written about Louis' life
and music, it is difficult to find any unexplored area of the man. Lil Hardin, pianist
with King Oliver's band, married Louis and
lived with him through the turning point of his
career. Her story is an interesting one in itself, but in her album of personal remi-
niscences,* Satchmo And Me,* *she throws some
illuminating sidelights on Louis in the early
days. The recording is in the form of a documentary, and the narrator's comments here are
in italics. Lil's account is notable for its frank-
ness and earthiness.*

* Lil Armstrong: Satchmo and Me. *Riverside RLP
12-120. Transcribed by the editors and reprinted
by permission of Orrin Keepnews, Riverside Records.*

LIL ARMSTRONG: "I REMEMBER POPS"

Boy, I'd heard so much from all the musicians about
King Oliver, King Oliver. So the first night he was in
town, he came over to Dreamland to meet us. King
Oliver and Johnny Dodds came over together that night,
and so he said to me he came to Chicago to work at the
Royal Garden and he said he'd be very glad if I could
come over and work with him. So I told him I'd have to
give a two-weeks' notice, and it was a thrill to me to
think that the great King Oliver wanted me to come and
play with him. So I asked him when he was to start,
and he told me, so I gave my two-weeks' notice and we
rehearsed and I joined him at the Royal Garden.

I didn't see the fellows much after they left work, so
I don't know too much about them, about their person-

45

ality at home or off the job; musically I could only say. Johnny was sober; Baby Dodds was kind of wild. He was kind of the playboy of the orchestra. King Oliver was sober too. He never smoked—he smoked cigars, but he didn't drink. None of them drank, hardly. Dutrey was a very business sort of a fellow. He was always buying property. Freddie Keppard was a man-about-town, I would say. He drank quite a bit and [was] a very good looking fellow with lots of girls—[as a] trumpet player, personally, I think he was better than King Oliver. I think he had a better tone; in fact, I know he did. I liked him better.

The band went to California, and after six months Lil returned to Chicago. She got a job at the Dreamland, and when King Oliver returned he asked Lil to join him again at the Royal Garden. There was also a new cornet player that Oliver had sent for from New Orleans, and the King wanted Lil to meet him.

When he sent for Louis to join him at the Royal Garden—I'm at Dreamland, and the second night that he's there he brings Louis over to the Dreamland to meet me, and I met him while I was playing. I was a little disappointed because all the musicians called him "Little Louis" and he weighed 226 pounds! And I said "Little Louis, wow, Little Louis."

. . . . .

While we were playing at the Royal Garden, a bunch of white musicians—10, 12, 15, sometimes 20—would come and they would all roll up right in front of the bandstand to listen, and I use to wonder to myself what they were listening to, what particular thing were they listening to. That's how much I knew about what we were doing. So they tell me that they were, Louis and Joe, they were some of Paul Whiteman's band and Bix was in the bunch. They were in that bunch that used to come, but I didn't know their names, never even asked who they were. You see the boys never talked to me anyway. They use to talk to Louis and King Oliver and Johnny, but they never said anything to me, never. Never a word was said, so naturally, I didn't know who they were. One fellow I remember, one fellow who was quite famous, Hoagy Carmichael. I remember he came and

46

sat in with the orchestra one night at the Garden. Yes, he came and played the piano. That's the only one I do remember his name that came. Several of them would sit in occasionally, not too much, but they would listen so intently that it was really funny to me because I didn't know what they were trying to get—what it was that they were trying to listen to. Now I know.

. . . . .

People were beginning to notice Lil's husband. As a matter of fact, some decided to try and cut him down to size. Lil remembers that particular night in Chicago so many years ago.

During the time that he was playing with me—well, word was getting around that Louis was a good trumpet player. So, one night Freddie Keppard came in to hear us and the bandstand was down low and Freddie stood there by the bandstand and he listened awhile, and then he said to Louis, "Boy, let me have your trumpet." So, Louis looked at me and I bowed my head, so Louis gave him the trumpet. So, Freddie he blew—oh, he blew and he blew and he blew and then the people gave him a nice hand. Then he handed the trumpet back to Louis. And I said, "Now get him, get him!" Oooh, never in my life have I heard such trumpet playing! If you want to hear Louis play, just hear him play when he's *angry*. Boy, he blew and people started standing up on top of tables and chairs screaming, and Freddie eased out real slowly. Nobody ever asked Louis for his trumpet again!

. . . . .

Louis was playing with Fletcher in New York at the Roseland. Lil joined him—saw that he was not billed and went back to Chicago to book him at the Dreamland.

I went to the Dreamland and I said I want to put a band in here. He said: "Oh yes, yes. Come in. Who've you got?" I said, "Well, I'll get some good musicians, but I want to bring my husband back from New York and I want him to be featured and I want $75 a week for him." So he said, "Well, nobody else is getting but $55." And I said, "I know, but he's coming back; he's coming back from New York and I want $75 and want his name out there in front." "Well, I think you're

47

crazy!" he said. "Nobody knows a thing about that guy yet." I said: "Never mind, you just put that up there. They know me and they'll come in." So I had him make a sign *Louis Armstrong, The World's Greatest Trumpet Player.* I wrote and told Louis: "Well, you can give Fletcher (Henderson) your two-weeks' notice and come on back home, because I got a job for you for $75 a week." And Louis didn't believe me and he didn't want to leave. He kind of liked playing with Fletcher. Louis, he wasn't anxious to be a star you know. He just enjoyed playing and he thought I was crazy with all that name stuff, putting his name out. He said I was real silly. So he said he wasn't coming back. So I said: "Well, I've already got the job and if you're not here by whatever the date was, if you're not here by this date, then don't come at all!" So then the next day I got a wire: "I will be there." So he came, and when he saw his name out there he said: "Girl, you are crazy! What do you mean calling me 'The World's Best Trumpet Player'? And I betcha I don't get $75 a week." I said: "I bet you do." So I got the contract and showed it to him, and he said, "Well, I still think you're crazy."

Press releases are usually noted for their excessive superlatives and lack of any genuine value. Here's a notable exception. Columbia Records, as part of its biographical service, issued a release culled from a lengthy taped interview conducted by George Avakian. This press release appeared in a French jazz magazine and an English jazz periodical as an exclusive interview, and in Down Beat *as a feature under Miles' byline. We are pleased to continue its career. It follows here in its entirety.*

(Self-Portrait of the Artist, *by Miles Davis. Columbia Records Biographical Service, Nov. 26, 1957. Reprinted by permission.*)

SELF-PORTRAIT
by Miles Davis

YOU want me to tell you where I was born—that old story? It was in good old Alton, Illinois. In 1926. And I had to call my mother a week before my last birthday and ask her how old I would be.

I started playing trumpet in grade school. Once a week we would hold notes. Wednesdays at 2:30. Everybody would fight to play best. Lucky for me, I learned to play the chromatic scale right away. A friend of my father's brought me a book one night and showed me how to do it so I wouldn't have to sit there and hold that note all the time.

My mother wanted to give me a violin for my birthday, but my father gave me a trumpet—because he loved my mother so much!

There was a very good instructor in town. He was having some dental work done by my father. He was the one that made my father get me the trumpet. He used to tell us all about jam sessions on the Showboat, about trumpet players like Bobby Hackett and Hal Baker. "Play without any vibrato," he used to tell us. "You're gonna get old anyway and start shaking," he used to say, "no vibrato!" That's how I tried to play. Fast and light—and no vibrato.

By the time I was sixteen I was playing in a band— the Blue Devils—in East St. Louis. Sonny Stitt came to town with a band and heard us play one night. He told me, "You look like a man named Charlie Parker and you play like him too. C'mon with us."

The fellows in his band had their hair slicked down, they wore tuxedos, and they offered me sixty whole dollars a week to play with them. I went home and asked my mother if I could go with them. She said no, I had to finish my last year of high school. I didn't talk to her for two weeks. And I didn't go with the band either.

I knew about Charlie Parker in St. Louis, I even played with him there, while I was still in high school. We always used to try to play like Diz and Charlie Parker. When we heard that they were coming to town, my friend and I were the first people in the hall, me with a trumpet under my arm. Diz walked up to me and said, "Kid, do you have a union card?" I said, "Sure." So I sat in with the band that night. I couldn't read a thing from listening to Diz and Bird. Then the third trumpet man got sick. I knew the book because I loved the music so much I knew the third part by heart. So

49

I played with the band for a couple of weeks. I had to go to New York then.

My mother wanted me to go to Fisk University. I looked in the *Esquire* book and I asked her, "Where's all of this?" Then I asked my father. He said I didn't have to go to Fisk, I could go to big New York City. In September I was in New York City. A friend of mine was studying at Juilliard, so I decided to go there too. I spent my first week in New York and my first month's allowance looking for Charlie Parker.

I roomed with Charlie Parker for a year. I used to follow him around, down to 52nd Street, where he used to play. Then he used to get me to play. "Don't be afraid," he used to tell me. "Go ahead and play." Every night I'd write down chords I heard on matchbook covers. Everybody helped me. Next day I'd play those chords all day in the practice room at Juilliard, instead of going to classes.

I didn't start writing music until I met Gil Evans. He told me to write something and send it to him. I did. It was what I played on the piano. Later I found out I could do better without the piano. (I took some piano lessons at Juilliard, but not enough.) If you don't play it good enough, you'll be there for hours and hours.

If you can hear a note, you can play it. The note I hit that sounds high, that's the only one I can play right then, the only note I can think of to play that would fit. You don't learn to play the blues. You just play. I don't even think about harmony. It just comes. You learn where to put notes so they'll sound right. You just don't do it because it's a funny chord. I used to change things because I wanted to hear them—substitute progressions and things. Now I have better taste.

Do I like composing better than playing? I can't answer that. There's a certain feeling you get from playing that you can't get from composing. And when you play, it's like a composition anyway. You make the outline. What do I like to play? I like *'Round About Midnight*. In fact, I like most any ballad. If I feel like playing it.

What do I think of my own playing? I don't keep any of my records. I can't stand to hear them after I've made them. The only ones I really like are the one I just made with Gil Evans (*Miles Ahead*), the one I
50

made with J. J. (Johnson) on my Blue Note date about four years ago, and a date I did with Charlie Parker.

People ask me if I respond to the audience. I wouldn't like to sit up there and play without anybody liking it. If it's a large audience, I'm very pleased because they are there anyway. If it's a small audience, sometimes it doesn't matter. I enjoy playing with my own rhythm section and listening to them. I'm studying and experimenting all the time.

I know people have some rhythm and they feel things when they're good. A person has to be an invalid not to show some sign—a tap of the finger even. You don't have to applaud. I never look for applause. In Europe, they like everything you do. The mistakes and everything. That's a little bit too much.

If you play good for eight bars, it's enough. For yourself. And I don't tell anybody.

Duke Ellington is today in his fourth or fifth renaissance. Throughout the four decades of his unprecedented career, Ellington has received full coverage in print. Following are excerpts from a four-hour interview the editors taped with Mercer Ellington for two distinct purposes: (1) to obtain a portrait of Mercer Ellington, a distinguished musician in his own right, and, (2) to see Ellington through the eyes of his son. We have attempted to retain the original flavor and stream-of-consciousness flow his recollections.

REMINISCING IN TEMPO
by Mercer Ellington

BEFORE MY TIME . . .

There are some pretty interesting things that I know about Ellington . . . things picked up from people who knew him before I was born. There was a guy by the name of Gump. He played piano by ear and had a sound like Ellington. In the beginning, it must have been Gump who was an influence on Ellington's playing. Then there was Mexico . . . nobody really knows where he came from. Ellington knew him only in New York. Jerry

Rhea was like a personal secretary to Ellington, his constituent. And also, at one time, was vocalist with the band. The fourth guy I'm trying to think of was called Black Bowie. Ellington knew Black Bowie and Jerry Rhea in the early days, when he was in Washington. These are the guys whose philosophy was identical to that of Ellington's, although they weren't musicians, nor have they at any time become publicly known.

What you see in Ellington today is very relative and very definitely due to the presence of these men in his life . . . especially Mexico, Jerry Rhea, and Bowie. Black Bowie and Ellington were teenagers together. I would guess they were friends from about 14 or 15 years old. Bowie realized that Ellington could play some piano, and for their various adventures they needed an automobile and some cash from time to time. Usually, Bowie got the car. But it was Ellington who provided the gas for it by playing the piano at different parties and things —a few dollars here and a few dollars there.

They went around and more or less had a social life together. It was in this period that Ellington began to form different thoughts about beautiful things—his imagination became great. He'd been born with a great imagination anyhow. But it was enhanced by a guy like Bowie, a guy who if he had only two dollars was able to feel he could live like a king. With this two dollars Ellington and Bowie would take situations and build them into things of grandeur. Maybe it was just a case of parking the car on the White House lawn . . . this would be equivalent to taking a cruise across the ocean or something.

Bowie was a real comrade . . . the man who had the earliest influence on Ellington. A man who reflected Ellington's kind of imagination. One day Ellington said to me; "You're going to St. Louis, and I want you to look up my worthy friend, Black Bowie." So I went to St. Louis, and down a dark street in a dirty old building, I found this meager office. The door, with the glass half broken out of the window, said *Daily Tattler*. Now, this was a newspaper that at one time existed in Washington through the auspices of Bowie. It had become popular in Harlem and quite a craze of the night-club set. It used to have all the little gossip that happened in the gin mills and hot spots. It had had its effect and its peak; now it was diminished. Yet it still lived with Bowie in this remote place. It sort of brought a flash of the Roaring Twenties back, just seeing that name on the door.

Bowie said, "I want you to meet some of the people that like Ellington," and we made the rounds of all the bars in St. Louis. We covered practically every bar, just to go in and shake hands with most of them, and every now and then a drink. And all these people, through Bowie, had become staunch Ellington supporters. They knew him as if they had grown up with him. They could tell how and why he got the name of Duke.

(In the early days, Ellington, even with what little he had, was impeccable as far as dress was concerned. He never wanted his pants to look unpressed and his shirts always had to be clean. If something happened he'd go back to change them.)

I think the thing that led to Bowie's demise and really to his virtual insignificance was that he fell victim to the one thing he had preached against all his life . . . he fell in love. This was the note I left Bowie on. This man who had had this hard-fast rule lived a lifetime to prove it was wrong. Then he just disappeared . . .

Traveling in the same party was Jerry Rhea. In a sense he was like the younger man around. Jerry doesn't come into the picture until the group had started. He was a 14-year-old running with the 18-year-olds, and that's a big difference. In a sense, Ellington influenced Rhea, but Rhea was Ellington's "salesman." Today Jerry is a beer salesman for the leading beer company in Washington. In those days he was the forerunner. For instance, if Ellington came into a joint, there was Jerry saying, "All right everybody, here comes Duke." And the funny thing is, the joint they wound up in after they came to New York was usually Mexico's speakeasy. So between Jerry selling him on one hand and Mexico talking about how great he was on the other, Ellington began to have his effect on New York City. The acclaim he got through these two guys, Jerome Rhea and Mexico, only worked for him *as an individual*. After all, he was playing piano in Elmer Snowden's band at the time. He was not yet a leader.

Today you would call Mexico's speakeasy an after-hours spot. Ellington would sit and play the piano for tips and things of that sort. Jerry made the people aware of the fact that they could have their choice of numbers, and Mexico was the one who served. Whisky came in two classifications in those days—No. 1 and No. 2. If you ordered a drink, you got No. 1. But if you came in and had more money to spend, you were allowed the oral privilege of ordering No. 2, thus showing everybody you were a big shot. Of course No. 1 and No. 2 were the same whisky.

So Ellington became aware of gimmicks and promotion, with the result that he began to learn how to convince people. Not necessarily how to convince them, *but how to make them want what you've got to give them,* instead of the other way around. This is the average attitude a musician has: give them what *they* want. In the early days Ellington was just this way. He had no particular regard for lessons or anything, musically. He just wanted to play things that were successful and brought good reactions from people; things that kept girls sitting on the piano bench while he played and entertained. What didn't bring good reactions, he threw out. Playing in Mexico's changed all that. He learned there what so few people know—so few leaders know—he learned *presentation,* one of his great assets all through his career.

ECHOES OF HARLEM

Even now, though Mexico is gone, you can still hear the echoes of his idea of No. 1 and No. 2 in Ellington. This is why I say this man had a tremendous effect on Ellington. He never scolded Ellington or told him he was wrong. He'd simply say, "A wise man would do so and so," and nothing was ever *wrong.* There was always a better choice or certain course of events. Mexico knew all the people that could lead him down the wrong road and Mexico used to steer him and give him knowledge as to who the real good influences were in New York and who the bad influences were. During these crazy Twenties, a guy who was just a musician could sit in a place in Harlem and get a fifty-dollar tip for playing just one tune . . .

GOIN' UP

He moved into the days when the Cotton Club became his stepping stone. He was going up. I say two things sent him on his way, the Cotton Club and his appearances in the Ziegfeld shows. The next important phase after Ellington had a band and got started was study, and the fact that he did it *himself*. He'd only read what he wanted. He wasn't what you'd call a prolific reader and he wasn't looking for any broad fields of knowledge. The only thing he wanted was to be able to write what he thought. He read different books on three-part harmony and four-part harmony, and finally developed his own five-part harmony. The first sign of things having any evidence of success was the fact that every once in a while I'd get a letter from my mother with a dollar bill in it. Later, we wound up having electricity in the house and a radio. Whenever he had a broadcast—a big event in our life—we were allowed to sit up, school night or not, and listen to the band. We'd hear the announcer come on with his great introduction for Duke Ellington. I remember this note of authority proclaiming Ellington. This really made me feel he was somebody. Then, the next summer I was allowed to travel with the band. I was eight years old, and we went to Salem, Mass.

IN A BLUE SUMMER GARDEN

In Salem I wanted to be a fireman because the guys around the fire house used to let me ride on the truck when they went out to a fire. So, this was a big thing. For the most part, I had no real outstanding desire. I mean I was too amazed. When you travel around at that age you're completely awed by so many things. Imagine, just the difference in towns between say, Washington, D.C. and Holyoke, Mass., and then to arrive in New York City and see the skyscrapers; to change schools from Washington, D.C. to the schools in New York City. This was quite a difference.

None of the family trips we took compared to the excitement of traveling with the band. Although, even on the road, I didn't see Ellington that much. You know, I worked with the band as assistant valet. I was about fourteen by then. Always, on summer vacations, he'd turn me over to a guy named Jonesy, who in the earlier days had been a waiter at the Cotton Club. When Ellington finally broke loose from the Cotton Club, Jonesy went with the band. They had a tune for him: *Stompy*

Jones. He was something else! Yeah, Jonesy was something else. He was the guy who was a complete devotee of Ellington. Anything Ellington did on or off the stage was the absolute gospel and that was it. He got his enjoyment in his work, and anything that surrounded it, and that was it. I mean, all he ever worried about was that everything was completely right and that the bandstand was set. When that was done, if there was something he wanted to do, then he'd do it. There's never been anyone since quite that dedicated. This is a man who was just drawn into the band away from a very good job. Don't forget—being a waiter in the Cotton Club in those days was a tremendous asset—those tips rolling in there and all the boys being big spenders.

HALF THE FUN

About the second day of the first summer in Salem, I was given the name "Brat." There are always one or two guys who have the knack of being able to connect sound with identification. Lester Young was like that. Pres had this terrific knack of naming things according to what they represented. When Ben Webster was talking about how *he* was king, and wanted to be called some big name, Pres just threw him back in his place by calling him "Beast," because he was always banging his chest. In those days, Otto Hardwicke in the band had this same knack. Regardless of what your feelings were in this situation, when Otto labeled you with something, that was it. You just had to accept it. Johnny Hodges was called "Rab" because everybody said he reminded them of the Easter Bunny—so that was it. No way he could shake it either. He just had it and that was the name that stuck. I began to know the guys, not for their names, but for their nicknames.

I remember the first time I realized the band could possibly make a mistake. They started on something and tricky Sam Nanton got messed up. He hit this wrong note—some way-off note on the trombone and it was so bad he had to get up off the bandstand and walk around. When they finally introduced me to him they were talking around, and when I got to Tricky I said, "I know *him* —he's the guy who hit the bad note!" No wonder they called me Brat!

Today all of that gang are my "uncles," because they

stopped me from using the nicknames and made me owe them the respect equal to a surname. I couldn't call the guys Mr. So-and-So, and yet I wasn't allowed to call them a straight first name. So it had to be Uncle Johnny, Uncle Harry, Uncle Toby, and the result is that with each of these guys I had a sort of a family relationship. That's how I began to know them.

JUST SCRATCHIN' THE SURFACE

When I was in high school, I went out with the band three or four summers running. In the process, I learned the instruments; each one of the guys showed me something. I started off on clarinet and saxophone. Barney [Bigard] taught me the clarinet, and I had a regular saxophone teacher, although Johnny [Hodges] used to show me some tricks of the trade.

Cootie [Williams] was responsible for getting me off the saxophone. He used to watch me blow from time to time, and once he said, "That boy's got natural chops!" And then he got this deal on a horn that was just being perfected, so for fifty bucks I got a new horn. That's the way I wound up playing the trumpet. A brass instrument seemed to be such a big thing in those days . . . such an important thing.

CARAVAN

Aside from the job and the money, it was the personal treatment that the band got that made the road worthwhile. There was always somebody ready to take the wives on a tour of the various places we visited. I remember when we hit Holyoke—that's the town with the ghosts—they were shown all the different houses that were supposed to be haunted, and given the gory details. Of course, they also saw the museums and things of that sort. When we hit Boston, Harry Carney's mother would always have the band out for a repast of some sort; it was always tremendous 'cause the food you ate came out of her backyard. Like we'd have ripe cabbage. His mother is still alive, and in very good shape, I might add. Don't ever take a stroll with her for about 10 or 20 blocks. She's a tall woman and she has a straw hat with a feather on it, and when she walks down the street, it flies straight up . . .

57

Ellington has always based his music on knowing the people who are its performers.

I played in the band for a while. Well, there are several ways you can put it . . . the war made trombone players scarce, and I was playing the E-flat horn. It looked more like a French horn than anything else. Ellington decided he'd let me sit back there and play trombone parts.

I think the first time Ellington ever heard me play a solo was at a dance out in Hempstead somewhere. I had developed this dance band with Leroy Lovett, and Ellington happened to come around. I had written a dance version of *Clair de Lune,* and put it into a fox trot. When we played it people liked it, and I had to play it over again. I don't know, maybe I satisfied Ellington, or convinced him I could play. That's when he gave me permission to join his band.

I stayed only a short spell. It's difficult for a man to join that band. There are many hardships, and I experienced them all, even though I knew most of the guys.

You know, I was the boss's son. The funniest thing was that I was caught right in the middle. Everything was friendly, but I wasn't the boss or even within his sight. When he left the bandstand, that was it. He went his way and I was left with the men. Oh, we ate dinner together and things like that. But I wasn't shown any more consideration than the average sideman in the band.

Of course, the Ellington band has always had absolute social standing throughout the country. Even today, an Ellington sideman can go to a town and spend from nine in the morning to six or seven at night, just visiting from house to house.

The size of Ellington's band has never been set. It started off as an eight-piece group and it grew to its present size because, as they went from place to place, when they realized a man *belonged,* he was hired. At one time the band had two bass fiddles. This was no particular design, it was just that these two bass players *belonged,* and the fact that they happened to co-exist was something else.

I don't know how Ellington ran into Ben Webster, but I think he heard him jamming one night and then asked him to come with the band. I remember that somewhere onstage, out on the road, in a theater—Ben had just joined the band—there were two statements that occurred within the same show. Ellington came off after Ben had just played something—I think it was later to become the solo for *Cottontail*—and said, "Man, he plays twice as much tenor as I thought he'd do!"

In the same set, they had played *Daybreak Express.* But it was *way up there,* and Ben had missed the whole first chorus. When Ben came off, he said to me, "Man, if you don't get on that express train on time, you *miss* it, don't you?"

Ellington wasn't even aware of the fact that Ben hadn't played; the only thing he retained out of the show was the tremendous solo Ben had played on *Cottontail.* The only thing that Ben had retained was the fact that Ellington had written some music that had gotten away from him.

And the result was that they both came offstage that day with greater admiration and respect for each other. As I say, the band grew. They picked up guys from place to place.

I Don't Know What Kind of Blues I Got

There was one guy who was all-encompassing, an anarchist of show business. I like to compare him to Thoreau because this guy owed nothing to nobody, and it was almost as if he hated success. His name was George Woods, and his most recent club was the place called The Red Rooster, right across the street from the Renaissance Ballroom on 138th Street and 7th Avenue. Only in recent years did he decide to stay still. It seems as soon as he'd go someplace, and the business would become profitable, George would eventually leave. He was the type of guy who almost took pride in being able to refuse money and status.

I think it was George—at least he was capable of it—who was once the proprietor of a joint called the Sawdust Trail. It was a speakeasy, after-hours joint, but one that moved from night to night. You could tell where it was, within two or three blocks, by the trail of sawdust. If you followed the sawdust, it led to some apartment, and that's where the club was tonight. Eventually George began to adopt a more normal way of life.

The Ellington family first met him when we moved to New York about 1930. The family took an apartment at 381 Edgecombe Avenue, just off Sugar Hill, which was brand-new then. Sugar Hill got its name because if you had a sweetheart, that's where you stashed her. Also, it took a lot of sugar to keep anything *going* up there. That's where the most expensive apartments were and your best neighborhood.

Two flights above the family apartment, Freddie Guy shared an apartment with George Woods. George was the first guy to show me magic tricks and things of that sort. Everything he said had some logic to it. George was the one who would get after me for different things which would be distasteful. He was the one I think who made me begin to realize that I shouldn't be as idealistic about Ellington as I wanted to be. In other words, Woods saw that one day this illusion that I had would be changed and he prepared me for the shock, so to speak . . . the shock of realizing that Ellington was another human being and not some person up on a pedestal. He gave me the idea of how a man could be susceptible to human failures. For instance, I couldn't understand why Ellington couldn't spend time with me—why he would have to sit up late, bang on the piano and sleep all day. I used to get up and wait around the room just to see him. And when he'd finally come out, he'd eat dinner quickly and go on to work. I could always see him at a distance; wherever he was I had the privilege of going. Of course, the kids in the neighborhood always thought that this was great, because here I was only 14 or 15 and I could go sit in the Cotton Club or be backstage in the downtown Paramount Theater and all that. Everything was so great and yet I felt . . .

This was something else. It was always a little difficult for him to adapt himself because it's different from having a baby and giving him a couple of pats on the head and not having to figure anything to say, as against having a child grow from a baby into a human being.

It was through George that what we now call *soul* was explained to me: that there is a greater value in certain kinds of knowledge gained through experience with people, than in education with its diplomas and degrees. You had to specialize in the matter of human relationships in order to gain this experience. It was George who taught me about Harlem . . .

TAKE THE "A" TRAIN

Here's Harlem that sits right in the middle of New York. You've got downtown New York, you've got Washington Heights, and you've got Harlem, an island apart.

When you cross 116th Street, say, from 116th to 155th Street, and possibly from Amsterdam Avenue over to Lenox, you find a basic philosophy and belief of a people—a culture which is very set and different in its way of life. There's pride within this culture. They do as much as they're done to. It's heterogeneous, yet it's apart from everything that surrounds it.

Harlem is a section of almost every city. Maybe some cities only have three people who belong to Harlem. Harlem has its primitive rites as much as, say, the inner areas of Africa and the Congo. But the Harlem George taught me had its own native heritage, and one not to be taken lightly. It just so happens that the guys who wound up in Harlem, whether they came out of jazz bands or wherever they came from, had a certain *thing*. I mean, if they'd been off someplace where instruments hadn't been manufactured for them, their music might have wound up on the pentatonic scale. They have a tendency to develop certain things and in a certain way, more emotional than philosophical in its nature.

George helped me understand that the music of Harlem is more related to *feeling* than rightness. Ellington had the same influence, but he was able to put it into greater form . . . you know, works like *Black, Brown, and Beige; Harlem; Liberian Suite;* and *New World A'Comin'*.

SOMETHING TO LIVE FOR

Harlem's primitive rites were reflected in the "jungle band." Ellington was among the first to understand both the heritage of Harlem and the fact that this was a new people, cosmopolitan, sophisticated. He had a jungle band in the early days, and, in a sense, he has a jungle band now.

He's still doing primitive material, but in a more sophisticated way. Take *The Mooche*, and more recently, *A Drum Is A Woman*.

Most people involved in jazz, who write about jazz, are

61

very conscious of the trends in the field. Most of them say that even the most significant figures in the last 10 or 15 or 20 years don't come up to Ellington or don't approach the pedestal to his throne. The reason they feel this way is these jazz figures don't seem to compose with depth or scope. The reason for this is probably because they don't have the same *frames of reference* Ellington had, or the same approach to life in *writing* music that he has.

In other words, I would say that a lot of the other guys had a more shallow existence. What I'm trying to say is they didn't have Black Bowie, Jerry Rhea, Mexico and George Woods; and they weren't able to remain unconfused by ideas which were away from what was normally being done. They weren't able to be *with* people who could rationalize and make these ideas logical to them. In other words, they were people who would succumb to a pointed finger of a moral code or musical theory code, saying, "You've broken the rule, so watch yourself—" or, *"Don't you dare!"*

Love You Madly

All of a sudden, I was someone who had to be spoken to. There was always just this little distance between us. He was never able to adapt himself as a father, and it got to a place where conversation was difficult. When I was first on the road with him, we didn't know each other well enough to really have anything to talk about. Gradually, however, he began to teach me music, which was one of the best things that could have happened. As time went by, it became more and more obvious that I could write with satisfaction only for his band. Well, I did do two or three things for Charlie Barnet, and tried a few for Basie, out of friendship. But right away Basie said, "Sorry, I can't use these. They're too close to Ellington." So all of a sudden I realized that I was enmeshed in a way of musical thought from which I wasn't really able to tear myself away. Therefore, if I couldn't write for the band, I either had to write for myself or nobody. This is sort of like a shell I got into I guess over the last ten years.

Everybody's always asking, "Is this the *real* Ellington? What is the real Ellington? Who is the real Ellington?"

Well, Ellington is a chameleon-type person. *This* is

62

the real Ellington. He changes. For instance, I've seen him leave a big dinner of some sort and wind up in a dive. And he is equally at home in either place. I've seen him talk to people of intelligence and people of ignorance, and keep the conversation going without embarrassing anyone, or making anyone self-conscious of his status.

Ellington was never one to get into the middle of a battle. He's never going to take up one side or the other. If two people differ, he'll sit there until the discussion has been settled, and then he'll probably say something that changes everything anyhow.

And he can get away with it because *this is Ellington . . .*

3. FICTION: Through a Glass, Darkly

THE OPENER

THE INTENSITY with which many jazzmen live and work, if it is to be captured at all in prose, must be captured with care and sensitivity, lest in print it turn into an unwitting satire of the truth. The appeal of the jazz scene, as we have already demonstrated, is ubiquitous. The challenge is unmistakable: to recreate in words the vitality, wit, fear, and love implicit in the music of the men. Some day it *will* be met, and met fully. In the meantime, we are left with a flawed miscellany of attempts, some dreadful, some promising, some brief but superb in parts; none really fulfilled works of art.

Jazz is something more than "a dedicated breed of lonely fanatics" and something less than the Sermon on the Mount. The delicate peak of the jazz novel still stands gleaming in the distance; the climbers, from Dorothy Baker (*Young Man With a Horn*) through John Clellon Holmes (*The Horn*) are perhaps distinguished more by the assault than the attainment.

The jazz short story has seemingly fared better. Each of the three pieces of fiction in this section captures something vital of the jazz world.

In his novel The Horn, *John Clellon Holmes
comes very close to scaling the peak (and
perhaps he actually* has) *in his unforgettable
first chapter, which initially saw the light of
print as a short story. With a lush, impressionistic palette of words he tells the classic once-
upon-a-time tale of the tribal duel. The young
warrior, driven neither by passion nor love,
but by the nameless song inside, attacks his
chieftain, long scarred with pain and glory.
But for Holmes (and for us) the time is The
Forties; the locale is The Street; the world is
Jazz . . .*

THE HORN
by John Clellon Holmes

CHORUS: WALDEN

> *"Men will lie on their
> backs, talking about the
> fall of man, and never
> make an effort to get up."*
> Thoreau

CONSIDER that it was four o'clock of a Monday afternoon,
and under the dishwater-gray window shade—just the
sort of shade one sees pulled down over the windows of
cheap hotels fronting the sooty elevateds of American
cities where the baffled and the derelict loiter and shift
their feet—under this one shade, in the window of a building off Fifty-third Street on Eighth Avenue in New York,
the wizened October sun stretched its old finger to touch
the dark, flutterless lids of Walden Blue, causing him to
stir among sheets a week of dawntime lying down and
twilight getting up had rumpled.

Walden Blue always came awake like a child, without
struggle or grimace, relinquishing sleep in accordance
with the truce he had long ago worked out with it. He
came awake with a sparrow stare, fast dissolving as the

64

world was rediscovered around him unchanged for his absence. He lay alone—without moving in the way a man used to waking beside the body of women will move, either toward her or away; lay, letting his water-cracked ceiling remind him (as it always did) of the gullies of shack roads back home where he would muddy his bare black feet when a child, and where, one shimmering cicada-noon, he had stood and watched a great lumbering bullock career toward him, and become a Cadillac-full of wild, zoot-suited city boys, pomaded, goateed, upending label-less pints, singing and shouting crazily at everything: "Dig 'at pick'-ninny! Dig the cotton fiel'! Dig the life here!"; to bump past him, gape-faced there in the ruts, and plunge on around the bend of scrub pines, where he had once mused over an ant hill in the misty Arkansas dawn—for all like some gaudy, led-astray caravan of Gypsies, creating a wake of rumor and head-shaking through the countryside.

Walden Blue slid long legs off the bed, and for a moment of waking reflection—that first moment, which in its limpid, almost idiotic clarity is nearly the closest human beings come to glimpsing the dimensions of their consciousness—he considered the polished keys and the catsup-colored neck of the tenor saxophone which, two years before, had cost him $175 on Sixth Avenue, becoming his after an hour of careful scales and haggling and of the gradual ease which comes to a man's fingers when they lose their natural suspicion of an instrument or a machine which is not their own, but must be made to respond like some sinewy, indifferent horse, not reluctant to be owned but simply beautiful in its blooded ignorance of ownership. For on this saxophone Walden Blue made music as others might make love a kind of fugue on any bed; Walden made music as a business, innocent (because love of it was what kept him alive) of just what others meant by their "business," implying as that might some sacrifice of most that was skilled and all that was fine in them. He considered his saxophone, in this first moment of waking, without pleasure or distaste, noting it with the moody, half-fond stare of a man at the tool he has spent much time, sweat and worry to master, but only so that he can use it.

Looking at it, he knew it to be also an emblem of some inner life of his own, something with which he

65

could stand upright, at the flux and tempo of his powers
—as others consider a physical feat an indication of man-
hood, and still others, a wound. To Walden the saxophone
was, at once, his key to the world in which he found himself, and the way by which that world was rendered im-
potent to brand him either failure or madman or Negro
or saint. But then sometimes on the smoky stand, between
solos, he hung it from his swinging shoulder like one
bright, golden wing, and waited for his time.

"Hey there," he said to himself reproachfully, dangling
his feet in an imaginary brook, for it was nearing three-
thirty, which meant the afternoon was slipping by; and so
he got up, stretching himself with the voluptuous grace
some musicians give to any movement, and went about
coffee-making. The electric plate was dead in one coil, the
pot itself rusty from weeks of four o'clock makings; and
without troubling his head about it, he used yesterday's
soggy grounds. Coffee had no taste or savor to him at
that hour: it was merely hot and black. He started his
day with it, and as though it poured something of its
nature into him, by the swirling night hours, amid smoke
and roar, he would be like it: hotter and blacker, if anything. The second scalding cup was as necessary to the
beginning of the day as the second shot of bourbon or
the second stick of tea was to its blissful morning end
someplace uptown, where, for sociability and personal
kicks, he would blow one final chorus for himself, with a
rhythm section of hardy, sweating souls collected from a
scattering of groups around town, and then, packing up,
go home empty of it all again. He drank his coffee back
on the bed, lean shanks settled down on it, naked as a
child; and each gulp re-established him in the world.

His mind was clear; in these first moments, scarcely a
man's mind at all, for he had no thoughts, just as he
rarely dreamed. One afternoon in L.A.—back nine years
ago, when bop was an odd new sound, and a name for
the jazz many of them had been blindly shaping, and
something else as well (a miraculous, fecund word, because no one then really understood its meaning, only
somehow knew)—he had sat on a similar bed over his
first cup, just like now, and out of the sweet emptiness
of his morning head a thought had come: that he was a
saxophone, as bright and shiny and potential as that, and
the night and his life would play upon him. Some after-

66

noons since then, he recalled recalling this thought, and often giggled secretly at its foolish accuracy. But never troubled his head.

But this afternoon something else was there. This morning—three or four o'clock at least, up at Blanton's on 125th Street, where, in the back, and after hours, they served coffee, and the musicians gathered to listen or play or talk that shop talk without which any profession in America would be thwarting to Americans—Edgar Pool had been inveigled to sit in with the house group (nothing more than rhythm upon which visitors could build their fancies), and as everyone turned to him in the drab, low-ceilinged room, giving him that respectful attention due an aging, original man whom all have idolized in the hot enthusiasm of youth, something had happened. And now Walden remembered.

There are men who stir the imagination deeply and uncomfortably, around whom swirl unplaceable discontents, men self-damned to difference, and Edgar Pool was one of these. Once an obscure tenor in a brace of road bands, now only memories to those who had heard their crude, uptempo riffs (their only testament the fading labels of a few records, and these mostly lost, some legendized already, one or two still to be run across in the bins of second-hand jazz record stores along Sixth Avenue), Edgar Pool had emerged from an undistinguished and uncertain musical environment by word of mouth. He went his own way, and from the beginning (whenever it had been, and something in his face belied the murky facts) he was unaccountable. Middling tall, sometimes even lanky then, the thin mustache of the city Negro accentuating the droop of a mouth at once determined and mournful, he managed to cut an insolently jaunty figure, leaning toward prominent stripes, knit ties, soft shirts and suede shoes. He pushed his horn before him; and listening to those few records years later, when bop was gathering in everyone but had yet to be blown, Walden, striving more with his fingers than with his head at that time, first heard the murmur of the sounds they were all attempting. Edgar had been as stubbornly out of place in that era, when everyone tried to ride the drums instead of elude them, as he was stubbornly unchanged when bop became an architecture on the foundation he had laid.

He hung on through fashions, he played his way when

67

no one cared, and made money as he could, and never argued. One night in 1938, in a railroad bar in Cincinnati, where the gang men came to drink their pay with their dusky, wordless girls (something in them aching only for dance), he sat under his large-brimmed hat and blew forty choruses of *I Got Rhythm*, without pause or haste or repetition, staring at a dead wall; then lit up a stick of tea with the piano man, smiled sullenly, packed his horn and caught the train for Chicago and a job in a burlesque pit. Such things are bound to get around, and when Walden saw him a year or so later (on another night at Blanton's), the younger tenors had started to dub him "the Horn," though never (at that time) to his face.

Edgar Pool blew methodically, eyes beady and open, and he held his tenor saxophone almost horizontally extended from his mouth. This unusual posture gave it the look of some metallic albatross caught insecurely in his two hands, struggling to resume flight. In those early days he never brought it down to earth, but followed after its isolated passage over all manner of American cities, snaring it nightly, fastening his drooping, stony lips to its cruel beak, and tapping the song. It had a singularly human sound—deep, throaty, often brutal with a power that skill could not cage, an almost lazy twirl on the phrase ends: strange, deformed melody. When he swung with moody nonchalance, shuffling his feet instead of beating, even playing down to the crowd with scornful eyes averted, they would hear a wild goose honk beneath his tone—the noise, somehow, of the human body; superbly, naturally vulgar; right for the tempo. And then out of the smearing notes, a sudden shy trill would slip, infinitely wistful and tentative.

But time and much music and going alone through the American night had weakened the bird. Over the years, during which he disappeared and then turned up, blowing here and there, during which, too late, a new and restless generation of young tenors (up from the shoeless deltas, like Walden, or clawed out of Harlem's back-alley gangs) discovered in his music something apt and unnamable—not the sound, but some arrow toward it, some touchstone—over the years which saw him age a little and go to fat, which found him more uncommunicative and unjudging of that steady parade of eager pianists and drummers that filed past behind him, the horn came down. Somehow it did not suggest weariness or compromise; it was more the failure of interest, and that strain of isolated originality which had made him raise it in the beginning out of the sax sections of those road bands of the past, and step solidly forward, and turn his eyes up into the lights. The tilt of his head, first begun so he could grasp the almost vertical slant of the mouthpiece, remained, the mouthpiece now twisted out of kilter to allow it; and this tilt seemed childishly fey and in strange contrast to his unhurried intent to transform every sugary melody he played and find somewhere within it the thin sweet song he had first managed to extract, like precious metal from a heap of slag.

Walden felt Edgar Pool threaded through his life like a fine black strand of fate, and something always happened. When he first heard him in the flesh—sometime back in 1941, in the dead center of war, after learning those few records by heart, after finding his own beginnings in Brahmin Lightcap's big band that came in with a smashing engagement in Boston, and went out six months later, a financial bubble, when the trumpet section grumpily enlisted in the Navy and most of the saxes were arrested on narcotics charges—after this, after waiting to hear Edgar, missing him in L.A. by a lost bus connection, getting hung up in Chicago, Walden had come into Blanton's one night, and heard a sound, and there was Edgar, horn at a forty-five-degree angle to his frame, playing behind Geordie Dickson as she sang *What Is This Thing Called Love?* with a tremble in her voice then that made you wonder. Something settled in Walden that night, and he decided to get out of the big bands, the bus schedules, the dance halls, the stifling arrangements; to get off the roads for a while; to stick around New York, which was his adopted pond after all; to give himself his head. It wasn't Edgar actually—just that aura of willful discontent around him: wanting a place, but not any place.

Since then Walden dug Edgar whenever he was around, puzzled and disturbed, but not until this morning in Blanton's had anything come out clear. Edgar had played with weary and indifferent excellence, noting neither Cleo —who played piano with Walden at the Go Hole every night but never got enough and, like so many young musicians (he was only eighteen), seemed to have no substantial, homely life but jazz, no other hours but night, and so hung around Blanton's till dawn with untiring smiles of expectation—nor the others who wandered in and out, listening to every other bar, gossiping and showing off their latest women. Edgar stood before them, down among the tables, for there was no proper stand, sax resting on one thigh, and Walden studied him for an instant with that emotion of startling objectivity that comes only when a man least expects or desires it. And for that moment he forgot his own placid joy at the night narrowing down to an end and to this hour among his own sort, at the sight of someone so inexplicably isolated from it all, though generally accepted as one pivot on which it turned.

Edgar fingered lazily, ignoring Cleo's solid, respectful chords, one shoulder swinging back and forth slightly, his chin pulled in. His hair was long over his large collar, he padded up and down on exaggerated crepe soles, and between solos he chewed a enormous wad of gum soaked in Benzedrine. They said he had "gone queer," but instead there was something soft and sexless about him. Then he smeared a few notes over a pretty idea—a crooked smile glimmering behind the mouthpiece, all turned in upon himself, all dark; and Walden alone seemed to catch the sinister strain of self-ridicule behind the phrase, behind the sloppy, affected suit, the fairy hip-swinging; and at that moment the presence of a secret in Edgar reached him like a light.

For if jazz was a kind of growing Old Testament of the Negro race—and of all lost tribes in America, too—a testament being written night after night by unknown, vagrant poets on the spot (and so Walden, reared on a strange Biblical confusion, often thought of it), then Edgar had once been a sort of Genesis, as inevitable and irreducible as the beginnings of things; but now, mincing, chewing, flabby, he sounded the bittersweet note of Ecclesiastes, ironical in his confoundment.

But just then Geordie Dickson flounced in with her cocker spaniel under one arm, two smirking white men guiding her, half-tipsy, between them. The sweaty faces around the room pivoted, and someone whispered hoarsely. For this was almost the first time in the ten years since something unknown had separated them that they had been in the same room. Their lives were fatefully,

70

finally intertwined, for Edgar had found her singing in a ginmill in Charleston (no more than sixteen then) and, probably with only a clipped word of command, had taken her away and brought her North—a sturdy, frightened, bitter girl, one-quarter white, raped at fourteen on a country lane by two drunken liquor salesmen, thrown into reform school where she was chained to an iron cot while her child was born out of her dead, finally released to find her family vanished, thrown back for pickpocketing in colored churches, released again in the custody of a probation officer who tried to get her into a whorehouse, and trying to keep off the streets with her voice when Edgar first saw her. He taught her some sense of jazz, got her the initial jobs, backed her on the records that followed, and took money from her when, all overnight, she became a sensation to that dedicated breed of lonely fanatic which jazz creates. Walden, among the others, had often stood in the vest-pocket clubs on Fifty-second Street during 1942, as the lights faded away and one spot picked her out—mahogany hair oil-bright, over one ear the large red rose still wet from the florist's, candle-soft eyes, skin the sheen of waxy, smooth wood—and heard the opening chords, on grave piano, of *I Must Have That Man*; and also heard, with the others, the slur, the sugar, the pulse in the voice, and had known, without deciding or judging, that it was right; and been dazzled too.

People turned wherever she went (although not anticipating a scene, as they did at Blanton's that morning), because she had the large, separated breasts of a woman who had spent hours leaning over her knees, working or praying; breasts that would be tipped with wide, copper-colored nipples; breasts that would not be moored; made for the mouths of children, not of men. In all her finery (off-the-shoulders gown, single strand of small pearls, the eternally just-budded rose), her flesh and the heavy-boned grace of her body alone had any palpable reality. There was a breath-catching mobility to her—nothing fragile or well bred, but that extraordinary power of physicality which is occasionally poured into a body. The deep presence of fecundity was about her like an aroma, something mindless and alive; that touch of moist heaviness (suggestive of savagery, even when swathed in lace) which is darkly, enigmatically female. She was a woman

71

who looked most graceful when her legs were slightly parted, who appeared to move blindly, obediently, from some source of voluptuous energy in her pelvis; whose thighs shivered in brute, incomplete expression of the pure urge inside her.

Edgar did not indicate by even the quaver of a note that the excitement and apprehension in the rest of the room had reached him. He played on, as if in another dimension of time, when she took a seat not ten feet from him, the spaniel squatting in her lap, wet nose over the edge of the table, eyes large. Neither did she look, but went about settling herself, nodding to acquaintences, chatting with her companions. She was arrogantly drunk, opulently sensual as only a woman in the candor of dissipation can be; and beside her Edgar looked pale, delicate, even curiously effeminate. She had always been strangely respectful of him, even when swarms of white men had fidgeted at her elbow, pleading to fasten her bracelets, even when easy money had turned her life hectic and privileged; she had looked at him, even then, with a tawny, resentful respect, like a commoner with a sickly prince.

Now she was drinking heavily out of a silver-headed, leather-jacketed pocket flask; her eyes grown flashing and wet. The spaniel lay on her thighs, subdued, and she poked and patted and cooed to him loudly, as if trying to goad him into a bewildered bark.

Edgar finished his chorus and gave it to Cleo on the piano, who never soloed, for whom the dreadful spaces of thirty-four open bars held no terrors, but small interest either; and then he slowly turned his back on her, a dreamy, witless grin weakening his face as he muttered nonsense with the drummer.

His absolute lack of recognition in these first moments was the surest sign to Geordie that he was electrically aware of her movements there in the room. Something in him was indestructible, some merciless pride with which he chose to victimize himself. Only he could smash or break it. Some said, after all, that he had gotten her on the morphine habit she threw only when, at the height of her glittering success, she had begun to miss engagements and ruin tunes; other rumors went that love between them had been a stunted, hot-house pantomime, always lurching on the shadowy edges of sensation—as queer and deformed as Edgar himself.

She began to chatter with vicious affectation when he took his reed into his mouth like a thumb and blew a windy yawp—trapped into the chatter as into everything else, because his placid, punishing indifference (not only to her but to all the real world) was yet another symbol of some incalculable superiority. Her mouth, as it snarled and quivered, was indescribably, cruelly sensual, as though she was about to faint from some morbid and exhilarating thought. But only her mouth had learned the tricks of contempt, brittleness and sophistication. Her eyes glowed steadily with something else, and as Walden looked at her, in these first moments that seemed supercharged with tension and thus unendurably long, he saw (as this morning he seemed fated to see everything that had been under his nose for years) the nature of that something else—saw that her long, shapely neck had started to wrinkle, that she had expensive powder in her armpits where there should have been soft, dark hair—and knew there was a flaw now where there had been none before, a flaw developed by a life that had carved a black cross on her forehead; and then sensed again the woman in her flesh, now gone slightly stale, and remembered that some said even the dog had licked it.

Edgar chose this moment to blow sweet, as a final passionless mockery of the auspiciousness of sentiment others might be feeling in that situation. His sound was disarmingly feeble, earnest, but meant to prove, by some inmost private irony, that he was, if so he chose, a timeless man. The limpid pathos of his song was somehow a denial of the past, a denial of any power over him but his peculiar self-abusive ability; and at that moment, just as Geordie's eyes drifted across and away from him, the saxophone, hanging limp against one thigh, stirred and came up, and there was for just that second a corresponding stir of vigor in his sound; and then he fell back into the vapid, thin tone, his horn descending, as if to say—and Walden heard—that he would be a slave to nothing, not even the genius inside him. His obsession was his last secret, the note he carefully never blew.

To Walden, he seemed a mask over a mask, all encrusted in an armored soul. Some said that Geordie had once stripped the masks away, one by one, with no

73

intent but desire, had had a hint of the inside, and had been driven wanton out of helplessness. The secret must have been (as it most always is) that his need was formless, general—a need which persists only because no satifaction can ever be fashioned for it; an inconceivable thing to a woman, a thing forever mysterious and infuriating to her; something peculiarly male, the final emblem of imperfection, impotence, but with a terrifying power to wound or create, the Jeremiah-like power of a fury at powerlessness.

So they were alone in all that room, absolutely locked together and alone, and yet steadfastly refusing to notice each other, and Walden knew that Edgar would blow all night if necessary, burst a lung, dredge himself to obliterate her—and not because he cared; not for her, but because of himself. Already somebody was thinking about how he could possibly describe it to the cats in his group the next night. "Man, it was positively the end!" would prove far too thin, and by the time word of it reached L.A., K.C., Chicago, it would be a kind of underground history, one of those nights that, passed from mouth to mouth, year upon year, become, in the alchemy of gossip, fabulous and Homeric.

Cleo, alone of everyone, refused to be drawn into the drama of their wills, but looked from Edgar to Geordie, not casually or with suspense as the others did, but with an expression of trembling, clear-eyed sorrow, his little hands automatically making the sad chords on which Edgar was shaping his humiliation of sadness, his lips saying softly over and over again: "Oh, man, what for? Oh, man, why? Oh, man, no!" Edgar only wiped a phrase across the words and wiggled his hips.

Walden, too, was struck dumb, all eyes, somehow horrified, for now Geordie's mouth was capped with straining avidity around the neck of the flask, the spaniel staring up at her with baffled dark eyes. Even Edgar watched this over his horn with a half-hidden, secretive sneer. And Walden, at that instant, suddenly thought of him as a Black Angel—something out of the scared, rainy nights of his childhood when his mother had tried to remember the Bible her mother had once, long ago in a bayou town, read to her, and had gotten it all mixed and filled it in herself in a droning, righteous whisper, till Satan carried a razor and Babylon was a place in

74

midnight Georgia, and the fallen angels were black bucks run wild through the county like the city boys in the Cadillac, and even Jehovah wore a Kluxer's sheet, and everyone was forever lost. Edgar was a Black Angel all right, and Walden suddenly knew. For like many people brought up on the Bible like a severe laxative, he often thought, without whimsy, about angels and suchlike. Not that he believed, that wasn't necessary; but sometimes when he played and stared up into a rose spotlight so as to concentrate, he thought about some possible heaven, some decent kind of life—and groped blindly like any man.

If he had better understood himself and the inconsolable ambiguity of men's aspirations, the unforgivable thing he did then might not have stunned him so. But he did not understand, and knew little of the concepts upon which men struggle to define their existence (although down in his heart waited a single note of music that he felt would shatter all discord into harmony), and so when he found himself suddenly beside Edgar, his horn clipped to its swing around his neck, and heard himself break into the pedestrian chorus of *Out of Nowhere* that Edgar was blowing, he was filled with the same sense of terror that had swept over him ten years before, the first time he had stood up before live, ominous drums and cut out a piece for himself. Only it was worse, because there was a complex protocol to "after hours," unwritten, inarticulate, but accepted by even the most beardless tyro with the second-hand horn for which he did not even own a case. There was a protocol, and it did not countenance an uninvited intrusion from the watchers, no matter who. On top of that, Walden (thought of among musicians as a "good, cool tenor," reliable, with sweet ideas and a feel for riffs, but one who had not yet found his way) was presuming upon Edgar Pool, revered from a distance by everyone who came later and blew more, whose eccentricities were accorded the tolerance due to anyone embittered by neglect, and whose lonely eminence as "the Horn" was beyond challenge, a matter of sentimental history. What Walden did, then, was unheard of.

But he started the next twelve bars nevertheless, keeping a simple tasty line. Edgar, reed still between loose lips, gave him a startled, then slyly amused glance, telling Walden, all in a flash, that for the audacity and the stupidity of the move he would do him the honor of "cutting" him to pieces, bar to bar, horn to horn. But the affront had shocked everyone else; the room was frozen, speechless; and Walden knew he was, in effect, saying to them: "I secede from the protocol, the law," and further (and this he did not know, though it was the truth of what he felt): "What I know must be done cannot be done within all that." But thereby he was placing himself outside their mercy and their judgment, in a no man's land, where he must go alone. Only Geordie was not transfixed; a slow, quivering smile had curled her lips, and her fingers had left the spaniel's ears.

Edgar leaped back easily, satirizing Walden's last idea, playing it three different ways, getting a laugh, horn hung casually out of one side of his mouth. The drums slammed in perfectly on top of Cleo's remonstrative chord, and Walden started to swing one shoulder, playing sweet when it was his turn, knowing they would take only six-bar breaks from then on, to tighten the time, and finally only three, when a man had to make himself clear and be concise; the last gauntlet when a misfingered note could be the end.

Edgar slouched there beside him, as if playing with one hand, yawping, honking, aping him; and only his beady eyes were alive, and they were sharp, black points of irony and rage. Walden looked into those eyes, and blew a moving phrase that once another Edgar might have blown, and was, at last, victim of the naïve core of his heart, the un-thought-out belief that it mustn't be Edgar's way. He looked at Edgar, loving him even in all his savage, smearing mockery, battling not him but the dark side of the Black-Angel soul; bringing light.

It got hotter, tighter, and Cleo, staring at Walden as at a barefoot man exulting on a street corner, laid down solid, uncritical chords for both of them, that it might be fair and just—all the time his innocent, dewy eyes on the side of sweetness, whoever would speak up for it.

Walden looked at Edgar, sweating now and gloomily intent, and blew four bars of ringing melody, so compelling that Edgar stumbled taking off, unable to recall himself (for "cutting" was, after all, only the Indian wrestling of lost boyhood summers, and the trick was getting your man off balance). And then Walden came back clear, and knew (now so beyond doubt, he almost

76

faltered) that his was the warmer tone, that this was what he had always meant; and so experienced a moment of incredible, hair-breadth joy.

The silence in the room came apart, because music was fair contest. The crowd unwillingly shifted the center of their prejudices, and between phrases Walden could hear Geordie crying sharply, "Blow! Blow!" but, looking out, found her rocking back and forth, her eyes narrowed now to bright wicks, and could not tell at whom she cried, and did not, he realized, consider himself her champion; but was only bringing light.

Edgar was shuffling forward, and blew four bars of a demented cackle, and for an instant they were almost shoulder to shoulder, horn to horn, in the terrible equality of art, pouring into each wild break (it felt) the substance of their separated lives—crazy, profound Americans, both! For America, as only they knew it who had wandered like furtive minnesingers across its billboard wastes to the screaming distances, turned half a man sour, hard-bitten, barren, but awakened a grieving hunger in his heart thereby.

America had laid its hand on both of them. In Edgar's furious, scornful bleat sounded the moronic horn of every merciless Cadillac shrieking down the highway with a wet-mouthed, giggling boy at the wheel, turning the American prairie into a graveyard of rusting chrome junk; the idiot-snarl that filled the jails and madhouses and legislatures; some final dead-wall impact. And in Walden, no sky-assaulter but open-eyed, there was the equally crazy naïvete that can create a new, staggering notion of human life and drive some faulty man before it through the cities, to plant an evangelist on every atheist Times Square, a visionary in any godless roadhouse; the impulse that makes cranks and poets and bargain-drivers; that put up a town at the end of every unlikely road, and then sent someone with foolish curiosity to see what was there.

This time Walden had the last chorus to himself, having earned it. By that same unspoken protocol, it was understood by everyone that he had "cut," and so Edgar stepped back—for though the victor might venture outside the law, the victim, having nothing left, must abide by it. And Edgar accepted. The crowd was on its feet when the drums signified by a final, ecstatic slam that

77

it was over, Geordie standing too, but in all the shouting and heated laughter there, she alone was motionless, grave.

Walden's moment of joy had gone off somewhere, and he felt a chill of apprehension, and swung on Edgar, one hand extended vaguely as if to right himself. But Edgar, unsnapping his horn, only glanced at him once— a withering, haunted look, a look he had probably never shown anyone before, leveled now at Walden, without malice, only as a sort of grisly tribute to his prowess and his belief. It was to be Walden's spoils: that bewildered stare in the eyes of another man, whose effort, even to punish himself out of pride, had been thwarted. It was a look which had a future, from which heavy, fatal consequences must proceed; and with it went a weak, lemonade grin, meant only to cover the wince of nausea; for Walden knew then that Edgar had horrified himself, like a drunk who sees, in the single, focused moment of hangover, the twitching, blotchy ruin of his own face, the shadow across the eyes—knowing all along that the horror will not fight down the thirst.

At that, Edgar turned, taking his horn and case, and limped away, pausing only at Geordie, not to touch her, but merely to peer at her for an instant, mutter something almost without moving those stony lips, and disappear into the crowd, making for the exit. Walden's hand still lay, half-spread, on the air.

Then Cleo was at his elbow, staring past him after Edgar, eyes moist with alarm, voice choked with shock as he exclaimed in an undertone, "Catch him before he dies! Catch him!" And he, too, ran away, still on the side of sweetness, knowing where it lay, looking neither to right nor left.

So Walden stood there alone in the light, isolated in his achievement, and by it, breathless and transformed, the way a man feels who has, on an impulse coming up from far down in his soul, totally altered his life all in a moment, and then looks up, stunned, to discover himself in a new moral position to everything around him. And in that dazzling isolation, only Geordie approached him, coming so close her fragrance swirled thickly through his head, and he saw that she was exhausted, sobered, and somehow resigned.

For just a second they were caught in an odd, impersonal affinity, and in that second, she whispered, "Don't worry. Don't you worry now. You know what he said to me? He only said, 'He sounded good.' Just that. Don't you worry now, honey."

She gave him a last wan, forgiving half-smile just as her escorts hurried up, one of them snuggling the sleepy spaniel, and Walden knew, for all the smile and for all the words, that she was worried nevertheless. But she turned and glided away then, leaving him standing there by himself, while people he had known for years clustered and exclaimed around him as though he was a notorious stranger, and he held his head up manfully under their praises . . .

Sitting on his bed, now, it all came back with blinding clarity between gulps of coffee; all of a piece, all in an instant, undamaged by sleep. He got up, shivering with the memory, to pour himself the second cup, and to realize, with dumb acceptance, that this was to be the first afternoon of his life.

He had brought the light all right, but the conflicts in a man's nature were not to be resolved by light alone. Edgar had fled in disgust and despair at what it had revealed, fled from the light because it was not for him any more. Walden was frozen, even now, hours later, by the power one man had over another; it sickened something trusting in him, even though he could not disbelieve the clear impulse that had prodded him to stand up. But the consequences of an action were endless, and he could not see the end of this particular one. He had taken a stand for once, and as he had discovered about his tone, so he had, for once and all, damned himself to going his way.

Then he knew that at some time, perhaps in the cramped second-sax chair of one of those tireless, all-but-forgotten road bands of the mythical past, this awful moment of human commitment must have been pushed up to Edgar too, and without thought or hesitation, Edgar had leapt in, cutting his road alone, and had blown, as himself, for the first time, and started, by finally tapping his sources and letting his sound out, toward that morning and Walden. That was the only secret, and Walden wondered, with all the astonishment of a new idea, what his end would be.

From now on, he realized as he stood before the bed,

79

suddenly amazed by his nakedness, there would be dreams through the mornings when he alone slept in the busy world, and all the irritations and responsibilities of age and work when he awoke. The armistice with sleep and discord had been forever broken. From now on he had to fight for his life and his vision, like every man.

At that, the quiet loneliness of self-knowledge descended over him like a prophetic hint of the shroud toward which all lives irrevocably progress. And pulling on his shorts, he remembered what Cleo had said just that morning.

"Catch him before he dies!"

And wondered if that was to be part of it, too. But putting the wondering aside for then, he set himself to dressing methodically. This was his first day in a strange, lonesome country, and one part of that, anyway, was knowing it could not be postponed any longer.

Tony Scott is representative of a new kind of jazzman. An acknowledged master of his chosen instrument, the clarinet, he is also a gifted photographer and a writer of rare sensitivity. His ear for language is impeccable; it springs from his understanding of jazz and love of its people. In the following short story, published here for the first time, Tony captures the final impact of Charlie Parker on a jazz follower, with a twist as darkly ironic as Bird's entire life.

(Printed by permission of the author.)

DESTINATION K. C.

by Tony Scott

"ONE NIGHT I went down to catch him at the Open Door and he didn't show. I heard he made it later, but I had to cut so's I could get up in time for my gig . . . man, can't you just feature me comin' in late to this gig? Sheeit, Mr. Railway Express himself would swoop down on me . . . this gig is dragging my butt. I'd like to take up a horn and learn to blow, man, all them fine chicks be chasin' me, all the cats be wantin' to buy me drinks, I'd stay high, hot damn, what a life . . . sleep everyday till

80

you feel like gettin' up, finish the gig at Birdland and go on up to an afterhour spot till squares like us is takin' off to make our daily bread with the daily news planted under our arms . . . no wonder musicians call us squares.

"If I could hit the numbers one time, just one time, I'd take off from this slave an' cop me a tenor sax an' take a few lessons an' learn one note real good an' make record dates with some funky rhythm an' blues outfit just to get some experience an' after that I'd get me a gig in Brooklyn so's no one would recognize me, 'cause when I hit the jazz scene ev'rybody be sayin' you heard that new cat wailin', he's crowdin' Bird. Sheeit . . . another time I went down to Birdland to catch him with strings an' he doesn't show up so Diz played with Bird's group and sounded the end . . . I waited till next set an' still no Bird, so I cut out. Man, was I drug.

"If I could blow me a horn I'd show up on the gig all the time, man, that's be kicks, just blowin' all the time . . . no worries, no boss watchin' over you . . . sheeit, record companies after you all the time, get your name in the Downbeat, playin' with JATP all over the world, man, how could you ever get drug. Them cats ballin' all the time an' I'm hung up down here workin' for Railway Express pushin' around ev'rything from a live snake to this coffin with some cat who's headin' for Kansas City.

"Sheeit, man, this cat shouldna' waited till he died before he went to Kansas City. What a jump town, I don't mean *now*, 'bout twenty years ago when Basie was at the Reno an' the cats used to blow all night an' day. Sheeit . . . that's where Bird came from, an' Pres, man, what a ball that musta' been; that musta been sumpin' else, blowin', ballin', an' booze, the three B's—"

"Hey, Spody, give me a hand with this coffin."

"Yeah, Joe, gotcha covered . . . you got to watch you mouth when you goin' south."

"Whadja say, Spody?"

"Nothin' man, just a little sayin' rhyme I picked up when I was young . . . real young . . . as I was sayin', that made two times I went to catch Bird an' he didn't show, so I'm pretty drug now 'cause I'm spendin' my hard-earned geets an' ain't catchin' my man in action, so three weeks ago I dug Bird comin' out'a Birdland an' I see the sign says Bird, Max, Mingus, Bud an' Blakey are cookin' together, so I follow Bird into the bar next door

81

and told him how I was drug 'cause he didn't show two times I was down to catch him and he apologized an' said for me to wait and he'd take me in with him. I wouldn't have said nothin' did I know he was goin' to die. Man, that drug me."

"Watch the end, lift it up a little higher . . . straight up, baby."

"So Bird says 'What kinda gig you got?' . . . so I told him . . . I'm down the Railway Express, an' he says, 'I'll be down to see you one day,' so I told him, man, what would you be doin' down at the Railway Express an' he says, 'I got friends ev'rywhere,' so I told him, Bird, anytime you come by, I'll take care of you."

"Easy does it, my man, lift up on your end real easy . . . that's it, my man, now slide it in, easy, easy . . . that's got it."

"But he never did show . . . you know, I had a feelin' he meant it . . . I was waitin' for him . . . he'll never show no more, he died a week after I saw him, worn out and tired at thirty-four . . . but the way he said it, I believed him. I don't know, I can't believe he's gone, nobody knew he was that tired, but man, a cat can only fight so long . . . he laid down a strong message . . . you know, I bet Bird woulda made it down to see me if he didn't die . . ."

"Let's go, Spody, you're treatin' this crate like a newborn babe. This guy is dead as a doornail."

"I know, Joe, but *this* cat is goin' back home to Kansas City and he deserves some special treatment, 'cause them Kansas City cats are liable to find out that we don't treat 'em right up here in New York and not send nobody up here no more; so take your time while I fix my man up here real comfortable like . . . solid. Ride easy, my man, you'll be home soon."

"Finished, Spody?"

"Yeah, Joe. Here comes Red with the check sheet . . . I'll see you later."

• • • • •

"Hey, Red, I'm checkin' in this coffin."

"O.K., Joe. How's Spody doin'?"

"He's O.K., but all he talks about is his friend, Bert he calls him, since this coffin came in. He died a couple weeks ago."

"Was he a close friend?"

"Naw, but he was very famous, one of those hotjive musicians."

"My kids musta heard him, they're crazy about that stuff. Give me a check on this loading clip."

"O.K. . . ."

"Destination: Brown's Funeral Home, 107 Van Dorn Street, Kansas City, Missouri . . ."

"Check."

"Contents . . . Charles Parker."

"Check."

James Baldwin is a young American novelist of stature. His superb short story, Sonny's Blues, *illuminates the constant problem of the outsider trying to comprehend a member of an alien world. In this story of brothers apart, perhaps the moral is: in order to understand a man, you have to know where he's been, where he is, where he's going . . . and why.*

(From Partisan Review, *Vol. XXIV, No. 3, Summer 1957. © 1957 by James Baldwin.)*

SONNY'S BLUES
by James Baldwin

I READ about it in the paper, in the subway, on my way to work. I read it, and I couldn't believe it, and I read it again. Then perhaps I just stared at it, at the newsprint spelling out his name, spelling out the story. I stared at it in the swinging lights of the subway car, and in the faces and bodies of the people, and in my own face, trapped in the darkness which roared outside.

It was not to be believed, and I kept telling myself that as I walked from the subway station to the high school. And at the same time I couldn't doubt it. I was scared, scared for Sonny. He became real to me again. A great block of ice got settled in my belly, and kept melting there slowly all day long, while I taught my classes algebra. It was a special kind of ice. It kept melting, sending trickles of ice water all up and down my veins, but it never got less. Sometimes it hardened and seemed to

83

expand until I felt my guts were going to come spilling out or that I was going to choke or scream. This would always be at a moment when I was remembering some specific thing Sonny had once said or done.

When he was about as old as the boys in my classes his face had been bright and open, there was a lot of copper in it; and he'd had wonderfully direct brown eyes, and great gentleness and privacy. I wondered what he looked like now. He had been picked up, the evening before, in a raid on an apartment downtown, for peddling and using heroin.

I couldn't believe it: but what I mean by that is that I couldn't find any room for it anywhere inside me. I had kept it outside me for a long time. I hadn't wanted to know. I had had suspicions, but I didn't name them, I kept putting them away. I told myself that Sonny was wild, but he wasn't crazy. And he'd always been a good boy, he hadn't ever turned hard or evil or disrespectful, the way kids can, so quick, so quick, especially in Harlem. I didn't want to believe that I'd ever see my brother going down, coming to nothing, all that light in his face gone out, in the condition I'd already seen so many others. Yet it had happened and here I was, talking about algebra to a lot of boys who might, every one of them for all I knew, be popping off needles every time they went to the head. Maybe it did more for them than algebra could.

I was sure that the first time Sonny had ever had horse, he couldn't have been much older than these boys were now. These boys, now, were living as we'd been living then; they were growing up with a rush and their heads bumped abruptly against the low ceiling of their actual possibilities. They were filled with rage. All they really knew were two darknesses, the darkness of their lives, which was now closing in on them, and the darkness of the movies, which had blinded them to that other darkness, and in which they now, vindictively, dreamed, at once more together than they were at any other time, and more alone.

When the last bell rang, the last class ended, I let out my breath. It seemed I'd been holding it for all that time. My clothes were wet—I may have looked as though I'd been sitting in a steam bath, all dressed up, all afternoon. I sat alone in the classroom a long time. I listened to the

84

boys outside, downstairs, shouting and cursing and laughing. Their laughter struck me for perhaps the first time. It was not the joyous laughter which—God knows why —one associates with children. It was mocking and insular, its intent was to denigrate. It was disenchanted, and in this, also, lay the authority of their curses. Perhaps I was listening to them because I was thinking about my brother and in them I heard my brother. And myself.

One boy was whistling a tune, at once very complicated and very simple, it seemed to be pouring out of him as though he were a bird, and it sounded very cool and moving through all that harsh, bright air, only just holding its own through all those other sounds.

I stood up and walked over to the window and looked down into the courtyard. It was the beginning of the spring and the sap was rising in the boys. A teacher passed through them every now and again, quickly, as though he or she couldn't wait to get out of that courtyard, to get those boys out of their sight and off their minds. I started collecting my stuff. I thought I'd better get home and talk to Isabel.

The courtyard was almost deserted by the time I got downstairs. I saw this boy standing in the shadow of a doorway, looking just like Sonny. I almost called his name. Then I saw that it wasn't Sonny, but somebody we used to know, a boy from around our block. He'd been Sonny's friend. He'd never been mine, having been too young for me, and, anyway, I'd never liked him. And now, even though he was a grown-up man, he still hung around that block, still spent hours on the street corner, was always high and raggy. I used to run into him from time to time and he'd often work around to asking me for a quarter or fifty cents. He always had some real good excuse, too, and I always gave it to him, I don't know why.

But now, abruptly, I hated him. I couldn't stand the way he looked at me, partly like a dog, partly like a cunning child. I wanted to ask him what the hell he was doing in the school courtyard.

He sort of shuffled over to me, and he said, "I see you got the papers. So you already know about it."

"You mean about Sonny? Yes, I already know about it. How come they didn't get you?"

He grinned. It made him repulsive and it also brought
85

to mind what he'd looked like as a kid. "I wasn't there. I stay away from them people."

"Good for you." I offered him a cigarette and I watched him through the smoke. "You come all the way down here just to tell me about Sonny?"

"That's right." He was sort of shaking his head and his eyes looked strange, as though they were about to cross. The bright sun deadened his damp dark-brown skin and it make his eyes look yellow and showed up the dirt in his conked hair. He smelled funky. I moved a little away from him and I said, "Well, thanks, but I already know about it and I got to get home."

"I'll walk you a little ways," he said. We started walking. There were a couple of kids still loitering in the courtyard and one of them said good night to me and looked strangely at the boy beside me.

"What're you going to do?" he asked me. "I mean, about Sonny?"

"Look, I haven't seen Sonny for over a year. I'm not sure I'm going to do anything. Anyway, what the hell can I do?"

"That's right," he said quickly, "ain't nothing you can do. Can't much help old Sonny no more, I guess."

It was what I was thinking and so it seemed to me he had no right to say it.

"I'm surprised at Sonny, though," he went on—he had a funny way of talking, he looked straight ahead as though he were talking to himself—"I thought Sonny was a smart boy, I thought he was too smart to get hung."

"I guess he thought so too," I said sharply, "and that's how he got hung. And how about you? You're pretty goddamn smart, I bet."

Then he looked directly at me, just for a minute. "I ain't smart," he said. "If I was smart, I'd have reached for a pistol a long time ago."

"Look. Don't tell me your sad story, if it was up to me, I'd give you one." Then I felt guilty—guilty, probably, for never having supposed that the poor bastard had a story of his own, much less a sad one, and I asked, quickly, "What's going to happen to him now?"

He didn't answer this. He was off by himself some place. "Funny thing," he said, and from his tone we might have been discussing the quickest way to get to Brooklyn, "when I saw the papers this morning, the first thing I asked myself was if I had anything to do with it. I felt sort of responsible."

I began to listen more carefully. The subway station was on the corner, just before us, and I stopped. He stopped, too. We were in front of a bar and he ducked slightly, peering in, but whoever he was looking for didn't seem to be there. The juke box was blasting away with something black and bouncy and I half watched the barmaid as she danced her way from the juke box to her place behind the bar. And I watched her face as she laughingly responded to something someone said to her, still keeping time to the music. When she smiled one saw the little girl, one sensed the doomed, still-struggling woman beneath the battered face of the semi-whore.

"I never give Sonny nothing," the boy said finally, "but a long time ago I come to school high and Sonny asked me how it felt." He paused, I couldn't bear to watch him; I watched the barmaid, and I listened to the music which seemed to be causing the pavement to shake. "I told him it felt great." The music stopped, the barmaid paused and watched the juke box until the music began again. "It did."

All this was carrying me some place I didn't want to go. I certainly didn't want to know how it felt. It filled everything, the people, the houses, the music, the dark, quicksilver barmaid, with menace; and this menace was their reality.

"What's going to happen to him now?" I asked again.

"They'll send him away some place and they'll try to cure him." He shook his head. "Maybe he'll even think he's kicked the habit. Then they'll let him loose"—he gestured, throwing his cigarette into the gutter. "That's all."

"What do you mean, 'that's all'?"

But I knew what he meant.

"I mean, that's all." He turned his head and looked at me, pulling down the corners of his mouth. "Don't you know what I mean?" he asked, softly.

"How the hell would I know what you mean?" I almost whispered it, I don't know why.

"That's right," he said to the air, "how would he know what I mean?" He turned toward me again, patient and calm, and yet I somehow felt him shaking, shaking as though he were going to fall apart. I felt that ice in my guts again, the dread I'd felt all afternoon; and again I watched the barmaid, moving about the bar, washing glasses, singing. "Listen. They'll let him out and then it'll just start all over again. That's what I mean."

"You mean—they'll let him out. And then he'll just start working his way back in again. You mean he'll never kick the habit. Is that what you mean?"

"That's right," he said cheerfully. "You see what I mean."

"Tell me," I said at last, "why does he want to die? He must want to die, he's killing himself, why does he want to die?"

He looked at me in surprise. He licked his lips. "He don't want to die. He wants to live. Don't nobody want to die, ever."

Then I wanted to ask him—too many things. He could not have answered, or if he had, I could not have borne the answers. I started walking. "Well, I guess it's none of my business."

"It's going to be rough on old Sonny," he said. We reached the subway station. "This is your station?" he asked. I nodded. I took one step down. "Damn!" he said, suddenly. I looked up at him. He grinned again. "Damn, if I didn't leave all my money home. You ain't got a dollar on you, have you? Just for a couple of days, is all."

All at once something inside gave and threatened to come pouring out of me. I didn't hate him any more. I felt that in another moment I'd start crying like a child.

"Sure," I said. "Don't sweat." I looked in my wallet and didn't have a dollar; I only had a five. "Here," I said. "That hold you?"

He didn't look at it—he didn't want to look at it. A terrible, closed look came over his face, as though he were keeping the number on the bill a secret from him and me. "Thanks," he said, and now he was dying to see me go. "Don't worry about Sonny. Maybe I'll write him or something."

"Sure," I said. "You do that. So long."

"Be seeing you," he said. I went on down the steps.

And I didn't write Sonny or send him anything for a long time. When I finally did, it was just after my little girl died, he wrote me back a letter which made me feel like a bastard.

Here's what he said:

Dear brother,

You don't know how much I needed to hear from you. I wanted to write you many a time but I dug how much I must have hurt you and so I didn't write. But now I feel like a man who's been trying to climb out of some deep, real deep and funky hole and just saw the sun up there, outside. I got to get outside.

I can't tell you much about how I got here. I mean I don't know how to tell you. I guess I was afraid of something or I was trying to escape from something and you know I have never been very strong in the head (smile). I'm glad Mama and Daddy are dead and can't see what's happened to their son and I swear if I'd known what I was doing I would never have hurt you so, you and a lot of other fine people who were nice to me and who believed in me.

I don't want you to think it had anything to do with me being a musician. It's more than that. Or maybe less than that. I can't get anything straight in my head down here and I try not to think about what's going to happen to me when I get outside again. Sometime I think I'm going to flip and never get outside and sometime I think I'll come straight back. I tell you one thing, though, I'd rather blow my brains out than go through this again. But that's what they all say, so they tell me. If I tell you when I'm coming to New York and if you could meet me, I sure would appreciate it. Give my love to Isabel and the kids and I was sure sorry to hear about little Gracie. I wish I could be like Mama and say the Lord's will be done, but I don't know it seems to me that trouble is the one thing that never does get stopped and I don't know what good it does to blame it on the Lord. But maybe it does some good if you believe it.

Your brother, Sonny

Then I kept in constant touch with him and I sent him whatever I could and I went to meet him when he came back to New York. When I saw him many things I thought I had forgotten came flooding back to me. This was because I had begun, finally, to wonder about Sonny, about the life that Sonny lived inside. This life, whatever it was, had made him older and thinner and it had deepened the distant stillness in which he had always moved. He looked very unlike my baby brother. Yet, when he

89

smiled, when we shook hands, the baby brother I'd never known looked out from the depths of his private life, like an animal waiting to be coaxed into the light.

"How you been keeping?" he asked me.

"All right. And you?"

"Just fine." He was smiling all over his face. "It's good to see you again."

"It's good to see you."

The seven years' difference in our ages lay between us like a chasm: I wondered if these years would ever operate between us as a bridge. I was remembering, and it made it hard to catch my breath, that I had been there when he was born; and I had heard the first words he had ever spoken. When he started to walk, he walked from our mother straight to me. I caught him just before he fell when he took the first steps he ever took in this world.

"How's Isabel?"

"Just fine. She's dying to see you."

"And the boys?"

"They're fine, too. They're anxious to see their uncle."

"Oh, come on. You know they don't remember me."

"Are you kidding? Of course they remember you."

He grinned again. We got into a taxi. We had a lot to say to each other, far too much to know how to begin.

As the taxi began to move, I asked, "You still want to go to India?"

He laughed. "You still remember that. Hell, no. This place is Indian enough for me."

"It used to belong to them," I said.

And he laughed again. "They damn sure knew what they were doing when they got rid of it."

Years ago, when he was around fourteen, he'd been all hipped on the idea of going to India. He read books about people sitting on rocks, naked, in all kinds of weather, but mostly bad, naturally, and walking barefoot through hot coals and arriving at wisdom. I used to say that it sounded to me as though they were getting away from wisdom as fast as they could. I think he sort of looked down on me for that.

"Do you mind," he asked, "if we have the driver drive alongside the park? On the west side—I haven't seen the city in so long."

"Of course not," I said. I was afraid that I might sound

90

as though I were humoring him, but I hoped he wouldn't take it that way.

So we drove along, between the green of the park and the stony, lifeless elegance of hotels and apartment buildings, toward the vivid, killing streets of our childhood. These streets hadn't changed, though housing projects jutted up out of them now like rocks in the middle of a boiling sea. Most of the houses in which we had grown up had vanished, as had the stores from which we had stolen, the basements in which we had first tried sex, the rooftops from which we had hurled tin cans and bricks. But houses exactly like the houses of our past yet dominated the landscape, boys exactly like the boys we once had been found themselves smothering in these houses, came down into the streets for light and air and found themselves encircled by disaster. Some escaped the trap, most didn't. Those who got out always left something of themselves behind, as some animals amputate a leg and leave it in the trap. It might be said, perhaps, that I had escaped; after all, I was a school teacher. Or that Sonny had, he hadn't lived in Harlem for years. Yet, as the cab moved uptown through streets which seemed, with a rush, to darken with dark people, and as I covertly studied Sonny's face, it came to me that what we both were seeking through our separate cab windows was that part of ourselves which had been left behind. It's always at the hour of trouble and confrontation that the missing member aches.

We hit 110th Street and started rolling up Lenox Avenue. And I'd known this avenue all my life, but it seemed to me again, as it had seemed on the day I'd first heard about Sonny's trouble, filled with a hidden menace which was its very breath of life.

"We almost there," said Sonny.

"Almost." We were both too nervous to say anything more.

We live in a housing project. It hasn't been up long. A few days after it was up it seemed uninhabitably new; now, of course, it's already run-down. It looks like a parody of the good, clean, faceless life—God knows the people who live in it do their best to make it a parody. The beat-looking grass lying around isn't enough to make their lives green, the hedges will never hold out the streets, and they know it. The big windows fool no one;

91

they aren't big enough to make space out of no space. They don't bother with the windows, they watch the TV screen instead. The playground is most popular with the children who don't play at jacks, or skip rope, or roller skate, or swing, and they can be found in it after dark. We moved in partly because it's not too far from where I teach, and partly for the kids; but it's really just like the houses in which Sonny and I grew up. The same things happen, they'll have the same things to remember. The moment Sonny and I started into the house I had the feeling that I was simply bringing him back into the danger he had almost died trying to escape.

Sonny had never been talkative. So I don't know why I was sure he'd be dying to talk to me when supper was over the first night. Everything went fine, the oldest boy remembered him, and the youngest boy liked him, and Sonny had remembered to bring something for each of them; and Isabel, who is really much nicer than I am, more open and giving, had gone to a lot of trouble about dinner and was genuinely glad to see him. And she's always been able to tease Sonny in a way that I haven't. It was nice to see her face so vivid again and to hear her laugh and watch her make Sonny laugh. She wasn't, or, anyway, she didn't seem to be, at all uneasy or embarrassed. She chatted as though there were no subject which had to be avoided and she got Sonny past his first, faint stiffness. And thank God she was there, for I was filled with that icy dread again. Everything I did seemed awkward to me, and everything I said sounded freighted with hidden meaning. I was trying to remember everything I'd heard about dope addiction and I couldn't help watching Sonny for signs. I wasn't doing it out of malice. I was trying to find out something about my brother. I was dying to hear him tell me he was safe.

"Safe!" my father grunted, whenever Mama suggested trying to move to a neighborhood which might be safer for children. "Safe, hell! Ain't no place safe for kids, nor nobody."

He always went on like this, but he wasn't ever really as bad as he sounded; not even on weekends, when he got drunk. As a matter of fact, he was always on the lookout for "something a little better," but he died before he found it. He died suddenly, during a drunken week end in the middle of the war, when Sonny was fifteen. He and Sonny hadn't ever got on too well. And this was partly because Sonny was the apple of his father's eye. It was because he loved Sonny so much and was frightened for him that he was always fighting with him. It doesn't do any good to fight with Sonny. Sonny just moves back, inside himself, where he can't be reached. But the principal reason that they never hit it off is that they were so much alike. Daddy was big and rough and loud-talking, just the opposite of Sonny, but they both had—that same privacy.

Mama tried to tell me something about this, just after Daddy died. I was home on leave from the Army.

This was the last time I ever saw my mother alive. Just the same, this picture gets all mixed up in my mind with pictures I had of her when she was younger. The way I always see her is the way she used to be on a Sunday afternoon, say, when the old folks were talking after the big Sunday dinner. I always see her wearing pale blue. She'd be sitting on the sofa. And my father would be sitting in the easy chair, not far from her. And the living room would be full of church folks and relatives. There they sit, in chairs all around the living room, and the night is creeping up outside, but nobody knows it yet. You can see the darkness growing against the window-panes and you hear the street noises every now and again, or maybe the jangling beat of a tambourine from one of the churches close by, but it's real quiet in the room. For a moment nobody's talking, but every face looks darkening, like the sky outside. And my mother rocks a little from the waist, and my father's eyes are closed. Everyone is looking at something a child can't see. For a minute they've forgotten the children. Maybe a kid is lying on the rug, half asleep. Maybe somebody's got a kid in his lap and is absent-mindedly stroking the kid's head. Maybe there's a kid, quiet and big-eyed, curled up in a big chair in the corner. The silence, the darkness coming, and the darkness in the faces frightens the child obscurely. He hopes that the hand which strokes his forehead will never stop—will never die. He hopes that there will never come a time when the old folks won't be sitting around the living room, talking about where they've come from, and what they've seen, and what's happened to them and their kinfolk.

93

But something deep and watchful in the child knows that this is bound to end, is already ending. In a moment someone will get up and turn on the light. Then the old folks will remember the children and they won't talk any more that day. And when light fills the room, the child is filled with darkness. He knows that every time this happens he's moved just a little closer to that darkness outside. The darkness outside is what the old folks have been talking about. It's what they've come from. It's what they endure. The child knows that they won't talk any more because if he knows too much about what's happened to them, he'll know too much too soon, about what's going to happen to him.

The last time I talked to my mother, I remember I was restless. I wanted to get out and see Isabel. We weren't married then and we had a lot to straighten out between us.

There Mama sat, in black, by the window. She was humming an old church song—Lord, you brought me from a long ways off. Sonny was out somewhere. Mama kept watching the streets.

"I don't know," she said, "if I'll ever see you again, after you go off from here. But I hope you'll remember the things I tried to teach you."

"Don't talk like that," I said, and smiled. "You'll be here a long time yet."

She smiled, too, but she said nothing. She was quiet for a long time. And I said, "Mama, don't you worry about nothing. I'll be writing all the time, and you be getting the checks . . ."

"I want to talk to you about your brother," she said, suddenly. "If anything happens to me he ain't going to have nobody to look out for him."

"Mama," I said, "ain't nothing going to happen to you or Sonny. Sonny's all right. He's a good boy and he's got good sense."

"It ain't a question of his being a good boy," Mama said, "nor of his having good sense. It ain't only the bad ones, nor yet the dumb ones that gets sucked under." She stopped, looking at me. "Your Daddy once had a brother," she said, and she smiled in a way that made me feel she was in pain. "You didn't never know that, did you?"

"No," I said, "I never knew that," and I watched her face.

"Oh, yes," she said, "your Daddy had a brother." She looked out of the window again. "I know you never saw your Daddy cry. But I did—many a time, through all these years."

I asked her, "What happened to his brother? How come nobody's ever talked about him?"

This was the first time I ever saw my mother look old.

"His brother got killed," she said, "when he was just a little younger than you are now. I knew him. He was a fine boy. He was maybe a little full of the devil, but he didn't mean nobody no harm."

Then she stopped and the room was silent, exactly as it had sometimes been on those Sunday afternoons. Mama kept looking out into the streets.

"He used to have a job in the mill," she said, "and, like all young folks, he just liked to perform on Saturday nights. Saturday nights, him and your father would drift around to different places, go to dances and things like that, or just sit around with people they knew, and your father's brother would sing, he had a fine voice, and play along with himself on his guitar. Well, this particular Saturday night, him and your father was coming home from some place, and they were both a little drunk and there was a moon that night, it was bright like day. Your father's brother was feeling kind of good, and he was whistling to himself, and he had his guitar slung over his shoulder. They was coming down a hill and beneath them was a road that turned off from the highway. Well, your father's brother, being always kind of frisky, decided to run down this hill, and he did, with that guitar banging and clanging behind him, and he ran across the road, and he was making water behind a tree. And your father was sort of amused at him and he was still coming down the hill, kind of slow. Then he heard a car motor and that same minute his brother stepped from behind the tree, into the road, in the moonlight. And he started to cross the road. And your father started to run down the hill, he says he don't know why. This car was full of white men. They was all drunk, and when they seen your father's brother they let out a great whoop and holler and they aimed the car straight at

95

him. They was having fun, they just wanted to scare him, the way they do sometimes, you know. But they was drunk. And I guess the boy, being drunk, too, and scared, kind of lost his head. By the time he jumped it was too late. Your father says he heard his brother scream when the car rolled over him, and he heard the wood of that guitar when it give, and he heard them strings go flying, and he heard them white men shouting, and the car kept on a-going and it ain't stopped till this day. And, time your father got down the hill, his brother weren't nothing but blood and pulp."

Tears were gleaming on my mother's face. There wasn't anything I could say.

"He never mentioned it," she said, "because I never let him mention it before you children. Your Daddy was like a crazy man that night and for many a night thereafter. He says he never in his life seen anything as dark as that road after the lights of that car had gone away. Weren't nothing, weren't nobody on that road, just your Daddy and his brother and that busted guitar. Oh, yes. Your Daddy never did really get right again. Till the day he died he weren't sure but that every white man he saw was the man that killed his brother."

She stopped and took out her handkerchief and dried her eyes and looked at me.

"I ain't telling you all this," she said, "to make you scared or bitter or to make you hate nobody. I'm telling you this because you got a brother. And the world ain't changed."

I guess I didn't want to believe this. I guess she saw this in my face. She turned away from me, toward the window again, searching those streets.

"But I praise my Redeemer," she said at last, "that He called your Daddy home before me. I ain't saying it to throw no flowers at myself, but, I declare, it keeps me from feeling too cast down to know I helped your father get safely through this world. Your father always acted like he was the roughest, strongest man on earth. And everybody took him to be like that. But if he hadn't had me there—to see his tears!"

She was crying again. Still, I couldn't move. I said, "Lord, Lord, Mama, I didn't know it was like that."

"Oh, honey," she said, "there's a lot that you don't know. But you are going to find it out." She stood up

96

from the window and came over to me. "You got to hold on to your brother," she said, "and don't let him fall, no matter what it looks like is happening to him and no matter how evil you gets with him. You going to be evil with him many a time. But don't you forget what I told you, you hear?"

"I won't forget," I said. "Don't you worry, I won't forget. I won't let nothing happen to Sonny."

My mother smiled as though she were amused at something she saw in my face. Then, "You may not be able to stop nothing from happening. But you got to let him know you's there."

Two days later I was married, and then I was gone. And I had a lot of things on my mind and I pretty well forgot my promise to Mama until I got shipped home on a special furlough for her funeral.

And, after the funeral, with just Sonny and me alone in the empty kitchen, I tried to find out something about him.

"What do you want to do?" I asked him.

"I'm going to be a musician," he said.

For he had graduated, in the time I had been away, from dancing to the juke box to finding out who was playing what, and what they were doing with it, and he had bought himself a set of drums.

"You mean, you want to be a drummer?" I somehow had the feeling that being a drummer might be all right for other people but not for my brother Sonny.

"I don't think," he said, looking at me very gravely, "that I'll ever be a good drummer. But I think I can play a piano."

I frowned. I'd never played the role of the older brother quite so seriously before, had scarcely ever, in fact, asked Sonny a damn thing. I sensed myself in the presence of something I didn't really know how to handle, didn't understand. So I made my frown a little deeper as I asked: "What kind of musician do you want to be?"

He grinned. "How many kinds do you think there are?"

"Be serious," I said.

He laughed, throwing his head back, and then looked at me. "I am serious."

"Well, then, for Christ's sake, stop kidding around

and answer a serious question. I mean, do you want to be a concert pianist, you want to play classical music and all that, or—or what?" Long before I finished he was laughing again. "For Christ's sake, Sonny!"

He sobered, but with difficulty. "I'm sorry. But you sound so—scared!" and he was off again.

"Well, you may think it's funny now, baby, but it's not going to be so funny when you have to make your living at it, let me tell you that." I was furious because I knew he was laughing at me and I didn't know why.

"No," he said, very sober now, and afraid, perhaps, that he'd hurt me, "I don't want to be a classical pianist. That isn't what interests me. I mean"—he paused, looking hard at me, as though his eyes would help me to understand, and then gestured helplessly, as though perhaps his hand would help—"I mean, I'll have a lot of studying to do, and I'll have to study everything, but, I mean, I want to play with—jazz musicians." He stopped. "I want to play jazz," he said.

Well, the word had never before sounded as heavy, as real, as it sounded that afternoon in Sonny's mouth. I just looked at him and I was probably frowning a real frown by this time. I simply couldn't see why on earth he'd want to spend his time hanging around night clubs, clowning around on bandstands, while people pushed each other around a dance floor. It seemed—beneath him, somehow. I had never thought about it before, had never been forced to, but I suppose I had always put jazz musicians in a class with what Daddy called "good-time people."

"Are you serious?"

"Hell, yes, I'm serious."

He looked more helpless than ever, and annoyed, and deeply hurt.

I suggested, helpfully: "You mean—like Louis Armstrong?"

His face closed as though I'd struck him. "No. I'm not talking about none of that old-time, down home crap."

"Well, look, Sonny, I'm sorry, don't get mad. I just don't altogether get it, that's all. Name somebody—you know, a jazz musician you admire."

"Bird."

"Who?"

"Bird! Charlie Parker! Don't they teach you nothing in the goddamn Army?"

I lit a cigarette. I was surprised and then a little amused to discover that I was trembling. "I've been out of touch," I said. "You'll have to be patient with me. Now. Who's this Parker character?"

"He's just one of the greatest jazz musicians alive," said Sonny, sullenly, his hands in his pockets, his back to me. "Maybe the greatest," he added, bitterly, "that's probably why you never heard of him."

"All right," I said, "I'm ignorant. I'm sorry. I'll go out and buy all the cat's records right away, all right?"

"It don't," said Sonny, with dignity, "make any difference to me. I don't care what you listen to. Don't do me no favors."

I was beginning to realize that I'd never seen him so upset before. With another part of my mind I was thinking that this would probably turn out to be one of those things kids go through and that I shouldn't make it seem important by pushing it too hard. Still, I didn't think it would do any harm to ask: "Doesn't all this take a lot of time? Can you make a living at it?"

He turned back to me and half leaned, half sat, on the kitchen table. "Everything takes time," he said, "and —well, yes, sure, I can make a living at it. But what I don't seem to be able to make you understand is that it's the only thing I want to do."

"Well, Sonny," I said, gently, "you know people can't always do exactly what they want to do——"

"No, I don't know that," said Sonny, surprising me, "I think people ought to do what they want to do, what else are they alive for?"

"You getting to be a big boy," I said desperately, "it's time you started thinking about your future."

"I'm thinking about my future," said Sonny, grimly. "I think about it all the time."

I gave up. I decided, if he didn't change his mind, that we could always talk about it later. "In the meantime," I said, "you got to finish school." We had already decided that he'd have to move in with Isabel and her folks. I knew this wasn't the ideal arrangement, because Isabel's folks are inclined to be dicty and they hadn't especially wanted Isabel to marry me. But I didn't

99

know what else to do. "And we have to get you fixed up at Isabel's."

There was a long silence. He moved from the kitchen table to the window. "That's a terrible idea. You know it yourself."

"Do you have a better idea?"

He just walked up and down the kitchen for a minute. He was as tall as I was. He had started to shave. I suddenly had the feeling that I didn't know him at all.

He stopped at the kitchen table and picked up my cigarettes. Looking at me with a kind of mocking, amused defiance, he put one between his lips. "You mind?"

"You smoking already?"

He lit the cigarette and nodded, watching me through the smoke. "I just wanted to see if I'd have the courage to smoke in front of you." He grinned and blew a great cloud of smoke to the ceiling. "It was easy." He looked at my face. "Come on, now. I bet you was smoking at my age, tell the truth."

I didn't say anything but the truth was on my face, and he laughed. But now there was something very strained in his laugh. "Sure. And I bet that ain't all you was doing."

He was frightening me a little. "Cut the crap," I said. "We already decided that you was going to go and live at Isabel's. Now what's got into you all of a sudden?"

"You decided it," he pointed out. "I didn't decide nothing." He stopped in front of me, leaning against the stove, arms loosely folded. "Look, brother. I don't want to stay in Harlem no more, I really don't." He was very earnest. He looked at me, then over toward the kitchen window. There was something in his eyes I'd never seen before, some thoughtfulness, some worry all his own. He rubbed the muscle of one arm. "It's time I was getting out of here."

"Where do you want to go, Sonny?"

"I want to join the Army. Or the Navy, I don't care. If I say I'm old enough, they'll believe me."

Then I got mad. It was because I was so scared. "You must be crazy. You goddamn fool, what the hell do you want to go and join the Army for?"

"I just told you. To get out of Harlem."

"Sonny, you haven't even finished school. And if you

100

really want to be a musician, how do you expect to study if you're in the Army?"

He looked at me, trapped, and in anguish. "There's ways. I might be able to work out some kind of deal. Anyway, I'll have the G.I. Bill when I come out."

"If you come out." We stared at each other. "Sonny, please. Be reasonable. I know the setup is far from perfect. But we got to do the best we can."

"I ain't learning nothing in school," he said. "Even when I go." He turned away from me and opened the window and threw his cigarette out into the narrow alley. I watched his back. "At least, I ain't learning nothing you'd want me to learn." He slammed the window so hard I thought the glass would fly out, and turned back to me. "And I'm sick of the stink of these garbage cans!"

"Sonny," I said, "I know how you feel. But if you don't finish school now, you're going to be sorry later that you didn't." I grabbed him by the shoulders. "And you only got another year. It ain't so bad. And I'll come back and I swear I'll help you do whatever you want to do. Just try to put up with it till I come back. Will you please do that? For me?"

He didn't answer and he wouldn't look at me.

"Sonny. You hear me?"

He pulled away. "I hear you. But you never hear anything I say."

I didn't know what to say to that. He looked out of the window and then back at me. "O.K.," he said, and sighed. "I'll try."

Then I said, trying to cheer him up a little, "They got a piano at Isabel's. You can practice on it."

And as a matter of fact, it did cheer him up for a minute. "That's right," he said to himself. "I forgot that." His face relaxed a little. But the worry, the thoughtfulness, played on it still, the way shadows play on a face which is staring into the fire.

But I thought I'd never hear the end of that piano. At first, Isabel would write me, saying how nice it was that Sonny was so serious about his music and how, as soon as he came in from school, or wherever he had been when he was supposed to be at school, he went straight to that piano and stayed there until suppertime. And,

101

after supper, he went back to that piano and stayed there until everybody went to bed. He was at that piano all day Saturday and all day Sunday. Then he bought a record player and started playing records. He'd play one record over and over again, all day long sometimes, and he'd improvise along with it on the piano. Or he'd play one section of the record, one chord, one change, one progression, then he'd do it on the piano. Then back to the record. Then back to the piano.

Well, I really don't know how they stood it. Isabel finally confessed that it wasn't like living with a person at all, it was like living with sound. And the sound didn't make any sense to her, didn't make any sense to any of them—naturally. They began, in a way, to be afflicted by this presence that was living in their home. It was as though Sonny were some sort of god, or monster. He moved in an atmosphere which wasn't like theirs at all. They fed him and he ate, he washed himself, he walked in and out of their door; he certainly wasn't nasty or unpleasant or rude, Sonny isn't any of those things; but it was as though he were all wrapped up in some cloud, some fire, some vision all his own; and there wasn't any way to reach him.

At the same time, he wasn't really a man yet, he was still a child, and they had to watch out for him in all kinds of ways. They certainly couldn't throw him out. Neither did they dare to make a great scene about that piano because even they dimly sensed, as I sensed, from so many thousands of miles away, that Sonny was at that piano playing for his life.

But he hadn't been going to school. One day a letter came from the school board and Isabel's mother got it —there had, apparently, been other letters, but Sonny had torn them up. This day, when Sonny came in, Isabel's mother showed him the letter and asked where he'd been spending his time. And she finally got it out of him that he'd been down in Greenwich Village, with musicians and other characters, in a white girl's apartment. And this scared her and she started to scream at him, and what came up, once she began—though she denies it to this day—was what sacrifices they were making to give Sonny a decent home and how little he appreciated it.

Sonny didn't play the piano that day. By evening, Isabel's mother had calmed down but then there was the
102

old man to deal with, and Isabel herself. Isabel says she did her best to be calm, but she broke down and started crying. She says she just watched Sonny's face. She could tell, by watching him, what was happening with him. And what was happening was that they penetrated his cloud, they had reached him. Even if their fingers had been a thousand times more gentle than human fingers ever are, he could hardly help feeling that they had stripped him naked and were spitting on that nakedness. For he also had to see that his presence, that music, which was life or death to him, had been torture for them and that they had endured it, not at all for his sake, but only for mine. And Sonny couldn't take that. He can take it a little better today than he could then, but he's still not very good at it and, frankly, I don't know anybody who is.

The silence of the next few days must have been louder than the sound of all the music ever played since time began. One morning, before she went to work, Isabel was in his room for something and she suddenly realized that all of his records were gone. And she knew for certain that he was gone. And he was. He went as far as the Navy would carry him. He finally sent me a postcard from some place in Greece, and that was the first I knew that Sonny was still alive. I didn't see him any more until we were both back in New York and the war had long been over.

He was a man by then, of course, but I wasn't willing to see it. He came by the house from time to time, but we fought almost every time we met. I didn't like the way he carried himself, loose and dreamlike all the time, and I didn't like his friends, and his music seemed to be merely an excuse for the life he led. It sounded just that weird and disordered.

Then we had a fight, a pretty awful fight, and I didn't see him for months. By and by I looked him up, where he was living, in a furnished room in the Village, and I tried to make it up. But there were lots of other people in the room and Sonny just lay on his bed, and he wouldn't come downstairs with me, and he treated these other people as though they were his family and I weren't. So I got mad and then he got mad, and then I told him that he might just as well be dead as live the way he was living. Then he stood up and he told me not to worry about him any more in life, that he was dead as far as I was concerned. Then he pushed me to the door and the other people looked on as though nothing were happening, and he slammed the door behind me. I stood in the hallway, staring at the door. I heard somebody laugh in the room and then the tears came to my eyes. I started down the steps, whistling to keep from crying, I kept whistling to myself, You going to need me, baby, one of these cold, rainy days.

I read about Sonny's trouble in the spring. Little Grace died in the fall. She was a beautiful little girl. But she only lived a little over two years. She died of polio and she suffered. She had a slight fever for a couple of days, but it didn't seem like anything and we just kept her in bed. And we would certainly have called the doctor, but the fever dropped, she seemed to be all right. So we thought it had just been a cold. Then, one day, she was up, playing, Isabel was in the kitchen fixing lunch for the two boys when they'd come in from school, and she heard Grace fall down in the living room. When you have a lot of children you don't always start running when one of them falls, unless they start screaming or something. And, this time, Grace was quiet. Yet Isabel says that when she heard the thump and then that silence, something happened in her to make her afraid. And she ran to the living room and there was little Grace on the floor, all twisted up, and the reason she hadn't screamed was that she couldn't get her breath. And when she did scream, it was the worst sound, Isabel says, that she'd ever heard in all her life, and she still hears it sometimes in her dreams. Isabel will sometimes wake me up with a low, moaning, strangled sound, and I have to be quick to awaken her and hold her to me, and where Isabel is weeping against me seems a mortal wound.

I think I may have written Sonny the very day that little Grace was buried. I was sitting in the living room in the dark, by myself, and I suddenly thought of Sonny. My trouble made his real.

One Saturday afternoon, when Sonny had been living with us, or, anyway, been in our house, for nearly two weeks, I found myself wandering aimlessly about the living room, drinking from a can of beer, and trying to

104

work up the courage to search Sonny's room. He was out, he was usually out whenever I was home, and Isabel had taken the children to see their grandparents. Suddenly I was standing still in front of the living-room window, watching Seventh Avenue. The idea of searching Sonny's room made me still. I scarcely dared to admit to myself what I'd be searching for. I didn't know what I'd do if I found it. Or if I didn't.

On the sidewalk across from me, near the entrance to a barbecue joint, some people were holding an old-fashioned revival meeting. The barbecue cook, wearing a dirty white apron, his conked hair reddish and metallic in the pale sun, and a cigarette between his lips, stood in the doorway, watching them. Kids and older people paused in their errands and stood there, along with some older men and a couple of very tough-looking women who watched everything that happened on the avenue, as though they owned it, or were maybe owned by it. Well, they were watching this, too. The revival was being carried on by three sisters in black, and a brother. All they had were their voices and their Bibles and a tambourine. The brother was testifying, and while he testified two of the sisters stood together, seeming to say, Amen, and the third sister walked around with the tambourine outstretched and a couple of people dropped coins into it. Then the brother's testimony ended and the sister who had been taking up the collection dumped the coins into her palm and transferred them to the pocket of her long black robe. Then she raised both hands, striking the tambourine against the air, and then against one hand, and she started to sing. And the two other sisters and the brother joined in.

It was strange, suddenly, to watch, though I had been seeing these street meetings all my life. So, of course, had everybody else down there. Yet, they paused and watched and listened and I stood still at the window. " 'Tis the old ship of Zion," they sang, and the sister with the tambourine kept a steady, jangling beat, "it has rescued many a thousand!" Not a soul under the sound of their voices was hearing this song for the first time, not one of them had been rescued. Nor had they seen much in the way of rescue work being done around them. Neither did they especially believe in the holiness of the three sisters and the brother, they knew too much

105

about them, knew where they lived, and how. The woman with the tambourine, whose voice dominated the air, whose face was bright with joy, was divided by very little from the woman who stood watching her, a cigarette between her heavy, chapped lips, her hair a cuckoo's nest, her face scarred and swollen from many beatings, and her black eyes glittering like coal. Perhaps they both knew this, which was why, when, at the rare times they addressed each other, they addressed each other as "sister." As the singing filled the air, the watching, listening faces underwent a change, the eyes focusing on something within; the music seemed to soothe a poison out of them; and time seemed, nearly, to fall away from the sullen, belligerent, battered faces, as though they were fleeing back to their first condition, while dreaming of their last. The barbecue cook half shook his head and smiled, and dropped his cigarette and disappeared into his joint. A man fumbled in his pockets for change and stood holding it in his hand impatiently, as though he had just remembered a pressing appointment further up the avenue. He looked furious. Then I saw Sonny, standing on the edge of the crowd. He was carrying a wide, flat notebook with a green cover, and it made him look, from where I was standing, almost like a schoolboy. The coppery sun brought out the copper in his skin; he was very faintly smiling, standing very still. Then the singing stopped, the tambourine turned into a collection plate again. The furious man dropped in his coins and vanished; so did a couple of the women, and Sonny dropped some change in the plate, looking directly at the woman with a little smile. He started across the avenue, toward the house. He has a slow, loping walk, something like the way Harlem hipsters walk, only he's imposed on this his own half-beat. I had never really noticed it before.

I stayed at the window, both relieved and apprehensive. As Sonny disappeared from my sight, they began singing again. And they were still singing when his key turned in the lock.

"Hey," he said.

"Hey, yourself. You want some beer?"

"No. Well, maybe." But he came up to the window and stood beside me, looking out. "What a warm voice," he said.

They were singing, *If I Could Only Hear My Mother Pray Again!*

"Yes," I said, "and she can sure beat that tambourine."

"But what a terrible song," he said, and laughed. He dropped his notebook on the sofa and disappeared into the kitchen. "Where's Isabel and the kids?"

"I think they went to see their grandparents. You hungry?"

"No." He came back into the living room with his can of beer. "You want to come some place with me tonight?"

I sensed, I don't know how, that I couldn't possibly say no. "Sure. Where?"

He sat down on the sofa and picked up his notebook and started leafing through it. "I'm going to sit in with some fellows in a joint in the Village."

"You mean, you're going to play, tonight?"

"That's right." He took a swallow of his beer and moved back to the window. He gave me a sidelong look. "If you can stand it."

"I'll try," I said.

He smiled to himself and we both watched as the meeting across the way broke up. The three sisters and the brother, heads bowed, were singing, "God be with you 'till we meet again." The faces around them were very quiet. Then the song ended. The small crowd dispersed. We watched the three women and the lone man walk slowly up the avenue.

"When she was singing before," said Sonny, abruptly, "her voice reminded me for a minute of what heroin feels like sometimes—when it's in your veins. It makes you feel sort of warm and cool at the same time. And distant. And—and sure." He sipped his beer, very deliberately not looking at me. I watched his face. "It makes you feel—in control. Sometimes you've got to have that feeling."

"Do you?" I sat down slowly in the easy chair.

"Sometimes." He went to the sofa and picked up his notebook again. "Some people do."

"In order," I asked, "to play?" And my voice was very ugly, full of contempt and anger.

"Well"—he looked at me with great, troubled eyes, as though, in fact, he hoped his eyes would tell me things

107

he could never otherwise say—"they think so. And if they think so. . . !"

"And what do you think?" I asked.

He sat on the sofa and put his can of beer on the floor. "I don't know," he said, and I couldn't be sure if he were answering my question or pursuing his thoughts. His face didn't tell me. "It's not so much to play. It's to stand it, to be able to make it at all. On any level." He frowned and smiled: "In order to keep from shaking to pieces."

"But these friends of yours," I said, "they seem to shake themselves to pieces pretty goddamn fast."

"Maybe." He played with the notebook. And something told me that I should curb my tongue, that Sonny was doing his best to talk, that I should listen. "But of course you only know the ones that've gone to pieces. Some don't—or at least they haven't yet, and that's just about all any of us can say." He paused. "And then there are some who just live, really, in hell, and they know it and they see what's happening and they go right on. I don't know." He sighed, dropped the notebook, folded his arms. "Some guys, you can tell from the way they play, they on something all the time. And you can see that, well, it makes something real for them. But of course," he picked up his beer from the floor and sipped it and put the can down again, "they want to, too, you've got to see that. Even some of them that say they don't—some, not all."

"And what about you?" I asked—I couldn't help it. "What about you? Do you want to?"

He stood up and walked to the window and remained silent for a long time. Then he sighed. "Me," he said. Then: "While I was downstairs before, on my way here, listening to that woman sing, it struck me all of a sudden how much suffering she must have had to go through— to sing like that. It's repulsive to think you have to suffer that much."

I said: "But there's no way not to suffer—is there, Sonny?"

"I believe not," he said, and smiled, "but that's never stopped anyone from trying." He looked at me. "Has it?" I realized, with this mocking look, that there stood between us, forever, beyond the power of time or for- giveness, the fact that I had held silence—so long! when

108

he had needed human speech to help him. He turned back to the window. "No, there's no way not to suffer. But you try all kinds of ways to keep from drowning in it, to keep on top of it, and to make it seem—well, like you. Like you did something, all right, and now you're suffering for it. You know?" I said nothing. "Well, you know," he said, impatiently, "why do people suffer? Maybe it's better to do something, to give it a reason, any reason."

"But we just agreed," I said, "that there's no way not to suffer. Isn't it better, then, just to—take it?"

"But nobody just takes it," Sonny cried, "that's what I'm telling you! Everybody tries not to. You're just hung up on the way some people try—it's not your way!"

The hair on my face began to itch, my face felt wet. "That's not true," I said, "that's not true. I don't give a damn what other people do, I don't even care how they suffer. I just care how you suffer." And he looked at me. "Please believe me," I said, "I don't want to see you —die—trying not to suffer."

"I won't," he said, flatly, "die trying not to suffer. At least, not any faster than anybody else."

"But there's no need," I said, trying to laugh, "is there? in killing yourself."

I wanted to say more, but I couldn't. I wanted to talk about will power and how life could be—well, beautiful. I wanted to say that it was all within; but was it? or, rather, wasn't that exactly the trouble? And I wanted to promise that I would never fail him again. But it would all have sounded—empty words and lies.

So I made the promise to myself and prayed that I would keep it.

"It's terrible sometimes, inside," he said, "that's what's the trouble. You walk these streets, black and funky and cold, and there's not really a living ass to talk to, and there's nothing shaking, and there's no way of getting it out—that storm inside. You can't talk it and you can't make love with it, and when you finally try to get with it and play it, you realize nobody's listening. So you've got to listen. You got to find a way to listen."

And then he walked away from the window and sat on the sofa again, as though all the wind had suddenly been knocked out of him. "Sometimes you'll do anything to play, even cut your mother's throat." He laughed and looked at me. "Or your brother's." Then he sobered. "Or your own." Then: "Don't worry. I'm all right now and I think I'll be all right. But I can't forget—where I've been. I don't mean just the physical place I've been, I mean where I've been. And, what I've been."

"What have you been, Sonny?" I asked.

He smiled—but sat sideways on the sofa, his elbow resting on the back, his fingers playing with his mouth and chin, not looking at me. "I've been something I didn't recognize, didn't know I could be. Didn't know anybody could be." He stopped, looking inward, looking helplessly young, looking old. "I'm not talking about it now because I feel guilty or anything like that—maybe it would be better if I did, I don't know. Anyway, I can't really talk about it. Not to you, not to anybody." And now he turned and faced me. "Sometimes, you know, and it was actually when I was most out of the world, I felt that I was in it, that I was with it, really, and I could play or I didn't really have to play, it just came out of me, it was there. And I don't know how I played, thinking about it now, but I know that I did awful things, those times, sometimes, to people. Or it wasn't that I did anything to them—it was that they weren't real." He picked up the beer can; it was empty; he rolled it between his palms: "And other times—well, I needed a fix, I needed to find a place to lean, I needed to clear a space to listen—and I couldn't find it, and I—went crazy, I did terrible things to me, I was terrible for me." He began pressing the beer can between his hands; I watched the metal begin to give. It glittered, as he played with it, like a knife, and I was afraid he would cut himself, but I said nothing. "Oh well. I can never tell you. I was all by myself at the bottom of something, stinking and sweating and crying and shaking, and I smelled it, you know? my stink, and I thought I'd die if I couldn't get away from it and yet, all the same, I knew that everything I was doing was just locking me in with it. And I didn't know," he paused, still flattening the beer can, "I didn't know, I still don't know, something kept telling me that maybe it was good to smell your own stink, but I didn't think that that was what I'd been trying to do—and—who can stand it?" and he abruptly dropped the ruined beer can, looking at me with a small, still smile, and then rose, walking to the window as though it were a lodestone. I watched his face,

110

he watched the avenue. "I couldn't tell you when Mama died—but the reason I wanted to leave Harlem so bad was to get away from drugs. And then, when I ran away, that's what I was running from—really. When I came back, nothing had changed, I hadn't changed, I was just —older." And he stopped, drumming with his fingers on the windowpane. The sun had vanished, soon darkness would fall. I watched his face. "It can come again," he said, almost as though speaking to himself. Then he turned to me. "It can come again," he repeated. "I just want you to know that."

"All right," I said, at last. "So it can come again. All right."

He smiled, but the smile was sorrowful. "I had to try to tell you," he said.

"Yes," I said. "I understand that."

"You're my brother," he said, looking straight at me, and not smiling at all.

"Yes," I repeated, "yes, I understand that."

He turned back to the window, looking out. "All that hatred down there," he said, "all that hatred and misery and love. It's a wonder it doesn't blow the avenue apart."

We went to the only night club on a short, dark street, downtown. We squeezed through the narrow, chattering, jam-packed bar to the entrance of the big room, where the bandstand was. And we stood there for a moment, for the lights were very dim in this room and we couldn't see. Then, "Hello, boy," said a voice, and an enormous black man, much older than Sonny or myself, erupted out of all that atmospheric lighting and put an arm around Sonny's shoulder. "I been sitting right here," he said, "waiting for you."

He had a big voice, too, and heads in the darkness turned toward us.

Sonny grinned and pulled a little away, and said, "Creole, this is my brother. I told you about him."

Creole shook my hand. "I'm glad to meet you, son," he said, and it was clear that he was glad to meet me there, for Sonny's sake. And he smiled, "You got a real musician in your family," and he took his arm from Sonny's shoulder and slapped him, lightly, affectionately, with the back of his hand.

"Well. Now I've heard it all," said a voice behind us. This was another musician, and a friend of Sonny's, a

111

coal-black, cheerful-looking man, built close to the ground. He immediately began confiding to me, at the top of his lungs, the most terrible things about Sonny, his teeth gleaming like a lighthouse and his laugh coming up out of him like the beginning of an earthquake. And it turned out that everyone at the bar knew Sonny, or almost everyone; some were musicians, working there, or nearby, or not working, some were simply hangers-on, and some were there to hear Sonny play. I was introduced to all of them and they were all very polite to me. Yet, it was clear that, for them, I was only Sonny's brother. Here, I was in Sonny's world. Or, rather: his kingdom. Here, it was not even a question that his veins bore royal blood.

They were going to play soon and Creole installed me, by myself, at a table in a dark corner. Then I watched them, Creole, and the little black man, and Sonny, and the others, while they horsed around, standing just below the bandstand. The light from the bandstand spilled just a little short of them and, watching them laughing and gesturing and moving about, I had the feeling that they, nevertheless, were being most careful not to step into that circle of light too suddenly: that if they moved into the light too suddenly, without thinking, they would perish in flame. Then, while I watched, one of them, the small, black man, moved into the light and crossed the bandstand and started fooling around with his drums. Then— being funny and being, also, extremely ceremonious— Creole took Sonny by the arm and led him to the piano. A woman's voice called Sonny's name and a few hands started clapping. And Sonny, also being funny and ceremonious, and so touched, I think, that he could have cried, but neither hiding it nor showing it, riding it like a man, grinned, and put both hands to his heart and bowed from the waist.

Creole then went to the bass fiddle, and a lean, very bright-skinned brown man jumped up on the bandstand and picked up his horn. So there they were, and the atmosphere on the bandstand and in the room began to change and tighten. Someone stepped up to the microphone and announced them. Then there were all kinds of murmurs. Some people at the bar shushed others. The waitress ran around, frantically getting in the last orders, guys and chicks got closer to each other, and the lights on the bandstand, on the quartet, turned to a kind of indigo. Then they all looked different there. Creole looked about him for the last time, as though he were making certain that all his chickens were in the coop, and then he—jumped and struck the fiddle. And there they were.

All I know about music is that not many people ever really hear it. And even then, on the rare occasions when something opens within, and the music enters, what we mainly hear, or hear corroborated, are personal, private, vanishing evocations. But the man who creates the music is hearing something else, is dealing with the roar rising from the void and imposing order on it as it hits the air. What is evoked in him, then, is of another order, more terrible because it has no words, and triumphant, too, for that same reason. And his triumph, when he triumphs, is ours. I just watched Sonny's face. His face was troubled, he was working hard, but he wasn't with it. And I had the feeling that, in a way, everyone on the bandstand was waiting for him, both waiting for him and pushing him along. But as I began to watch Creole, I realized that it was Creole who held them all back. He had them on a short rein. Up there, keeping the beat with his whole body, wailing on the fiddle, with his eyes half closed, he was listening to everything, but he was listening to Sonny. He was having a dialogue with Sonny. He wanted Sonny to leave the shore line and strike out for the deep water. He was Sonny's witness that deep water and drowning were not the same thing—he had been there, and he knew. And he wanted Sonny to know. He was waiting for Sonny to do the things on the keys which would let Creole know that Sonny was in the water.

And, while Creole listened, Sonny moved, deep within, exactly like someone in torment. I had never before thought of how awful the relationship must be between the musician and his instrument. He has to fill it, this instrument, with the breath of life, his own. He has to make it do what he wants it to do. And a piano is just a piano. It's made out of so much wood and wires and little hammers and big ones, and ivory. While there's only so much you can do with it, the only way to find this out is to try to make it do everything.

And Sonny hadn't been near a piano for over a year. And he wasn't on much better terms with his life, not the life that stretched before him now. He and the piano stammered, started one way, got scared, stopped; started an-

113

other way, panicked, marked time, started again; then seemed to have found a direction, panicked again, got stuck. And the face I saw on Sonny I'd never seen before. Everything had been burned out of it, and, at the same time, things usually hidden were being burned in, by the fire and fury of the battle which was occurring in him up there.

Yet, watching Creole's face as they neared the end of the first set, I had the feeling that something had happened, something I hadn't heard. Then they finished, there was scattered applause, and then, without an instant's warning, Creole started into something else; it was almost sardonic, it was *Am I Blue*. And, as though he commanded, Sonny began to play. Something began to happen. And Creole let out the reins. The dry, low, black man said something awful on the drums; Creole answered, and the drums talked back. Then the horn insisted, sweet and high, slightly detached perhaps, and Creole listened, commenting now and then, dry, and driving, beautiful and calm and old. Then they all came together again, and Sonny was part of the family again. I could tell this from his face. He seemed to have found, right there beneath his fingers, a damn brand-new piano. It seemed that he couldn't get over it. Then, for awhile, just being happy with Sonny, they seemed to be agreeing with him that brand-new pianos certainly were a gas.

Then Creole stepped forward to remind them that what they were playing was the blues. He hit something in all of them, he hit something in me, myself, and the music tightened and deepened, apprehension began to beat the air. Creole began to tell us what the blues were all about. They were not about anything very new. He and his boys up there were keeping it new, at the risk of ruin, destruction, madness, and death, in order to find new ways to make us listen. For, while the tale of how we suffer, and how we are delighted, and how we may triumph is never new, it always must be heard. There isn't any other tale to tell, it's the only light we've got in all this darkness.

And this tale, according to that face, that body, those strong hands on those strings, has another aspect in every country, and a new depth in every generation. Listen, Creole seemed to be saying, listen. Now there are Sonny's blues. He made the little black man on the drums know it, and the bright, brown man on the horn. Creole

114

wasn't trying any longer to get Sonny in the water. He was wishing him Godspeed. Then he stepped back, very slowly, filling the air with the immense suggestion that Sonny speak for himself.

Then they all gathered around Sonny and Sonny played. Every now and again one of them seemed to say, Amen. Sonny's fingers filled the air with life, his life. But that life contained so many others. And Sonny went all the way back, he really began with the spare, flat statement of the opening phrase of the song. Then he began to make it his. It was very beautiful because it wasn't hurried and it was no longer a lament. I seemed to hear with what burning he had made it his, with what burning we had yet to make it ours, how we could cease lamenting. Freedom lurked around us and I understood, at last, that he could help us to be free if we would listen, that he would never be free until we did. Yet, there was no battle in his face now. I heard what he had gone through, and would continue to go through until he came to rest in earth. He had made it his: that long line, of which we knew only Mama and Daddy. And he was giving it back, as everything must be given back, so that, passing through death, it can live forever. I saw my mother's face again, and felt, for the first time, how the stones of the road she had walked on must have bruised her feet. I saw the moonlit road where my father's brother died. And it brought something else back to me, and carried me past it; I saw my little girl again and felt Isabel's tears again, and I felt my own tears begin to rise. And I was yet aware that this was only a moment, that the world waited outside, as hungry as a tiger, and that trouble stretched above us, longer than the sky.

Then it was over. Creole and Sonny let out their breath, both soaking wet, and grinning. There was a lot of applause and some of it was real. In the dark, the girl came by and I asked her to take drinks to the bandstand. There was a long pause, while they talked up there in the indigo light, and after awhile, I saw the girl put a Scotch and milk on top of the piano for Sonny. He didn't seem to notice it, but just before they started playing again, he sipped from it and looked toward me, and nodded. Then he put it back on top of the piano. For me, then, as they began to play again, it glowed and shook above my brother's head like the very cup of trembling.

4. JAZZ POETRY: Rhyme Without Reason?

THE OPENER

ONE of the most peculiar directions jazz has taken in recent years has been toward a mixture of poetry-reading to a background of jazz. Generally acknowledged to have begun in San Francisco, the fad spread to the East, but met with mixed critical and audience approval.

Right on the heels of jazz-poetry came improvised drama to jazz, improvised opera to jazz, prose readings to jazz, and so many other variations on the jazz-poetry theme that one musician was moved to say, following a grueling session of blank verse and blanker improvisation, "What'll they do next . . . weight-lifting to jazz?"

Some of the more publicized efforts have been contributed by poets Lawrence Ferlinghetti, Alan Ginsberg, Kenneth Rexroth, Kenneth Patchen, Langston Hughes, Jack Kerouac, and artist-poet William Morris. The last-named pair are represented in this section.

Reports of the death of this trend, though frequent, have been grossly exaggerated. Poetry readers seem to be multiplying in direct proportion to the swelling of the ranks of the "beat generation" and the coffee houses they frequent in our major cities.

Reporter Bob Rolontz of The Billboard *has followed the course of jazz-poetry with amused bewilderment. After gathering several note-books full of impressions, he sat down, gritted his teeth, and wrote this piece for* The Jazz Review.

(The Jazz Review, *Feb. 1958. Reprinted by permission.*)

WHATEVER BECAME OF JAZZ AND POETRY?

by Bob Rolontz

DURING the past decade, there have been many new and radical jazz movements. Some have flowered and prospered. Many have fizzled out like damp squibs. Few, however, have fizzled out so dismally as the jazz-poetry movement which, a year ago, [1957, Ed.] came bravely out of the West like a young Lochinvar. Today, it is difficult to understand the high seriousness with which it was greeted. If any jazz style ever bordered on the comic, it was this fusion of jazz and poetry; as presented in the East, it bordered on the farcical.

Prior to the outbreak of the jazz-poetry movement, there had been a number of attempts to fuse the two idioms. In the 1920's, poet Langston Hughes recited poetry with piano backing, and Kenneth Rexroth experimented with poetry and jazz about two decades later in Chicago. Perhaps the world of jazz was not as sensitive as it is today, because these early experiments caused hardly a ripple as compared with the excitement generated by the 1957-58 jazz-poetry brouhaha.

Jazz-poetry, unlike many other art forms, did not spring spontaneously into being. Rather, it was carefully planned. As put succinctly by Kenneth Rexroth, "It is very important to get poetry out of the hands of the squares. If we can get poetry out into the life of the country, it can be creative. Homer, or the guy who recited Beowulf, was show business. We simply want to make poetry part of show business." [1]

[1] Liner Notes, *Poetry Readings In The Cellar,* Fantasy LP 7002.

In other words, although many musicians took to it avidly, it was the poets, not the musicians, who started the jazz-poetry movement.

The new jazz-poetry began in San Francisco, a city often called "the Paris of the younger generation." It is logical that this city, currently undergoing a "cultural renaissance," should have been the birthplace. San Francisco has become a gathering place for many of our writers and poets, including such contemporary personalities as Kenneth Rexroth, Kenneth Patchen, Alan Ginsberg, Lawrence Ferlinghetti and Jack Kerouac. It has many jazz clubs, and a number of modern jazzmen work and live there much of the time. Further, it is the mother city of the intriguing group of young men and women known as the "beat generation," or, in the vernacular, as b.g.'s or beatniks. There are links among all three groups, but perhaps the strongest is the attention paid to avant-garde movements by all three.

Since there were poets who wanted to read their poetry to jazz, musicians who wanted to play music to this poetry, and an audience who wanted to hear the mélange, there was little difficulty in getting the jazz-poetry movement going. Although it is questionable how much the "beatniks" know of either jazz or poetry, they came to listen and returned to listen again. Soon there were clubs with regular jazz-poetry readings flourishing in San Francisco.

In addition to attempting to enlarge the audience for modern poetry as Rexroth wanted to do, some poets believed that by reading to a jazz accompaniment they were adding to the poetry itself. There is an interesting dichotomy here on the part of the poets. Some felt that their conventional poetry, poetry originally written to be read without music, was enhanced when music was added. Others felt that poetry should be written especially to be read to music. Lawrence Ferlinghetti reportedly holds the singular distinction of writing the ". . . first poem in the English language written specifically to be read with a jazz accompaniment." [2] The poem is *Autobiography*.

Jazz musicians, too, were caught up in the spreading appeal of the verses. Allyn Ferguson's Chamber Jazz Sex-

[2] *Ibid.*

118

tet contributed to the alliance of jazz and poetry via its work supporting Kenneth Patchen's poetry readings on a Cadence recording issued last fall. In commenting on jazz-poetry, Ferguson stated, "The final product should be conceived in terms of the poet's interpretation of the text . . . the music . . . composed to the poet's readings . . . and designed to fortify the emotional material of the poetry." [3]

Tenor-man Bruce Lippincott expressed his feelings about jazz in relation to poetry by calling it a "different approach to jazz . . . responding—not in a preordained way—but in a kind of question and answer—sort of a relative pitch way. The music becomes visual and broader . . . it has a new dimension." [4]

It wasn't long before word of the success of the jazz-poetry readings reached the ears of the canny eastern club owners, who immediately began playing their part in the avant-garde movement. In New York City, the Half Note, the Village Vanguard, and the Five Spot all got into the act. By March, all three clubs were featuring poets reading their poetry to jazz.

The Half Note went wild for poets. Deciding that if one poet did well in a San Francisco club, a group of poets would do sock business in New York, the club auditioned a score of poets for the job. The owner of the Half Note, Mike Canterino, rounded up his poets by placing a sign in his window which read, "Poets Wanted." (In spite of business in the poetry line being only so-so lately, the Village always seems to have its share of poets.) Canterino held two auditions for his poets; one private, one public. How did Canterino, admittedly no student of the metered line, select the poets he intended should be heard publicly? He had them recite their works and chose those he thought would interest his clientele. "Anything a bit off-color," said Canterino, "I cut out. After all, I run a family place."

Three or four poets declaimed their imagery on a fateful Monday night, backed by a small, competent modern jazz group. There was no rehearsal; the musicians were just supposed to fall in behind the poets.

Canterino felt that the audience reaction and the opin-

[3] Liner Notes, *Kenneth Patchen Reads His Poetry,* Cadence LP 3004.
[4] *Poetry Readings In The Cellar.*

119

ions of various jazz critics would help him determine which of the poets would get the nod to become regular performers at the club. The best description of that night, according to one judge and critic, is, "eerie, man, eerie. . . ." The poets not only failed to impress those who had come into the club innocently expecting jazz, but also so disturbed the leader of the jazz group by their odd meter that he jumped off the bandstand while a poet was reading, shouted, "I can't stand it," and was seen no more that performance. As a final blow, the jazz-poetry fans came to the Half Note as spectators, not customers, and retired to a small saloon next door to drink twenty-five cent beers between the readings.

The Half Note gave up jazz-poetry.

The Vanguard and the Five Spot were more cautious. The Vanguard, under the watchful eye of owner Max Gordon, began jazz-poetry readings with one of the luminaries of the San Francisco literary revival, Jack Kerouac. The author of the much-acclaimed novel, *On The Road,* lasted all of two performances. His short run was due not to the fact that he didn't draw well, but rather that the large crowd of "beatniks" who appeared were either unable or unwilling to spend money. They came and listened, but they forgot to order.

After Kerouac, the Vanguard booked Langston Hughes (not a member of the San Francisco set) for Sunday afternoon readings, and made out satisfactorily for a while with a non-"beat" (but more affluent) audience.

At the Five Spot, owner Joe Termini kept to a Sunday afternoon jazz-poetry pattern too. He used local poets, some fairly well known, but in spite of names like James Grady and Arthur Weinstein, the poets didn't draw too well.

Thus, as of March of last year, jazz-poetry had made little progress in New York clubs. Was it that easteners were too sophisticated to fall for a fad, or was jazz-poetry too delicate a bloom to survive the transplant from San Francisco to New York? Not at all, said Kenneth Rexroth in one of the popular magazines. It just hadn't been handled correctly in New York, and most of the people involved had no idea of what they were doing. Given some rehearsal with the musicians, the right poet and the right poetry, he continued, jazz-poetry could have real meaning. Rexroth, successful via this formula

CHARLIE MINGUS

COLEMAN HAWKINS

Photos by Ed Hamilton

Album covers reproduced by courtesy of the record companies

at The Cellar in San Francisco, was booked into the Five Spot for two weeks.

The Five Spot, one of New York's more *outré* jazz clubs, usually attracts a fairly wild-looking crowd of jazz aficionados. College girls in shorts rub shoulders with long-haired painters in mottled dungarees. Village girls in leotards, men in sweaters and leather jackets—their eyes shaded by dark glasses—sailors, cadets, and the Madison Avenue cool crowd, have all made the Five Spot their own. It is home for both the "beatnik" and the serious jazz student.

Rexroth opened at the Five Spot in April, backed by Pepper Adams' jazz group. For the two weeks he was there, reading his own and others' poetry in a loudly serious metered style, the club enjoyed two of the best weeks it had known. Who, however, were the enchanted? Not the jazz critics or the reviewers or the jazz students or the "beatniks." During Rexroth's engagement at the club, the audience was composed mainly of neatly dressed people who almost certainly worked at publishing houses and had charge accounts at Scribner's. He knocked out the poetry fans—but he lost the jazz buffs.

The final straw for the whole jazz-poetry movement may have occurred last summer. In July, Kenneth Patchen appeared on a coast-to-coast TV show reading his poetry to the backing of the Allyn Ferguson Jazz Sextet. The show was similar to the album that Patchen and Ferguson had cut for Cadence. The next day, *New York Times* TV critic Jack Gould not only slaughtered the program, but hammered at the whole jazz-poetry movement as well. While he was at it, he also attacked Patchen's poetry. (We jazz reviewers usually objected only to the lack of fusion between the forms, and felt we could let the literary critics handle the quality of the poetry.)

While the jazz-poetry movement was at fever pitch, the record companies edged into the picture too. Cadence Records released its Kenneth Patchen set; Fantasy released one by Rexroth. Evergreen issued an LP featuring San Francisco poets, and Dot released an alum called *Word Jazz* with the voice of deejay Ken Nordine. Nordine's explanation of word jazz came out like this: "A thought followed by a thought followed by a thought, ad infinitum. . . ." [5] As if to stress the humorous aspects of the matter, the second Ken Nordine album was titled, *Son of Word Jazz*. There were other scattered albums and singles of jazz-poetry by other companies and other poets. Rumor has it that no one broke down any record-shop doors trying to purchase these albums.

Jazz-poetry is now back in San Francisco, except for scattered cultish pockets of resistance in the East. Occasionally, there are jazz-poetry readings in New York City, but they appear to have little more than curio value. With the notable exception of Rexroth, who has been booked back into the Five Spot this winter, jazz-poetry has had weak box office. More important, although jazz-poetry spread from the West Coast to the East and back again, it left little impress of its visit except for the employment it gave to poets who, at one time, appeared to be more in demand at jazz clubs than musicians. It is doubtful if jazz-poetry will receive much attention in the next encyclopedia of jazz.

Maybe it should have been sung.

[5] Liner Notes, *Word Jazz*, Dot LP 3075.

Time *magazine described William Morris as "The storm center of this culture crisis . . . who can make with both the words and the brushes." In this section, Morris is represented with a special article discussing his philosophy as a jazz poet. His paintings demonstrate the impact of jazz on his pictorial work.*

BEAT AND JAZZBEAT
by William Morris

i like jazz that swings swinging sounds are always in-fluencing creative artists & people especially younger people   as i said i like jazz that swings & i mean swings with a cool swing   take mulligan he swings   most west-coasters swing   being one myself doesnt mean a thing charley bird parker swung like crazy   i meet him once he was something else not just as a musician but as a man that really loved his fellows   parker is from the east so its not really important what color creed or haircut you have

getting back to personal influence in the early fifties
jazz first came to me an awakening it was in jail or
to be more correct it was the sheriffs honor rancho before that i had listened to all types of music but cats
there at the rancho told me about progressive sounds
& i started to understand what modern musicians were
putting down since then this kind of music was always
with me other kinds left me cold & i wanted to be cool
    how often i painted to wayout sounds from records
swinging with the modern jazz quartet sonny rollins kon-
tiz giuffre miles & that sweet horn clifford brown & so
many others
    jazz became more than a thread in my life it was too
strong a thing to be left out of my work one of my
paintings is named requiem for bird a tribute for the
end alto who sent me & will always send me a man
who was beat & great take my poetry although i have
never written a jazzpiece or poem that is concerned totally with music it still comes in as these examples will
show some lines from a poem entitled swing with the
world
like/this means world is not square/this is all old hat
stuff/columbus proved it/personally the flat earth society is my party/if sides are to be taken/sides/how
about this crazy mulligan side/mr m is all there/except
some part of him/which is off dreaming about some
firengine red halfnote/alright world/what are you going to do for me . . .
    & from another long poem cantiba high:
my helen my paris/you live today/with other eyes/
your bodies still are golden/you listen to coltrane in the
night/how like ulysses/his long horn moans from the
black sea/coming through the black mist/black ships
are counted by poets
    & later on in the same poem:
oh swing me into sounds/of modern jazz quartet/going
so far out/color music/ah music/the word brings back
your hair/the color was music/small wonder i should
telephone/three thousand miles to get things straight
/i mean about your hair/you must never cut it . . .
    jazz swings & so does poetry & on occasion they swing
together i have read with jazzmen on a halfdozen gigs
& i know some poets that really go when they make it
with jazz kerouac & jack micheline are good enough ex-
123

amples   david meltzer jon adams hugh romney & older
poets like rexroth & kenneth patchen are all making it
with jazz on both coasts working with such musicians as
monk, mingus, al francis & many others

jazz poetry requires a meeting of minds   i am looking
forward to doing an lp on jazzpoetry & i feel not every
poet or. musician can do it well   hard work can i am
sure result in these two contrasting mediums making it
together   whatthehell we are often trying to say the same
thing   the purists in both fields tend to fail in matters of
imagination   when experiments stop progression stops
with it   i am all for action whether it be poetry painting
or just balling   it all goes to jazz   i am all for action
with a solid beat in it & it will swing baby & i mean
swing

---

*The reading of poetry to jazz easily bridged
the gap between the espresso house and the
recording studio. Among those who made
the uptown trek to the recording studios was
leading spokesman of the "beat generation"
Jack Kerouac. However, Jack did not have an
easy time getting his voice on records.*

Gilbert Millstein, whose New York Times
review of On The Road *brought Kerouac his
first serious recognition, played a leading role
in what turned out to be a cause célèbre.*

*Millstein, in chronicling the checkered his-
tory of Kerouac's jazz-poetry LP, wrote:
"Originally,* Poetry For The Beat Generation,
*a collaboration in which Jack Kerouac reads his
poetry to the piano accompaniment of Steve
Allen, was produced by another company.
Some months after it was recorded and shortly
before it was placed on sale (130 of the albums
had been distributed to reviewers and others),
the president of Dot Records, Randy Wood,
stopped both pressing and distribution, de-
claring that certain passages were 'in bad
taste,' certain lines 'off color,' and that, as
reported in* Variety, *he would not only not
permit his children to listen to it, but that
'his diskery would never distribute a product
that's not clean family entertainment.'"*

Veteran jazz-record producer, Bob Thiele,

124

then eastern artist and repertoire director for Dot Records, soon left that firm to become president of his own company, Hanover-Signature Records, under whose banner Kerouac's Poetry For The Beat Generation was finally released, unexpurgated and sans furor.

Kerouac, himself, has written of the recording session, "I came up to New York from Florida for the date, which we arranged by mail, and went into the studio to meet Steve at 1 p.m. He was there. I was carrying a huge suitcase full of untyped manuscripts of prose and poetry. I said, 'What'll I read?' He said, 'Anything you want.' He sat down and started to stroke chords on the piano. They were pretty. I reached into my suitcase as if blindfolded and picked out something and showed it to Steve, who glanced at it briefly, and said, 'Okay.' He started to play the piano, making a sign to the engineer. They turned the tape. I started to read. Between cuts I kept giving Steve some of my pint of Thunderbird, which he drank with a charitable gaiety. He was nice. We finished the session in an hour. The engineers came out and said, 'Great, that's a great first take.' I said, 'It's the only take.' Steve said, 'That's right,' and we all packed up and went home."

The poetry read on the recording, like Kerouac's synopsis above, is more notable for its humor than its incisiveness. We have selected two poems, transcribed from the recording, which demonstrate Kerouac's abiding interest in jazz.

(Quotes from liner notes of Poetry For The Beat Generation [Hanover HML-5000] by Gilbert Millstein reprinted by permission of the author and Hanover Records, Bob Thiele, president. The poems, Deadbelly and Charlie Parker, copyright © 1959 by Jack Kerouac, were originally printed in Mexico City Blues, an anthology of poetry by Jack Kerouac published by Grove Press, Inc., and were also recorded by Jack Kerouac in a Hanover-Signature Record Corp. album. Transcribed from the record by the editors.)

CHARLIE PARKER
by Jack Kerouac

Charlie Parker looked like Buddha.
Charlie Parker who recently died laughing at a jug-
        gler on TV
after weeks of strain and sickness
was called the perfect musician
and his expression on his face
was as calm beautiful and profound
as the image of the Buddha
represented in the East—the lidded eyes
the expression that says: all is well.

This was what Charlie Parker said when he played:
        all is well.
You had the feeling of early-in-the-morning
like a hermit's joy
or like the perfect cry of some wild gang at a jam
        session
Wail! Whap!
Charlie burst his lungs to reach the speed of what
        the speedsters wanted
and what they wanted was his eternal slowdown.
A great musician
and a great creator of forms
that ultimately find expression
in mores and what-have-you.

Musically as important as Beethoven
yet not regarded as such at all
a genteel conductor of string orchestras
in front of which he stood proud and calm
like a leader of music in the great historic World-
        night
and wailed his little saxophone
the alto
with piercing, clear lament
in perfect tune and shining harmony
Toot!

As listeners reacted
without showing it
and began talking

126

and soon the whole joint is rocking and talking
and *everybody* talking—
and Charlie Parker
whistling them on to the brink of eternity
with his Irish St. Patrick Patootlestick.
And like the holy mists
we blop and we plop
in the waters of slaughter and white meat—
and die
one after one
in Time.

And how sweet a story it is
when you hear Charlie Parker tell it
either on records or at sessions
or at official bits in clubs
(shots in the arm for the wallet).
Gleefully he whistled the perfect horn
anyhow made no difference . . .

Charlie Parker forgive me.
Forgive me for not answering your eyes.
For not having made an indication
of that which you can devise.
Charlie Parker pray for me.
Pray for me and everybody.

In the Nirvanas of your brain
where you hide—
indulgent and huge—
no longer Charlie Parker
but the secret unsayable Name
that carries with it
merit not-to-be-measured
from here to up down east or west.

Charlie Parker:
lay the bane off me
. . . . and everybody.

DEADBELLY

by Jack Kerouac

> Old Man Mose
> early American jazz pianist

127

had a grandson
called
Deadbelly.
Old Man Mose
walloped the rollickin' keyport—
Wahoo Wild Hosts! pianny—
with monkeys in his hair
drooling spaghetti, beer and beans
with a cigar mashed in his countenance
of gleaming happiness.
A furtive madman of old sane times.
Deadbelly don't hide it.
Lead killed Leadbelly.
Deadbelly admit
Deadbelly modern cat
Cool!
Deadbelly, man,
Craziest!

Old Man Mose is dead
but Deadbelly get ahead.

5. BLUES: They Died of Everything

THE OPENER

BIG Bill Broonzy died in Chicago on August 15, 1958.
Billie Holiday died in New York City July 17, 1959. Les-
ter Young died in New York City on March 15, 1959.
Charlie Parker died in New York City March 12, 1955.

Four people lived and died. They are connected only
by three things: their art, their greatness, and the blues.

The blues . . . they sang them, they played them, they
lived them.

At the very center of jazz is the blues;
Chameleon-like, of changing hues;
To know them is to have paid your dues . . .

(*The Blues,* poem by Burt Korall, from liner notes of *The
Blues Is Everybody's Business* (Coral CRL 59101). Reprinted
by permission.)

The first thing a human being learns in life is to cry. As Big Bill Broonzy lay dying, he mourned, "Young people have forgotten how to cry the blues." Throughout his sixty-one years, Bill Broonzy never forgot how to cry the blues. Broonzy's close friend, veteran jazz writer and blues authority, Studs Terkel, has caught in words the vigor and the sadness, the dimensions and the essence of the blues . . . which were the essence of the life of William Lee Conley Broonzy.

(The Blues, Big Bill Broonzy; (EmArcy Records MG 36137) liner notes by Studs Terkel, author of Giants of Jazz, *reprinted by permission Art Talmadge, president, Mercury, EmArcy Records. The notes were written shortly before Broonzy's death.)*

THE BLUES . . . BIG BILL BROONZY

by Studs Terkel

IF THE BLUES is a poetic remembrance of things past— or of today's trauma—small wonder Big Bill Broonzy is a most natural bard. He has no forgettery.

> I was in a place one night
> They was all havin' fun
> They was all buyin' beer and wine
> But they would not sell me none.

It was 1947. Or was it '48? Four of us in a jalopy were passing through a pleasant Indiana town on our way to Purdue. Lafayette, it was. We were thirsty. We saw a tavern, a workingman's hangout. Bill tossed a casual glance, almost imperceptibly. He smiled. "Uh-uh. They won't serve me. You guys go on in." He was outvoted. After all, these were hard-working guys, decent men. Bill had no right to jump to conclusions. As we entered, all conversation ceased. Shot and a beer was the order for four. The pudgy gent behind the bar was genial enough. Politely, he murmured: "I can serve three of you."

> They said if you white, you all right
> If you brown, stick aroun'

129

But as you black
Mmm, mmm, brother, get back, get back, get back.

The profane gibberish three of us mumbled is of small matter. We were licked as we slunk out, X-rayed as we were by the hostile eyes of good, solid workingmen. One man laughed softly. It was Bill. We were losers, the three of us without and the wretched clods within. Only Bill was the winner, a laughing winner.

> You know I can't lose
> Baby, I can't lose
> Not with this moppin' broom I use.

Big Bill, porter. Aside from work in railroad gangs, led by Sleepy John Estes and Leadbelly among others; plow hand; cook, molder; preacher; piano mover. Mover and Shaker.

> I was born in Mississippi
> Arkansas is where I'm from.

"Man I worked for in Arkansas, all his kids went to college. Come home doctors, lawyers, girl a school teacher. I wished I could go to college someday. Well, I did. I went to college in Ames." He wasn't kidding. At Iowa State, he landed a job as campus janitor.

It's Big Bill's razor-whet, lovely sense of irony that's enabled him to overcome. Cheated, euchred, gypped, triple-crossed most of his livelong days—by men and by fate—he's invariably come up with an ace.

On a visit to his mother (born in slavery, died in 1957 at the age of 102), he drove his big second-hand car into a filling station. Just outside Little Rock. The red neck was about to get nasty. A black man in what appeared to be a luxury auto . . . "Whose car is this, boy?" Came the deadpan retort: "Man I work for. My boss." The answer satisfied the white American. But if this black man owned that car . . . boy!

Double-talk? Sure. You must understand one thing, though. Bill spoke the truth, *his* truth. Always, Big Bill has been *his* own boss. No matter how humiliating the circumstance, he never allowed himself to be humiliated. A servant, often; servile, never. Neither has he been belligerent. Just Bill The Man, rich in his own secret humor. Sure, he's made adjustments, but they've been of *his* choosing. He has borne his dignity as gracefully as his guitar.

> I love you, baby
> But I sure ain't gonna be your dog.

Not just a woman he's singing about. Life itself. As for his feelings toward members of the fair sex, Leporello's *Madamina* could easily have applied to the roving Bill. One difference: the blues singer was far more gentle than the Spanish Don. He evinces a genuine affection for women.

> My suitcase packed, my trunk's already gone
> Now you know about that, baby
> Big Bill won't be here long . . .

No scenes, no recriminations. Never has Big Bill sung of bad women. They've all been good, warm-hearted. Some less than others. Some more so.

> Willie Mae, don't you hear me callin' you
> If I don't get my Willie Mae
> I declare there ain't no other woman will do.

Fond memories. Sly ones, too. Consider his way of kidding phonies and pretenders. Often, he's tossed darts at caste—even among his own people.

> She said her mother was a Creole
> And an Indian was her dad.

The dark-skinned singer remembers being denied admission to the church to which his light-skinned grandmother belonged. And so he speaks a universally ethnic truth. (How often the nose of the German Jew was out of joint when he encountered the Polish Jew! Till Mr. Schicklegruber refused to be selective in this matter. How the blonde Florentine passed by the swarthy Calabrian! And in what tone of voice did the "lace curtain" Irish refer to the "turkeys"?)

Unfortunately, in his latter years, Big Bill's poetry and mother-wit have been less than appreciated in some quarters. Trying to hide his hurt, he has recounted the numerous times Anatole Broyard's hipsters have hooted him, walked out on his blues. And young jazz fans who should know better. Cool children of a cool evening can be awfully cold. "Place I work for in Buffalo, man pays me off first night. First set. He says they don't like what you singin'. Who wants to hear that old-time stuff? Nobody's gonna pay to hear that these days."

Duke never walked out on Big Bill. Nor did Count. They know. That's why they're the artists they are.

He's lost track of the exact number of blues he's written; some 360, give or take a half-dozen. So many he has handed to others. "Why not? If it suits 'em better'n me, why shouldn't they have it?"

And he insists on keeping green the memory and song of his friends no longer here. "Leroy Carr, he's gone. Big Maceo, he's gone. Jim Jackson, Richard M. Jones, ol' Lead, they're gone. If I don't sing their blues, who will? Maybe the blues'll die someday. But I'll have to die first."

And what of Tampa Red talking to himself? And Memphis Minnie shouting somewhere in the darkness? Does anybody really give a hoot out there? Who cares? In the Age of Indifference, of bland Ivy and Jivy Leaguers on the make, jazz fans all, according to the Gospel of *Playboy,* to care deeply is archaic. Moldy. To these careful young men who couldn't care less, Big Bill says: "I care."

He missed out on a critical appointment with the doctor not long ago.

"What happened, Bill?"

"There's a kid just come up from Mississippi. Gotta lot of blues. Went over to talk with 'im about copyright so's he don't get gypped like I done."

To keep the blues alive . . . Big Bill Broonzy is dedicated. For they are a piece of a man and he is something of a man. In this Period of the Pipsqueak, that's really something.

Billie Holiday. "By the time she found fame and fortune as a jazz singer," wrote her biographer William Dufty, "Billie was emotionally exhausted, spent. At an age when other kids were picking out graduation dresses, Billie's future was already behind her." She lived unending variations of the blues. As Burt Korall wrote, "Billie Holiday so illuminated human situations as to give the listener a rare, if frightening, glimpse into the realities of experience. Where others fear to tread, she reached out and touched; where others mask their eyes, she defiantly kept hers open. Lady moved in and out of sharp corners; she was marked, cruelly cut, and finally lost to us."

(Liner note quotations from The Billie Holiday Story *(Decca DXB 161) and* The Blues Are Brewin' *(Decca DL 8701), reprinted by permission.)*

BILLIE'S BLUES
by Burt Korall

IN THE TENDER, impressionable years of her youth, Eleanora "Billie" Holiday was deeply touched and influenced by the records of Louis Armstrong and Bessie Smith. They initiated a lasting love for the ways and means of both these figures of jazz vocal stature. The horn-like qualities of Louis, the earthiness and regality of "The Empress of the Blues" left their mark; the blues, a prime concern of both, cut deeply into the Holiday heart and mind, assuming a large portion of reality for her as she proceeded through the maze that has been her life.

The blues are the marrow of jazz, "a base, like the foundation to a building," as Jimmy Rushing has phrased it. First vocally projected, later evolving into an instrumental form, the blues are not the only source or means of expression for the jazz vocalist, but certainly a most compatible one.

Rooted to the blood lines of one segment of our population, equally functional and cogent to all, the blues are a summing up of work songs, spirituals, field hollers, min-

133

strel songs, etc., and have evolved from a comparatively pristine vocal simplicity to an often vigorous instrumental complexity, reflective of the changes that have taken place in American music. And despite the passage of time and the advances made in technique, the basic frame, the essential strength of the form, generally has not been affected, though distortion has occurred in various spheres, notably in the area of *rock* and *roll.*

The spectrum of human feeling has been well delineated within the blues framework—usually twelve bars of music based on three basic chords in dramatic stanza form: a line, a repeat, a punch line. The emotional qualities projected are dependent upon the practitioner's bent and the tenor of the blues material in treatment. As has been pointed out by jazz critics and musicians, the blues are not necessarily blue.

Critic Whitney Balliett has written: "They can be sad, miserable, low-down sad. They can be angry-sad. They can be haunting. They can be lilting, salubrious, joyous, bubbling. They can be wildly exuberant. They can be funny, sardonic and even nasty. They can be ironic. They can be dirty. . . ."

The blues can underline environment, area, degree of sophistication; however, for all this, it is the unique construction and sound of blues melodies, the power and reality of blues lyrics—poetry, if you will—that mark it as a form of capital importance.

In antiquity, the human voice came first; the instruments followed. In jazz, the same pattern was repeated. The blues were sung, and the instrumentalists assimilated manners and mannerisms, eventually growing beyond vocal blues, which have not paralleled instrumental blues in development to complexity.

The twenties and thirties brought wide recognition for the blues, a discovery by the many of what had been important to the few. The blues singers—Ma Rainey and the Smiths—came on; and later, Joe Turner, Jimmy Rushing and others. Intermarriage, exchange of values between the jazz vocal and instrumental performer, was prevalent. Out of this emerged a tradition epitomized by Louis Armstrong—that of the instrumentalized jazz singer who adopted the *feel,* phraseology of a jazz horn (thereby adding an emotional extra to the reading of a

134

lyric story) and often approached impressionism, the end justifying the means.

Teddy Wilson recently said of Billie Holiday: "You can feel her singing, like another instrument."

In *Hear Me Talkin' To Ya*—Hentoff and Shapiro—(Rhinehart), Billie made her position clear: "I don't think I'm singing, I feel like I'm playing a horn. I try to improvise like Lester Young, like Louis Armstrong or someone else I admire. What comes out is what I feel."

Very much a product of the jazz *ambiance*, Lady Day has derived much of her artistic strength and found more than her share of pain and sadness in this milieu. Her life has been more concentrated and searingly lived than a mere statement of her numerical age can attest. At least partially because of this, she has developed an ability to make her vocal pictures shimmer with truth.

Born in Baltimore, Maryland, 43 years ago, she has walked a road that has been arduous and unstintingly real. Working at eleven, singing by the time she was fifteen, Billie moved on a conveyor belt through a youth that hardly existed.

She was "discovered" by John Hammond and Benny Goodman. A series of record appearances in the thirties brought recognition beyond the inner circle of friends, musicians and critics. Stints with the Count Basie and Artie Shaw bands in 1937 and 1938 further established her position with the public. Then two years at New York's Cafe Society Downtown established her as a solo attraction.

Through the early and mid-forties, the singer was most often seen and heard on Manhattan's 52nd Street: a voluptuous figure, attractively gowned; the ever-present gardenia setting off a well-structured, aloof yet demanding face.

Since then, Billie frequently has worked the concert hall circuit. Still a singer of great influence, she often has fallen victim to a chaotic personal life. But despite her "troubles," she continues to sing songs that mean something to her, infusing them with an aura and a satisfying taste of the blues center of her personality. Lady brings to songs an alternately bitter and sweet sound and limber, horn-like phrasing. Most important, she offers candor, musicality and personal revelation of a striking sort. For all her sacrifices at various altars, she never has abandoned her artistic values.

When the subject under discussion is a musician as well known as Lester Young, the problem of capturing his enigmatic personality is heightened. Working without the usual biographical basics, Metronome's editor, Bill Coss, stroked a rapid sketch of Young, and gave us a glimpse of the personality behind his jazz mask. Much of the secret side of Young emerges in this piece, as blunt as a telegram, yet as rhythmic as a poem.

(Lester Young, *reprinted from* Metronome, *Oct. 1955, by permission of Bill Coss, editor.)*

LESTER YOUNG
by Bill Coss

THE SOLEMN, slow, slouching enigma of jazz, Lester Young, who, more than anyone else, bridged the gap from "our music" to Bird, still stands astride the jazz world today—one foot in New Orleans, the other on Broadway, at 51st or 52nd Street. In either place, in all places, he presents the swinging, light, fluent, smoky sound, his almost tip-toe walk, his colorful expressions, his phlegmatic exterior. This mask which covers him is a product of the particular price he paid for his own bid for individuality: "I won't call names, but they used to take me down to the cellar and play Hawk's records for me . . . you dig? . . . and asked me couldn't I play like that . . . But I hardly even listened most of the time, 'cause I knew I wasn't goin' that way." The way he did go was filled with rebuffs: "The critics used to call me the honk man . . . Mike Levin said I had a cardboard sound and that I couldn't play my horn . . . You dig? . . . That made it harder to play my horn . . . That's why I don't put the kids down . . . They're all playing . . . It depends on whether you dig them." Along with all the other things that hurt Prez were the always prevalent rumors; things like people saying that he couldn't read: "I sure hate to read . . . When I was twelve years old I

136

tried to get by in my daddy's band just on my ear, but he threw me out when he dug . . . So I got mad and practiced and came back and cut everyone else on the band . . . And I read Mundy's scores on Basie's band." In these early years, Prez had the oddest kind of musical heroes—Jimmy Dorsey and Frankie Trumbauer: "I finally decided on Trumbauer as the one who floored me the most . . . but, you see, he was playing alto or C-melody sax and, in copying all his records, that's how I developed my sound." Now that he's served his sentence he seems still to pay more; the sensitivity has deepened, the mask has become more firmly himself. Not so much so that he won't tip it from time to time, revealing sudden warmth, humor, shrewdness. As a rabid Giant fan, for example, now "waiting for next year," he is an incessant, though modest, gambler: "I will bet you thirteen dollars of my money," is his usual expression. Or his happiness in playing: "Still kicks." Or about his imitators: "I listen to records I made, only I'm not sure they're mine, and I don't even know if it's me." Or about being booked with his friend Paul Quinichette on the same Birdland show—this to his manager Charlie Carpenter: "Lady Carp, if I go up there and play me, I'm playing him, and if I play something else, that isn't what the people came to hear." (Incidentally, he feels that Paul and "maybe Eager" come closest to him.) But sometimes the mask tilts instead of tipping and reveals confusion and hurt: "That singing that everybody talks about—I'm just being funny . . . But I sing lyrics with my horn, and I'd like to play those slow ballads—but the people make so much noise . . . by the time you play a chorus and a half you wish it was long over . . . Not like that everywhere . . . Funny, they come in to hear, but I guess they get goin' on the drinks . . ." Or about imitators: "So many guys doing Bird—just running chromatics . . . just running chromatics." But he goes on what seems to be his tired way, enlivening life for many of us, shrouding his inner self from the probes of the world around him, occasionally indulging in the bizarre (his eyes glow with secret humor at the mention of water-pistol fights at Birdland), enjoying his lovely wife and sprouting son, his modest brick home, his mid-afternoon nap (he sleeps very few hours at a time) and the constant and sometimes simultaneous din of television set and record player. The coolness disappeared for just a moment during the afternoon of this interview. Bob Crosby's show was over and Prez, a jazz immortal, paid instant, enthusiastic tribute: "That Bob Crosby . . . he's still wailing." And so, of course, is Prez.

Bird lives! Everywhere you turn in modern jazz—soloists, composers, arrangers—Charlie Parker's tremendous influence is felt. Bill Coss writes of Charlie Parker with clear-eyed understanding of the man and the world he made.* At the time this was written, contractual commitments to another record company made it impossible for Coss to mention Parker by name. Although it undoubtedly added to the difficulties of writing the piece, it resulted in heightening the impact of the work. In unraveling a bit of Parker's tangled life, Coss weaves into the fabric of the piece some of the people and the places involved in the beginnings of the Bop Era.

* Jazz At Massey Hall (*Debut Records DEB-124*), liner notes reprinted by permission of Charles Mingus, president.

CHARLIE PARKER
by Bill Coss

WHEN Sparrow jumped last, not the jump described in Elliot Grennard's short story, *Sparrow's Last Jump,* which described only one of many jumps, it was like no Babe Ruth, no Lou Gehrig at home plate in Yankee Stadium heaped with gifts from loyal fans. There was no fanfare for a final performance in a brilliant career, no warm oratory, no cushion for his retirement.

Instead there was an upsetting debacle in a night club and an anticlimactic, shrouded, fizzle of a death four days later.

And now, perpetuating a life which seemed purposely ended, there are stories about a tame bird who visits in a musicians' bar, a feather which floated from the ceiling of Carnegie Hall. There are men who went back to their wives, some who left them; some musicians who

138

are hastening to become pretenders to his throne, others who are content to blow seance sessions with him.

None of this seems strange, however, no matter how twisted, for this was a man who led adulators to grow fat or lean according to his own diet decisions. Young men used narcotics because he was rumored an addict; others changed their instruments because they could never hope to equal him; others copied their mannerisms, their hair styling, their clothes, their eating habits —in short, their lives—from this creature to whom they very nearly gave worship.

A strange God. A creature wanting and suggesting self-destruction; a familiar of every evil by his own admission; a companion of quantities of good, for what reason he could never fathom.

What did he worship, this one who was worshipped? His art, of course; his genius, if you'll allow a qualified use of that word. But both of these things were part of him, left and right arm, necessary, things he could not do without; things he was not allowed to do without, regardless of how he tortured his body or mind. They were his life, and in their frustration he found a reason, among other things, for ending what hardly pleased him.

It never let him rest, so the worship was more forced than not; he did attempt several times to disregard it, but it never let him rest; it pulled his lazy body and pushed his lazy mind, somehow tearing him from mediocrity and thrusting him into clarity and brilliance of expression. He paid it reed service, nothing else.

Since pleasure and frustration were so evenly matched within his talent, he turned, or so it seems—perhaps he only made it seem so—to the talent's reward, to money as an object of worship. "Bread," he said. "That's your only friend."

At the same time, almost as a parallel line, he worshipped himself, even though, again by his own admission and his actions, which were far more eloquent, he hated himself. Then as God and his servant, as the adored and the adoring, finding both wanting, he did as the religious have always done; he made sacrifice, being at once penitent, victim and deity. None were appeased, none were satisfied, the victim was more burnt than offering,

139

but it was over and there could be no more bowing of head, no more scraping of soul.

There was "Sparrow," "Bop," "Charlie Chan," or what have you; the terms are nearly interchangeable for most jazz listeners. A man of many aliases of all kinds, he lived his life as bop did, sometimes foolishly, sometimes mystically, and sometimes with an impatient yet eloquent expressiveness.

Before those years were finally spent, the New Jazz Society of Toronto decided to reunite as many of the early bop greats as they could. Early in 1953, the club's officers approached several musicians in the hope of running a mammoth jazz concert in Massey Hall in Toronto, which would feature both this bop giant's quintet and a number of Canadian jazz musicians who had formed a large band.

Running into early trouble, the club finally contracted with bassist Charlie Mingus to bring such a group to Canada in May. Mingus convinced Charlie Chan, Dizzy Gillespie, Max Roach and Bud Powell that this would benefit one and all. (Perhaps it's only of passing interest, but one sidelight of the trip is that, having arrived at LaGuardia airport, they discovered that only five of their party of seven, swelled by the presence of Mingus' wife and Birdland's Oscar Goodstein, could take the pre-arranged flight, that two would have to wait for a later plane. By some process of figuring they decided to leave Chan and Gillespie behind, then spent many hours in Toronto wondering if they would ever come. For those who knew them, the fascination in the story lies in wondering what Dizzy and Charlie did at LaGuardia airport for those several hours; waiting was hardly common to either of them and that is an uncommonly difficult place in which to wait.)

In Toronto, the quintet performed brilliantly with asides for individual temperaments. And, fortunately, there was a tape machine present to record most that came to pass. The asides are often more felt than heard: Chan's unusual amount of interpolations on *Perdido;* Chan blowing Bud off of his back on *Things Just One Of Those Things,* Ed.]; Chan seemingly furious on his early choruses of *(Salt) Peanuts* as if he were scolding the clowning Gillespie, whom he had announced before the tune as "my worthy consituent."

One can wonder if the use of that word was deliberate or not.

Asides aside, they blew music of startling quality that night. These were no golden days of bop, this commemorates no zenith of a style, but it is eloquent music played by five exceptional musicians, something of a distinction in jazz-recording circles as a general rule.

This was a quintet that bop built, a quintet which had largely built bop, excepting Mingus, possibly, who had spent most of the early bop years on the West Coast. And the fascination of the music, of the revolution it was, is more than equalled by the personal mark it made on each one of these. Two choruses, a release, and now this will be the last chorus.

First there was our Sparrow; his the most obvious tragedy. Then there is Dizzy Gillespie who early developed a mask for his protection: a beard and all that, a rug, a variety of nonsense, and finally the tilted horn. A pretending clown prince, he occasionally plays that clown with sweet dignity, he can always play, clown or no, with exceptional brilliance.

Bud Powell, driven mad by beauty or a policeman's club, has influenced whole scores of pianists. He has no influence over himself. Only the final tragedy is missing; he is still alive.

The seemingly impassive Max Roach, who has a disciplined relentlessness made hard by years of privation and insecurity. Some kind of strength has somewhat protected Max, has kept him whole, while not wholly sparing him scars.

Charlie Mingus, who is less disciplined and more restless, made, not hard, but suspicious by years of privation and insecurity. But, like Max, less touched by the burden of the bop years than the rest. Potentially the richest of these talents, he is yet to fully mature, though his present is more than most futures.

And coda: This is an album liner? Where are the adjectives? How come no excitement? What kind of a cast is that?

A plaster cast, of course, formed for a crippled world; formed by a crippled world. A cast which matches each line of body, which alternately promises healing and disintegration, which preaches and curses, gives both

141

good and bad, strength and itches. A cast which, in short, plays both sides against the middle.

And in this playing there is exquisite workmanship, seldom matched, artistry which will survive any last jump, and eloquence that is as exact as it is exacting whether speaking of life or death. There are the adjectives; not many of them; all that are needed in the presence of so much that is excellent; all of it truly dramatic whether in music, death or life.

At three o'clock in the morning, the world seems to grind to a halt. This is a timeless time when yesterday was yesterday, tomorrow will be tomorrow, and there is no today. This is the Greenwich mean time of the blues. Jake Trussell's poem limns the time, place, and sound.

(From After Hours Poetry, © *1958 Kingsville Publishing Co., Kingsville, Texas; reprinted by permission of the author. Jake Trussell is sports editor and columnist of the* Kingsville Record, *jazz disc jockey at KINE, and frequent contributor to leading jazz publications.)*

3 A. M. JAZZ CLARINET
by Jake Trussell

Play it like the night
    Play it with the clouds low down and black

And the rain falling across a dull street lamp
    Play me a wet street and the dark houses

And the woman by the corner that goes with it.
    Play it way down,

Way down deep and then bring it up as the rain
                gusts harder
    Bring it up until the woman steps into a doorway

And there is nothing left but the wet street and the
                dark houses
    Up until the lamp is nothing but a smudge
And the black is all there is.

142

6. HUMOR: Louder and Funnier

HUMOR in jazz is exaggerated, understated, and improvised endlessly on a few basic themes.

The jazz vocabulary itself is a major source of humor (to a jazzman *bread* is money, *ridiculous* is wonderful, and *dig* the most useful verb ever invented.) Caricature also plays a large role in the humor of jazz. But too often these elements—caricature and the jazz language—seem to sum up the musicians to the public at large.

Cruel reference is often made to the most negative aspects of jazz life. Despite the poor taste of jokes based on narcotics, Jim Crow, bearded boppers, and stereotypes of the musicians themselves, the fact is that these are actually weak and distorted reflections of true jazz humor.

What is true jazz humor? Some random samples appear on the following pages.

Like its language, true jazz humor is satirical, earthy, spontaneous, and genuinely witty. Above all, it is topical. It has even become chic today to identify oneself with the language of jazz and its humor.

And who but a jazzman could say of Zsa Zsa Gabor, "Man, what key is *she* in?"

Jazz humor is often acid. For instance, when a critic starts swinging on a jazz institution or major personality or, better still, another critic, his copy fairly sizzles. When Tom Scanlan, jazz critic of the Army Times, *got his back up over the coming Newport Jazz Festival recently, he rapped out a column that was pungent, crackling, and pulled no punches. What's more, it was funny, too.*

(From Jazz Music, © *1959, Army Times Syndicate; in* Army Times, *January 31, 1959; reprinted by permission.)*

AN EVENING OF COMEDY
by Tom Scanlan

JAZZ today has growing pains. Much like a typical adolescent, it takes itself too seriously and is badly in need of some good, clean fun. For that reason, I hereby suggest that one of the evening programs at the Newport Jazz Festival this summer be devoted to "A Night of Comedy." And to give this suggestion some kind of impetus and direction, here are a few ideas for such a hilarious program.

Tenor-men Sonny Rollins, John Coltrane, John Griffin and Ornette Coleman will compete in a "bad note" contest. The one who plays two choruses in a row without hitting a clinker wins a special award from *Metronome* magazine.

Thelonious Monk will attempt to play the piano (if he's in the mood).

A critics' panel will discuss jazz piano. Critic Barry Ulanov will explain why Phineas Newborn is the successor to Art Tatum "with a clear title to the throne." Critic Martin Williams, of *Down Beat* and *The Jazz Review,* will explain why Art Tatum "obviously had limited melodic invention." And Paul Sampson, jazz columnist for the *Washington Post* and *Times-Herald,* will explain why Thelonious Monk is "his favorite pianist after (sometimes before) John Lewis." In so doing, Sampson will explain Monk's "thorough musical grounding."

144

John Lewis will attempt to play the piano with both hands at the same time.

Jazz critics Nat Hentoff and George Frazier will meet in a boxing ring with typewriters oiled. If Frazier writes "I kid you not" or "I tell you true" before Hentoff uses words like "minimal" or "arcane" or "egregious" or "spare," he will lose. If the reverse happens, Hentoff will be the winner. If Frazier quotes a Latin phrase at the same time Hentoff quotes Elizabethan verse, the bout will be declared a draw.

After explaining what the name of *Metronome* magazine is this month, *Metronome* (or *Jazz Today* or *Music U. S. A.* or whatever it is) editor Bill Coss will explain why the results of the annual *Metronome* poll, published in the January issue, "was a particularly satisfying poll, more filled with quality than we can remember having happened for many years," a poll "that justifies our faith in our readers and fills us with personal satisfaction."

Chet Baker, third-best male jazz singer according to the *Metronome* poll (Louis Armstrong was not in the top ten), will sing.

George T. Simon, writer and associate producer of the Timex all-star jazz shows on television, will explain how to produce a good jazz show on television. During Simon's lecture, 50 drum soloists and 100 other musicians will be present for demonstrations, and Jane Morgan and Jaye P. Morgan will sing. Dakota Staton will also be on tap for imitations of Dinah Washington, Sarah Vaughan, Ella Fitzgerald, *et al.*

Jimmy Giuffre, clarinet virtuoso according to *Metronome, Down Beat* and *The Jazz Review,* will attempt to demonstrate his clarinet technique by playing a Goodman solo. Any Goodman solo. Or a DeFranco solo. Any De-Franco solo. Or a Hucko solo. Any Hucko solo.

Several of the poll-winning guitarists will attempt to demonstrate unamplified rhythm guitar.

Eddie Condon and Mezz Mezzrow will throw their biographies at one another.

French critic Hugues Panassie will explain how Bobby Hackett is "somewhat lacking in swing," how Benny Goodman "has a tone that is inclined to be thin," how Jack Teagarden is "sometimes a little corny and sentimental,"

and why Mezz Mezzrow is unqestionably one of the greatest of all jazz musicians.

Another French critic, Andre Hodeir, will explain the
five ages of jazz (primitive, old-time, preclassical, classical, modern), making plain just how this pigeon-holing
works and just who decides on how to pigeon-hole whom
where.

The publishers of *The Encyclopedia of Jazz* will recite
the "more than 200 compositions" Leonard Feather has
written, and Feather will appear briefly to explain why
Elvis Presley is included in *The Encyclopedia of Jazz.*

Now, I think that would be a real fun-type evening.
Later, after the belly laughs, and in the event people may
want to hear some music, we could have an All-Non-
Metronome band, made up of musicians who didn't get
enough votes to be listed in the top ten on their instru-
ments. People like Benny Carter, Edmund Hall, Peanuts
Hucko, Bud Freeman, Harry Edison, Buck Clayton, Billy
Butterfield, Teddy Wilson, Joe Bushkin, Louis Armstrong.
You know, jazz musicians.

---

*Here's Jack Kerouac again . . . in a breaking-up
mood.*

DAVE BRUBECK

by Jack Kerouac

The New Orleans *New York Club*
wishes to announce
the opening of new sessions
and new fields
DADDY-O!

Dave Brubeck's the swingingest!

And I wish to say
farewell to Al Smith
HELLO, DAVE.

Sometimes jazz humor can come from an entirely unexpected source. Witness the following excerpts from a young boy's diary.

(Play The Melody, Stupid, by Dari Brubeck, Columbia Records press release, Dateline/Jazz. Reprinted by permission.)

FATHER TO SON:
"PLAY THE MELODY, STUPID"
by Dari Brubeck

DARI BRUBECK, eldest son of jazz pianist Dave Brubeck, accompanied father halfway around the world this year [1958, Ed.] on a State Department-sponsored tour of Europe and Asia. Unlike his father, who set his images to music for a new Columbia album, *Jazz Impressions of Eurasia,* eleven-year-old Dari jotted down *his* ideas in a school tablet (complete with Mickey Mouse on the cover):

"Dad had to go to east Berlin to get permission to catch a train to Poland in the communist zone. Mom, Mike and I went to a hotel and waited for 3 hours. Mom got worried. Finally he came back we went to the train station and just barely on time we got on the train. Dad asked the conductor what the first stop was the conductor answered Frankford. We're on the wrong train yelled Dad loudly. It was to late the train was moving. So we waited for the train to stop but when we came to Frankford it turned out everything was alright. It was Frankford on the Oder **not** Frankford on maine. Finally we got to our distonation. When we got off the train and we heard (in English) Welcome to Poland.

The name of the town we stayed in was Szcezin C Stateeno. We got on a old bus. The seats were wet and cold. Ellie Morells stuck her foot in the gas tank which was under the floor, but there was a big hole in the floor. Mom asked Ellie to look on her leg and see if we had enought to make it to Szcezin. When the bus started I warned Ellie not to get sucked down into the gas tank. After we got underway the bus kept making rumbling noises which sounded like a sort of huveh-huvvveh. So we started betting when it would fall apart. Thursday and Friday were taken so I took Monday (it was Saturday).

We never found out who won. We arrived at 5 a.m. and hit the sack.

The next day Mike and I got up about 11. I was on my way to the mens room when I saw Adams. He asked if we would breakfasts. I told Mike to get dressed. Mike and I went down and ate ham and eggs under the American flag. At the breakfast table I met the man who will be the anouncer for some of the concerts. His name is Roman Voshco. Roman took us around the town. It wasn't a town with a lot to see in it he said. But for Mike and I there was plenty. We could see the people. After all it isn't every American boy that sees Poland! There were alot of ruins from the war. Roman showed us a fotoplastican. A fotoplastican is a very large dark room built around a pillar which takes up most of the space. There is a ring of chairs all around this pillar. You can sit in the chair and look trough little windows in the pillar and you see pictures of far off places. Later that day we went to the hall where Dad would be playing that night. To look at the building from the outside it didn't look like the best hall, but inside is what counts so we went in.

Looking at it from the inside 'it's the most.' It was very modern in desighn. The walls were painted gaily and the hall it self was good.

That night Mike and I attended the concert. We were back stage. Then Roman asked us if we would play. Mike and I were reluctant, but everybody convinced us that it would be O.K. I was a little scared but I came through. We were interduced and Mike walked out on stage with me following. Just as I was all the way out on stage, and Mike sat down on the drum stook, Dad exclaimed 'Oh God.' I took off, but Dad grabbed me and I sat down by Dad and he whispered "Play the melody stupid!" I played the melody. Paul came in and we jelled pretty well. Joe stood up by Mike and helped him and told him to 'wale. Mike did, he whanged away on the off-beat, and to come to think of it didnt sound to bads."

Ira Gitler is a serious young man about jazz. But in addition to writing analytical pieces about music and the men who create it, he often takes time out to indulge his sense of humor with limericks that swing. He has annotated Prestige jazz albums for nine years, has written for the major magazines in the music industry, and was anthologized in the British jazz book, Just Jazz. *Among other activities, he is presently reviewing jazz records and contributing serious and humorous articles to* Down Beat.

GITLIMERICKS
by Ira Gitler

1.

Once decried as rock 'n Rollins
now one of critics' li'l darlins
Sonny may have evolved his style
but he was cookin' all the while.

2.

It's very flukey
  when Pat Suzuki
    sings at a festival of jazz
'Cause whatever she's got
  (and a lot it's not)
    jazz doesn't need what she has!

3.

The hipster is a groovy guy
  colorful and laughable
    he's always fallin' by.

The hippy is overdone
  over-hip and he ain't no fun.

But one who is hip
now *he's* the man
he's always cool
and never a flip

I'm wise to you cats
  you'll skip one and two

149

focus on three
   and nod, "That's me."

4.

Little girls
chasing cats
falling down on their prats.

Called camp followers,
they're verbally abused
but not before they're physically used

One girl follows ballplayers
her sister, sailors seeks
but *these* chicks
   are something else—
they're musician freaks!

5.

Young tenormen working out of their Coltrane bags,
   playing Stitt-like runs and Rollins' lags.
Everyone's created in some image
   that's a beginning, we know
But you've got to come out of the scrimmage
   with a face of your own to show.

Ferris A. Benda, former jazz-record reviewer for Popular Knitting *and the* Poultry Growers & Feed Annual, *is widely known as a freelance writer, and has just completed the operation manual for the 1958 Pontiac. In addition to his present occupation writing liner notes for the Kellogg Cereal Co., he is active as an annotator and is compiling a complete discography of songs beginning with the word "the."*

Although Mr. Benda may be best remembered for having compiled and edited a complete listing of the personnel of all the Charlie Barnet bands, he has been influential in the recording industry, too. It was he who fought for the labeling of records in the center, around the hole, instead of at the circumference in white ink. And it was also Mr. Benda who suggested that Leonard Feather open an Encyclopedia of Jazz Room, and book talent alphabetically.

His appraisal of the current plight of the record industry appears below. It was written on yellow manila paper with a Smith-Corona portable typewriter at about twenty-three words a minute. It is unedited and unspliced.

(From Music '58, *published by Maher Publications, Inc., and reprinted by permission.)*

IS THE PHONOGRAPH RECORD HERE TO STAY?

Despite some feranstance in the coduviator, it seems likely to be semarilated.

by Ferris A. Benda

BEFORE phonograph records are manufactured at .54 rpm, and what we now call a 12-inch LP can be covered in a single groove, it's time to assess what we have to determine if we've drained it of its potential.

It's indicative that *Down Beat*'s reviewing staff gave the Civil War two stars because of the lack of empathy on the part of the Confederacy, who admittedly had some sparkling soloists but just couldn't seem to get any depth into their charts.

151

And how about that one-star rating these same reviewers gave the recent satellite launching fiasco at Cape Canaveral, reasoning as they did that it would have been far more dramatic, and quite possibly successful, if the rocket experts had dispensed with the Vanguard missile and the fuel and merely teed up the U.S. Sputnik and let the President loft it into orbit with a four wood.

There's also been a pretty general putting down of Maria Callas and Renata Tebaldi because they don't sing with a beat.

And how about this current controversy over who discovered the roots, and how far back you have to go before you play modern . . . or start to swing?

There's even talk now about whether a drummer actually needs drums to keep the rhythm going.

What about the academic question of the ability to improvise *vs.* a beard?

And will *Saints* finally become the national anthem?

These are questions all of us will have to face up to before too much longer. While you've read the preceding paragraphs, Gerry Mulligan has recorded with three different groups for two labels.

What I'm driving at is that the whole industry is standing still. The critics are becoming jadded with today's recorded output. They're looking for something new to review.

And the public, too, seeks new faces, new ideas, new sounds.

Something has to be done—and fast—to keep jazz from becoming lost in the shuffle. More will have to be done to keep records popular.

It's time for some sober thought. Or, at least, some thought.

Where, for instance, were the a&r men recently when Eddie Condon tuned a tenor banjo for a participant in a rock-and-roll session at Columbia? It's this kind of offbeat thing that the critics can get their teeth into. An offguard, swinging moment like this is worth at least four studio sessions.

And what ever happened to the fellow at RCA-Victor, the one with the gray-flannel tie, who memoed George Marek on doing an LP called *Sounds from Flushing in Hi-Fi,* to feature nearly 100 fixtures, including the entire section of eighteen in the men's room at Grand Central

Station? And that unusually musical one on the fifth floor of the Merchandise Mart in Chicago.

There are plenty of great ideas lying around just waiting to be picked up and rolled down the alley to see if they'll make a strike.

When, for instance, is Columbia going to stop sitting on that tape of Dave Brubeck ordering egg roll in a Chinese restaurant? How about that Capitol series of Benny Goodman inserting a new reed with commentary by Sol Yaged?

And what about those old Vocalions?

Now, I'm sure we're all agreed something must be done. But just what it is has been plaguing a&r men for months. One bright young a&r man with circles under his eyes and a girl friend who only last week told him some terribly distressing news, has been toying with the idea of taking a group like the Jazz Messengers or the Jazz Lab and having them record themes from, say Beethoven's *Fifth* or Haydn's *Clock Symphony* or Verdi's *Aïda* or Tchaikovsky's *Fourth*. This is not without merit.

It's not with merit, either, but it does show that he's thinking.

He is the same man who conceived the forthcoming *Turk Murphy Reads James Joyce* LPs, which will be issued in a very limited edition, indeed.

And enterprising no end is the record executive who has compiled a series of LPs on riverboats. The first few tracks are fine, but LP after LP of paddlewheels churning through brackish water can be pretty dismal. However, there's some interest on Vol. 3, track 5, when an engineer falls overboard and the passengers sing *Rock of Ages*.

There's also something to be said for the thought behind the recent conversation LP, by which you can play solo piano.

Actually, what the industry needs is something so startling and different that people will forget stereo tape and wide-screen movies, and will concentrate on LPs again. A price cut could do it.

But we have to get away from gimmicks. No more LPs like that one with Stan Kenton playing charts backwards. Or that Basie set of just endings. Let's stop thinking static. Think fluid!

There's a lot, too, that can be done with the LP package. Liner notes, for instance, could be solicited from such as Ernest Hemingway, T.S. Eliot, and Sherman Adams, to name just a few. They couldn't come up with any less information than on some liners today.

Record labels could be jazzed up, too. There's a report that Riverside is considering having all their labels written by Henry Miller. This makes for a completely functional LP. No part is wasted.

Album covers have made great strides. Some fashion models with obviously arrested puberty have brought the cover art question right down to the ultimate. There is no place left to go but into outright obscenity, or possibly X-ray plates.

The musicians are doing their part. They're not only experimenting with new and different instrumentation, but also with alien instruments. On a recent session, a Dixieland drummer used a goat bladder filled with helium instead of drums. It worked out fairly well, although it did keep rising to the ceiling when he was needed for four-bar breaks.

And there's currently a West Coast trumpeter who is experimenting with his mouthpiece in a violin. What he expects to accomplish is anyone's guess, but it will be unique . . . if at all.

Decca is reported to be seriously considering issue of an LP of music created by a cage of orangutangs, recorded live at the Bronx Zoo. It's pretty atonal, however, and may be considered too far out for release at this time.

It all remains a problem, then. And just sitting there with a headache doesn't help at all.

Ideas of all kinds are needed to make this thing go.

And, with any kind of a push, we can be back to 78s in no time at all.

Publicist-writer Elliot Horne has long observed the jazz scene and listened to its sounds. Some of the sounds have been musical, others have been verbal. With a good ear for both, Horne has compiled the latter into an up-to-date, often outrageously colorful dictionary for the modern cat. One word of warning: don't try to memorize these because, chances are, by the time you do, they'll be obsolete.

(Revised for The Jazz Word *by Elliot Horne from an article which originally appeared in the magazine section of the* New York Sunday Times, *Aug. 18, 1957. Reprinted by permission of the* New York Times *and the author.)*

THE ARGOT OF JAZZ

by Elliot Horne

A BAD FACE—A hipster's version of Rasputin; he's capable of infamous treacheries. A no-good cat who'd beat his mother for beer money.

A BOX—A hopeless square to whom hip is hep and jazz means nothing.

A FIG—A traditionalist; a cat for whom jazz sort of ended with the swing era. For him Mulligan's a stew, Parker a coat, and yes, sir, he remembers Paul Desmond. Wasn't he a cowboy actor in the movies?

A MOLDY FIG—The swing era was avant-garde stuff for this guy. He spells jazz "J-A-S-S" and reminisces passionately on jugs, washboards and riverboats. His record collection reeks of formaldehyde and the musician he digs must be dead for quite some time.

A VEST—From "greasy vest"; a rundown, even dirty cafeteria or restaurant. "A spoon," from "greasy spoon" is just as bad.

ALWAYS IN THE CELLAR—A horn man who always blows in a low register.

AX—Any musical instrument, even a piano.

BALL—Fun, a good time; also sexual intercourse.

BEAR—An unattractive girl.

BEARD—An avant-garde type; also a hipster.

155

BEHIND THE COTTON CURTAIN—The South, deep in as the X in Dixie.

BELLS—Vibraphones.

BLOW—To play a musical instrument, any instrument. Thus, "He blows fine piano." Also to perform any act: "He blows great conversation," "she blows scrambled eggs from endville." "Endville" (obs.) means the best.

BLOWS FOR CANINES—Plays long successions of high notes; screeches.

BOGUE—Fake, phony, false, bogus.

BOOMS—Drums. See also Hides.

BOX—Piano.

BREAD—Money. See also Geets, Green and "M."

BUG—To annoy, bother.

BUSTED—Arrested.

BUSTER—Generic for a guy with no future and not much of a past, either.

CAT—A male.

CHARTS—Musical arrangements. See also Maps.

COOL—Reserved, calm, relaxed.

COMMERCIALS—Request numbers. Usually played by dance bands. Some hot bands pointedly ignore requests and will play a blues, for example, if asked for *Rosetta*.

COPPIN zz's—Taking a nap, nodding (from cartoon argot—from circles above cartoons containing word, descriptive).

CRAZY—An exclamation of approval.

CRUMBS—A small sum of money; also called "small bread."

CUT—To take leave; to outdo.

CUTTING A TAKE—Explaining a point. In the recording business, literally to make a record.

DRAG—To bore; a disappointment.

ENDS—When a hipster buys clothes he begins with his Ends; his shoes. Formerly "kickers," "footpads" and "bottoms."

EYES TO COOL IT—The desire to relax, to get away from it all. To have eyes for anything is to want something, thus, "I got eyes to dig some sack time," meaning, "I'd like to get some sleep."

FALL—(up, in, by, etc.) To show up, enter, arrive.

FAR OUT—Extremely advanced; gone; they don't run trains there any more. In music, modern jazz.

FINGER POPPER—A cat (musician or hipster) who is swinging.

FINK—An objectionable person.

FUNKY—Originally evil, smelly; now earthy, bluesy, gutsy.

FUZZ—The cops.

GAS—Great. It's a gas!

GEETS—Money.

GIG—Work; also a job.

GOOD LOOKIN' OUT!—The guy tips you to both ends of a daily double; the blind date he gets you looks like Monroe. That's good lookin' out!

GO-IT-ALL—An automobile. See also Rubber, Short, and Wheels.

GREASE—To eat.

HANGIN'—Waiting around; sweating out a decision.

HAVE YOU SEEN MY HAT?—Have you seen my girl, chick, broad, rib?

HE SURE DID SPEAK—He played well or he blew great.

HE'S CLOSE, MAN!—The musician has done just about everything attainable on his ax; the cat digging him has been reached, *i.e.,* the guy blowing has hit a nerve.

HEAVY CREAM—A fat girl.

HIDES—Drums.

HIP—In the know.

HIPPY—Generic for a character who is supercool, overblasé, so far out that he appears to be asleep when he's digging something the most.

I'M SORRY, MAN—Expression of disagreement; bewilderment; failure to reach any conclusion.

J.C.—James Caesar Petrillo, former president of the American Federation of Musicians.

LAME—Square, but not hopelessly so. If you're lame you can learn.

LATER—Goodbye.

LEONA—Generic for Buster's wife, who is always deriding him for being nowhere.

LIVING ROOM GIG—A guest appearance on television. A gig is middle-musicianese for any job.

LOOSE WIG—A completely uninhibited, really way-out musician.

LYING—Playing the notes as written, rather than improvising on a theme; dogging it; playing with a sweet band rather than a hot one.

MAKE IT—Adequate, succeed; also, sexual conquest.

MAPS—Musical arrangements.

MEAN—The best; the greatest. See also Terrible, and Tough.

MEET—A jam session. Thus, "Fall in, man, we're gonna make a meet in the p.m."

"M"—Money.

MONKEY—A music critic. (He sees no music, hears no music, digs no music.)

MOTHER—(n) the greatest.

OOFUS—A dope; the kind of person who shows up at Newport with a ticket for Carnegie hall.

OUT SACK—An attractive dress, a knockout.

PAD—Home.

PIPE—A saxophone.

PLEADING A FIVE—When one cat refuses to get up on the stand and blow with another. Derived from pleading the Fifth Amendment or refusing to talk.

PUT ON—To tease, tongue-in-cheek deception.

SCENE—Any place where musicians play or gather; by extension, any place persons meet or any event they attend. Thus, "Let's make the country scene this week end."

SECURITY CATS—Television or radio musicians under contract who work regularly, preferring the security of a salary to gigging around with a band on different jobs.

SHE'S NUTS—The girl is a doll

SHORT—An automobile.

SHUCKING—Bluffing, faking, vamping, playing chords when a cat doesn't know the melody.

SIS—A girl.

SKY—A hat.

SMALL PIPE—Alto saxophone. Also, Big Pipe for baritone saxophone.

SPANK THE PLANK—Shake hands. Gimme some skin. Gimme five. Hello there!

SPLIT—To take leave.

SPLOUD!—High-spirited; happy; wild.

SOMETHING ELSE—A phenomenon so special it defies description. Thus, when asked if the music was great (or a gas), a cat may reply, "No, man, not that; it was something else."

STIFFIN' 'N' JIVIN'—Showing off or blowing high with lots of sound effects but not much musicianship.

TASTE—Usually a drink or some money. Can mean a portion of anything good.

TERRIBLE—The best; the greatest.

THE EARS ARE MOVING—A responsive audience.

THE MAN—The leader of a band.

THE MARBLE PAD—An asylum. Not to be confused with a crazy pad.

THE MASS GASSER—Billy Graham.

THE NOOSE IS HANGING—All the musicians are primed for a cutting session, *i.e.,* each man will attempt to outdo or cut the others.

THE SNAKE—The subway.

THE TIME BOX—Jail. Also "slammer."

THERE'S NO MORE ROOM—An individual or a group (musicians or otherwise) are too much.

THEY REALLY WALK—The rhythm section really swings.

TOUGH—The best; the greatest.

TWISTED—Confused, mixed up, way too far out.

VEIN—The double bass.

VINES—Clothes. Formerly "threads."

WAIL—To play, blow, or perform outstandingly. By extension, to do anything very well.

WANTS THE MOON—A cat who takes a melody for a wild ride, trying to do things his horn won't or can't.

WHEELS—An automobile.

WHIFFER—A flute.

WIG—To flip. Also, an intelligent cat.

WHO'S TAKING CARE OF BUSINESS?—Who's on the stand tonight?

YOU GOT IT ALL—The answer to "What's new?" when a cat means "Nothing, man."

7. SKYHOOK: From Nowhere to Nowhere

THE OPENER

GARY Kramer's study of the problem of narcotics in jazz, written especially for *The Jazz Word,* is, in every sense, a pioneering effort. Much has been said about The

Problem, but invariably from a moralistic or a superficial point of view.

Kramer, a serious student of jazz and its creators, a former *Billboard* reporter, and now with *Atlantic Records,* had been waiting a long time to put into print this searching, probing, well-documented analysis.

Skyhook contains no sure-fire answer or remedy for The Problem. But, it does bring into sharp focus some of the roots of The Problem, and illuminates some of the areas to be explored in reaching its solution.

If Kramer has done nothing more than place The Problem in honest perspective, his contribution has been of immeasurable value.

SKYHOOK: NARCOTICS AND JAZZ

by Gary Kramer

JAM SPOT RAIDED AS "THRILL CLUB
FOR JAZZ-STRUCK YOUNG GIRLS"

MINNEAPOLIS—More than 50 Minneapolis musicians and their friends were snatched by detectives from a jam session at the Harlem Breakfast Club and thrown into jail to languish there until the following noon. The charge: the club is a "thrill" place for jazz-struck young girls and their "reefer-smoking" musician friends.

WITH a certain irritating frequency, John Doe out in the suburbs of some big city in America opens up his morning newspaper and is jolted by a story like the one above. John Doe doesn't hear any jazz on the radio, he wouldn't dream of going near the "joints," he is not offered accounts of *musical* activities of jazzmen in the papers—but every so often an isolated item of scandal on the police blotter hits the local press or wire services and then a picture of *jazz* springs full-born from his imagination: a sordid, jumbled world in which narcotics addiction, illicit sex, criminal behavior and social anarchy run rampant.

Sensational stories like the one above sadden everyone interested in jazz, not only because of the grossly

The author acknowledges with gratitude the helpfulness of discussions on this subject with Charles Winick, Maxwell T. Cohen, Wallace Nottage and Kenneth Marshall.

erroneous picture it presents of musicians and the jazz world in general, but because such incidents lead to "crack-downs" and "clean-up" campaigns in which jazz, and the important things people are trying to do through art form and a constructive cultural force are railroaded jazz, suffer. Those who believe in jazz as a distinctive into having to defend vices and evils presumably allied to jazz—and sometimes it seems completely futile to keep protesting that there is no generic relationship between the two.

The quasi-official spokesmen for jazz have systematically tried to debunk the stereotyped public image of the jazz musician as a drug user. They insist that only a small minority of jazz musicians are addicts, and that drugs play no more of a role in jazz circles than they do in the private lives of people in any other professional group. Their point of view is that it is grossly unfair to judge the lot by the misadventures of a few, unrepresentative individuals.

Jazz magazines are performing a valuable service in placing the narcotics situation in better perspective. A great danger lies in minimizing the problem, however. What is really gained by trying to cover up the fact that use of marihuana and narcotics has been very widespread in certain periods of jazz history? This is a well-documented fact and is commonplace knowledge to anyone who has kept up any serious association with the jazz world. Examine a list of all the musicians who have run afoul of the law on this charge between, say, 1945 and the present! The roster is neither small nor unrepresentative. It makes, in fact, an abridged jazz Who's Who.

People who have a vested interest in jazz cannot be blamed for not wanting to publicize the past or present involvement of musicians and fans with drugs. This is, after all, a *national* problem that affects all age, economic, social and professional groups to some degree. Current information indicates that the jazz musician group is not the only highly addicted professional category (the medical profession, for example, shows a comparatively high addiction statistic)—but because musicians live in the public eye and have a special appeal to young people, they have a special problem in this connection.

The narcotics problem is many kinds of a problem. To present the public-relations angle of it first is perhaps to emphasize the least important part. Of more consequence is the individual musician and what happens to him once caught up in the narcotic habit. We can never measure what has been lost already through the premature deaths of several of jazz's most important artists, through careers blighted at particularly productive points in certain individuals' lives. The suffering, physical and mental, of the addict is of such a degree that it ought to engage our sympathy and motivate understanding, no matter how great our repugnance to the narcotic's "twilight world."

Nobody knows how many jazz musicians are drug users, either by number or by percent. We do know that too many are for the best interests of jazz. It is a known occupational hazard, and ought to be acknowledged as such. Instead of sensationalizing the issue, as the general press continually does, or pooh-poohing it, as many jazz writers are inclined to do, it would be better if a serious attempt were made to establish the extent of addiction and usage among jazz musicians and vigorously encourage scientific study of the sociological, psychiatric and legal aspects of the problem. Nothing would help jazz more than would a display from *within* the jazz world of a conscientious concern to obtain and circularize the real facts. Lacking these, as we do, the musician can be defended against a prejudiced public only with counterpropaganda.

ADDICTION
Addiction is the compulsive use of a habit-forming drug. Through repeated consumption of narcotic drugs like heroin, morphine or opium, the addict loses self-control over the drug and has an overwhelming desire or need to obtain the drug. His body is physically dependent on the drug, for deprived of it, the agonies of the abstinence syndrome are brought on. The addict is also emotionally and psychologically dependent on drugs, since they supply him with his prime satisfactions in life, and in the end they become the focus of his existence.

Drug *use* and addiction are not synonymous. It is important to realize that there are nonaddicting drugs—of which marihuana and cocaine are examples—and that the use of them may play a completely different role in the life of the user than do addicting drugs. Cases are known, too, of addicts who controlled their use of drugs carefully enough so that they were able to use drugs over a period of many years and lead a "normal," useful life, undetected by anyone and without being drawn into the addict subculture.

SOCIAL BACKGROUND OF THE JAZZ MUSICIAN

How marihuana and narcotics come into the jazz world in the first place is explained by the origin of the jazz musician himself. His social background provides the first key. From the twenties on, a high percentage of the jazz musicians, indeed, a majority of them, have been Negroes. The typical Negro musician either grew up or lived most of his early life in the Negro slum quarters of New York, Chicago, Detroit and a handful of other large cities in the North. Even those jazzmen originally from the South typically came to these same Northern cities at an early enough age to come under the same environmental influences. Because of segregated housing practices, the Negro professional musician, even after achieving a measure of financial success, generally is forced to remain a resident of the same racial ghettoes in which he spent his childhood.

In just those districts of New York, Chicago and Detroit where one finds the heaviest concentration of childhood (and present) homes of Negro musicians, one also finds the ratio of drug addiction very high, in comparison with the ratio for the general population of the city. This does not mean that drug use is "contagious" or that proximity to drug users makes it easier for nonusers to come under their influence. It *does* mean that certain oppressive features of life in slum neighborhoods, commonly experienced, weigh heavily on a significantly large number of individuals living there. When the pressures become unbearable, these individuals become vulnerable to drug use and/or the associated pathologies of *Street Corner Society*,[1] all of which stimulate and promote one the high incidence of drug addiction in neighborhoods

[1] William F. Whyte, *Street Corner Society*. Chicago: University of Chicago Press, 1943. A classic study of the conditions of living in a deteriorating Northern urban slum.

another: prostitution, sexual irregularities, gambling, rackets, gang warfare, anti-authority behavior, etc.

It is still not sufficiently appreciated by white people, even the basically sympathetic ones, what a destructive effect the routine life experience of the Negro has on his personality. For that reason, they do not understand where they are forced to live. The Negro typically has to contend with congested living quarters, absence of privacy, poor sanitation, limited conveniences of living, and an unstable, female-dominated family life at home. In school, the youngsters experience indifference or rejection by teachers working in overcrowded, understaffed conditions. Looking for work, the Negro is held back by both prejudice and his own difficulty of acquiring the educational and professional qualifications necessary to get the job. In his leisure hours, he experiences, even in a sophisticated city like New York, galling humiliations in restaurants, clubs and social gatherings. The harsh treatment of Negroes at the hands of the police and the courts adds yet another touch of gloom to this dismal picture.

The cumulative effect of such a life experience on the personality all too often is low self-esteem, withdrawal and disorientation from conventional society. Some individuals, struggling with repressive forces beyond their control, can express themselves finally only in acts of hostility and aggression.[2] This is the background necessary to understanding the high incidence of drug use in slum areas. These same conditions help explain the disproportionately high number of Negroes in over-all crime rates, in statistics of hospitalization for mental diseases, tuberculosis, alcoholic psychoses, illegitimate births, deliquency and so on. Wiping out drug users and suppliers, without wiping out discrimination and the other stroy the basic situation that encourages widespread drug social inequities of the Negro's daily life, would not destroy there; it would only throw him on to the other pathologies of Street-Corner Society.

All this is by way of making it understood that many Negro musicians have had their first experience with

[2] Statistics that document these generalizations will be found in Abram Kardiner and Lionel Ovesey, *The Mark of Oppression: A Psychosocial Study of the American Negro.* New York: Norton, 1951, pp. 51-64. The entire book is a brilliant study of the effect of caste and class on the individual Negro personality.

drugs long before coming into the jazz world proper. That the drug is easily accessible at a very early age to those growing up in the slums can be deduced from the high arrest figures of adolescents there. For example, while a majority of census tracts of New York had not a single teen-aged resident apprehended or treated for drug addiction in the period 1949-1952, in most parts of Harlem, more than 10 per cent of the boys 16 to 20 years old had been apprehended or treated in the same period. Presumably the actual figure is somewhat higher, since some, of course, would evade the attention of the law. A Chicago study of arrests for drug use showed that roughly 16 per cent of all Negro boys born in Chicago in 1931 had by 1951 been arrested for narcotics violations.[3]

Many musicians continue in adult life a practice originating in adolescence. Earlier anxieties brought on by economic instability, racial discrimination, sexual and emotional inadequacy, are not immediately obliterated by a certain amount of acceptance as a jazz musician. People who *were* able to solve their problems to their own satisfaction early in life by "getting high" have a strong inducement to continue to do so later on, as long as the original conditions for the anxieties persist. And they plainly do, in the case of many musicians.

The high rate of drug use in depressed urban neighborhoods is not to be construed as evidence of a more permissive attitude to drug use on the part of the community proper. The churches, schools, and civic and political organizations in an area like Harlem, for example, are far more sensitive to the narcotics problem than their counterparts elsewhere—and precisely because they live so close to it. Anyone who has either had an addict in the family or observed a case of addiction at close hand knows very well the financial burden and emotional

[3] John A. Clausen, "Social Patterns, Personality, and Adolescent Drug Use," article in *Explorations in Social Psychiatry*, ed. by Alexander H. Leighton, John A. Clausen and Robert N. Wilson. New York: Basic Books, 1957, p. 238.
These statistics show an alarming degree of adolescent drug use among Negroes. They may cover up the true extent of adolescent drug use in middle- and upper-class white neighborhoods, however. Negroes are more "vulnerable" to arrest, and as a consequence usually are shown in a poor light in statistics comparing them to other groups better able to camouflage crime incidence in their neighborhoods.

drain that it is—and could hardly take an indifferent attitude to its use by others as yet unaddicted. For various reasons, however, the family and conventional institutions have a weaker influence on the young in depressed neighborhoods. The adolescent often feels strong ties only to his peer group, which may be a gang. He is a realist, and his possibilities of "amounting to" something in life have to be achieved in terms of the Street-Corner Society described before. All this conditions him to accepting the basic premises of the drug subculture.

Sociology provides only the first key. The narcotics problem is by no means confined to the socially victimized residents of Harlem and Chicago's South Side. In jazz, in particular, drug use knows no color lines. As for white musician addicts, we are confronted by the puzzling fact that in many cases, their early economic and social background is quite "respectable" and comfortably bourgeois. In the final analysis, only detailed and intimate knowledge of the individual musician allows us to understand his own special relationship to drugs.

SOME STEREOTYPED REASONS FOR DRUG USE

Almost all musician users, if questioned about their first use of drugs, give the impression that it started in a very casual, uncalculated way. They would have you believe that the motivation was purely hedonistic; they were looking for a new "kick," as if it were nothing different than going to bed with some new broad. There is an expression of this attitude in Champion Jack Dupree's *Junker's Blues:*

> Some people call me a Junker
> 'Cause I'm loaded all the time
> I just feel happy
> And I feel good all the time.
>
> Some people say I use the needle
> And some say I sniff cocaine
> But that's the best old feeling in the world
> That I've ever seen.
>
> Say goodbye, goodbye to whiskey
> Lordy, so long to gin.

166

I just want my reefers.
I just want to feel high again.[4]

It seldom happens that one begins using drugs on one's own initiative. It is usually done at the urging of someone you love or respect. The circumstances under which the "initiation" takes place are generally not sensational in any way. This contributes, too, to the feeling of many addicts that there was nothing of special significance about their first step into the drug orbit. Insofar as use is limited to moderate smoking of marihuana, which is nonaddicting and over which self-control can be exercised, the hedonistic "kick" may be the true aim.

If a jazzman first begins taking drugs early in his professional career, he may feel that drug use has a connection with his playing. Some musicians believe that drugs have an almost magic ability to stimulate their creative and technical powers, and have used this as a ground for insisting that musicians are entitled to special consideration in the matter of drug use.

What really happens to the musician who "turns on" and then goes on to the bandstand and blows? Mezz Mezzrow, in his autobiography, *Really The Blues,* gives this description of what happened to him after taking his *first* marihuana cigarette:

> The first thing I noticed was that I began to hear my saxophone as though it was inside my head. All the other instruments sounded like they were way off in the distance; I got the same sensation you'd get if you stuffed your ears with cotton and talked out loud. Then I began to feel the vibrations of the reed much more pronounced against my lip, and my head buzzed like a loudspeaker. I found I was slurring much better and putting just the right feeling into my phrases—I was really coming on. All the notes came easing out of my horn like they'd already been made up, greased and stuffed into the bell, so all I had to do was blow a little and send them on their way. The phrases seemed to have more continuity to them and I was sticking to the

---

[4] Champion Jack Dupree, *Blues From The Gutter,* Atlantic LP 8019. *Junker's Blues,* by Champion Jack Dupree, is reprinted by permission of Progressive Music Publishing Co., Inc. Copyright 1959.

theme without even going tangent. I felt I could go on playing for years without running out of ideas and energy. There wasn't any struggle. I began to feel very happy and sure of myself. With my loaded horn, I could take all the fist-swinging, evil things in the world and bring them together in perfect harmony.[5]

Not only did Mezzrow feel that he personally reached Olympian heights, but he would have us believe that the audience also caught the divine spark from his marihuana-inspired playing:

The people were going crazy over the subtle changes in our playing; they couldn't dig what was happening but some kind of electricity was crackling in the air and it made them all glow and jump.[6]

The audience became "one solid, mesmerized mass." One girl, it seems, got completely hysterical and lost control of herself. While listening to Mezzrow, she put on an impromptu obscene dance, "all the time screaming, 'Cut it out! It's murder!' but her body wasn't saying no."[7]

This may all be a lot of poppycock. That marihuana or any narcotic ever made much of a musician out of Mezz Mezzrow would certainly be a thesis hard to defend. If his playing had the Dionysian effect he describes above, it is more than likely that plenty of "pot" was circulating among the members of his audience as well as among the musicians on the stand. Nevertheless, it is important to note that Mezzrow's attitude has been repeatedly voiced by jazzmen, and it is still to be heard today. Many first-rate musicians have *believed* that their playing was greatly improved as a result of "getting high." They say that they have an enormously heightened sensitivity in regard to sound, rhythm, timing and motor coordination. They often assert that drugs "relax" them and remove inhibitions.

Two published experiments tend to prove that marihuana and the addicting drugs are cruelly self-deluding on this score. Dr. C. Knight Aldrich administered the Sea-

[5] Milton (Mezz) Mezzrow, *Really The Blues.* New York: Random House, 1946, pp. 72-73.

[6] *Id.* at p. 73

[7] *Id.* at p. 75

shore Test to twelve former users of marihuana while they were under the influence of pyra-hexyl compound, a marihuana-like synthetic which gives a psychological effect identical to marihuana. The group, which included two professional musicians, took the Seashore Test three different times, under "normal" circumstances and while under the "influence" of pyra-hexyl compound.

The Seashore Test tests ability to recognize differences in pitch, dynamics, time, timbre and identification of rhythm patterns. Eight of the patients thought they did better on the tests while "high"; none recognized a loss of efficiency. In point of fact, none of the men taking the test improved his score while "high"; the general performance was much worse.[8]

A group of experimenters, headed by Dr. Edwin G. Williams, later confirmed the results reported by Dr. Aldrich. This research team also gave marihuana users the Seashore Test under controlled conditions, and reported poorer performance while "high" and also noted that patients who took the test *thought* they had done better while artifically stimulated. Dr. Williams' group gave the marihuana users a battery of tests, of which the Seashore Test was only one. The results showed that use of marihuana makes comprehensive and analytical thinking more difficult, and an adverse effect was noted on accuracy in those tests which require concentration and dexterity.[9]

These experiments, of course, did not test specific *jazz* qualities, nor were they conducted with a significant sample of jazz musicians. However, they are in line with the present consensus of jazz critics: that drug use (including marihuana, but especially true of the addicting drugs) substantially interferes with the disciplines necessary for best performance. The musician user himself undoubtedly *feels* better and feels his playing is better when "high," but there is no correlation between this and good performance. A special case, of course, would be the addict on whom the effects of the abstinence

[8] C. Knight Aldrich, "The effect of a synthetic marihuana-like compound on musical talent as measured by the Seashore Test," *U. S. Public Health Report,* vol. 59 (1944), pp. 431-433.
[9] Edwin G. Williams *et al.,* "Studies on Marihuana and Pyra-Hexyl Compound," *U. S. Public Health Report,* vol. 61 (1946), pp. 1059-1082.

syndrome have come to be so extreme that he is all but ineffective unless he is stimulated by the drug.

PERSONALITY AND THE MUSICIAN USER

Defense of the use of drugs for "kicks" or for its supposed stimulation for better playing are ordinarily cover-ups for a more deep-seated motivation for use. Neither of these factors induce the average jazz musician to indulge in even one marihuana cigarette. Why narcotics use becomes a part of the behavior pattern of some musicians and not of others is a complex problem that so far has not been illuminated by much solid research. The answer appears to lie in an understanding of the make-up of the individual personality and an infinity of variables in his life-experience.

Psychiatrists look on the repeated use of either marihuana or the addicting drugs as an index to a long-established pattern of anxiety and maladjustment. They say that drug use, even on the conscious level, is not casual and it is certainly not a kind of innocent pleasure-seeking. Much as addicts like to insist that their "troubles" all started with taking drugs (thus establishing a convenient scapegoat for a wide variety of difficulties that they usually get into because of their irresistible urge for the drug), investigation shows that before that step, there was already more trouble in the addict's past than he could cope with. Adolescent addicts typically show serious emotional problems involving their family and their peers—participation in gangs, truancy and other school-adjustment problems, delinquency and tangles with the law—long before first use of drugs. The accompanying insecurities and feelings of low esteem and inadequacy establish the need for the kind of escape that a drug can give.

Studies of a group of young men at the Federal hospital for narcotics addicts at Lexington, Kentucky, found that *all* showed marked evidence of psychopathology. Nearly half were classified as incipient or overt schizophrenics. The others were said to show "delinquency dominated disorders" and "inadequate personalities." The researchers concluded, "The adolescent opiate addict functions below his intellectual capacity or potential. Both consciously and unconsciously, his emotional responsivity is constricted and/or controlled. . . . Acute-

170

ly sensitive to the malignant and rejective aspects in his interpersonal environment, he responds with sociopathic attitudes and behavior."[10]

If all addicts are sick, to greater or lesser degree, the question arises, "In the case of musician addicts, what are the special qualities of the jazz world that contribute to his being influenced to use drugs? Is there something 'sick' about the jazz environment itself?" The truth is that jazz, during most of its history, *has* been connected with most of the delinquent aspects of Street-Corner Society—but at the same time, it must be said that jazz *also* offered a legitimate and rather unique means of transcending an atmosphere of squalor and evil.

The night-club world of the jazz musician is a highly special one. It is a subculture with its own values, some of them independent of (and occasionally, even contrary to) those of conventional society. It is not "sick" *per se*. Living continuously in such an environment has its special dangers, however, and they can have an acute effect on both musicians and people who follow jazz seriously as fans.

The difficulty of gaining *entrée* into the jazz world is the first reef on which the inexperienced can conceivably founder. If one becomes a jazz musician at all, the first attempts to get into the field ordinarily occur while one is still in the teen years. The decision to be a jazz musician is in itself a conscious attempt to "escape" an otherwise unattractive environment, in many cases. John Clellon Holmes, speaking of Cleo, an 18-year-old piano player in his novel, *The Horn,* describes the situation well in telling how he, "like so many musicians, seemed to have no substantial homely life but jazz, no other hours, but night."

It is difficult for a young musician to enter the field in the first place, and it is not easy to find stable employment in the apprentice years, even if one does have above-average talent. To make matters worse, jazz periodically goes through "lean" stretches, sometimes a number of years long, making the life of a young would-be jazz musician a grueling test of endurance. It is easy to

[10] Donald L. Gerard and Conan Kornetsky, "Adolescent opiate addiction: a study of control and addict subjects," *Psychiatric Quarterly,* vol. 29 (1955), p. 479.

see how important it is, under these circumstances, for a young musician to gain recognition from those who have "made" it. It is equally clear how easily he can be misled if he knows that some jazz star whom he idolizes is an addict. A young, emotionally immature person will be influenced to "identify" totally with some older musician he admires—and he may feel that taking drugs, as the older man does, is part and parcel of gaining acceptance in his group.

The same thing can sometimes be seen in operation among young people who are not practicing musicians, but fans. They often show a strong urge to identify with a famous musician who is a known addict—sometimes not in spite of, but *because of* his addiction. Charlie Parker and Billie Holiday become their own private symbols of social defiance. Some of this hero-worship need not be taken too seriously; it is typical youthful "fad" behavior, a part of the eternal aspiration of the young to be "hip" and a class apart from the "squares." When emulation of the idol leads to the point where the devotee also begins to take addicting drugs, however, then obviously a more serious personality problem is manifesting itself.

The responsibility of the older, established musician can be seen to be a very heavy one. To both the younger musicians and to the youthful fans, his example can be decisive, for better or worse. It is not amiss to comment that some very influential musicians have not only been thoughtless in this regard, there have been cases where some used their power with deliberate malevolence. The fictional character of Edgar Pool, a jazz musician in *The Horn,* who takes a perverted pleasure in "turning on" the singer, Geordie, was obviously drawn from real life. People familiar with addicts are aware that some of them get some kind of twisted psychic reward out of making "junkies" of others.

In addition to whatever emotional satisfaction an addict gets from "swelling the ranks," an economic angle is also involved. Some musicians, in a position to do so, have used their influence in a subtle way to see that available work went to fellow-addicts and that the non-addict was barred. There have been situations where it was to one's financial advantage to be "one of the boys." An important incidental feature of an all-addict group

172

is that more lines of supply are made available, which is to the mutual advantage of all.

At the more extreme stages of addiction, the addict is completely submerged in the drug culture. A sense of moral obligation is obscured in him by his total preoccupation with obtaining and using drugs. At that point, even music becomes of secondary interest to him; it may finally come to mean little more than a quick source of income to sustain drug use. A kind of willful "point of no return" occurs when the musician quits playing and hocks his horn.

THE JAZZMAN IN (OR OUT OF) SOCIETY

Studying the habits of professional musicians, we observe that drugs seem to have played different roles in different historical periods. One drug tends to be used more frequently than another, and seemingly, for different reasons. Charles Winick has suggested that there is a typological connection between the kind of music a jazzman plays, his acceptance (or nonacceptance) by society—and the specific drug he uses.[11]

Nonacceptance by society has more often than not been the situation with which the jazzman has had to contend. This has always been an important factor in encouraging drug use among jazz musicians. Toward the end of the twenties, jazz suffered its own private kind of Depression. Lack of work and lack of public interest had come suddenly and it hit the musicians hard. Mezzrow describes the situation in Chicago:

> The nights were coming to be long shimmying chains of muggles for us, reaching from nowhere all the way to nothing-doing, each one longer and knottier than the last. The weed was the only thing that kept us going, no jive.[12]

The preferred drug of the twenties seems to have been marihuana, although a variety of others were used, too. Nobody seems to have regarded smoking marihuana as especially scandalous. Its use was very widespread, and it is not surprising that references to it oc-

[11] Charles Winick, "Narcotics Addiction and Its Treatment," *Law and Contemporary Problems,* vol. 22 (1957), p. 15.
[12] Mezzrow, *op. cit. supra* note 5, at p. 164.

cur in the titles of several well-known jazz discs of the late twenties and the thirties: *Golden Leaf Strut* (Original New Orleans Rhythm Kings, 1925), *Muggles* (Louis Armstrong, 1928), *The Viper's Drag* (Cab Calloway, 1930), *Tee Rollers Rub* (Freddie "Redd" Nicholson, 1930), *Chant of The Weed* and *Reefer Man* (Don Redman, 1931, 1932), *Sendin' The Vipers* (Mezz Mezzrow, 1934), *A Viper's Moan* and *Jerry The Junker* (Willie Bryant, 1935), *You'se A Viper* (Stuff Smith, 1936), and *Tea and Trumpets* (Rex Stewart, 1937). Certain lines referring to drugs could also be cited in popular songs of the period by Irving Berlin, Cole Porter and others. The wonderful song by Arthur Johnston and Sam Coslow that we know as *Lotus Blossom* was originally entitled *Marihuana*.

Jazz musicians needed something to offset the desperate condition in which they found themselves after "hot" jazz all but died in the late twenties. Marihuana helped them reconcile themselves to an intolerable reality, they insisted. This use of marihuana as a kind of psychological crutch suggests a potential danger that lies within this drug, so often defended by musicians as nonhabit-forming and "practically harmless." One asks, "If marihuana is nonaddicting, why is it that so many people who smoke it spend so much of their time seeking and using marihuana? They act as if they can't live without it." The truth seems to be that many people who smoke marihuana, while not physically dependent on it, are "hooked" by circumstances in life to feel a need for the escape that it can give. The more this becomes the habitual way of facing up to problems, the more the marihuana user is conditioned to identify with the drug subculture. Being "hooked" in *that* sense establishes a basis for experimenting with the addicting drugs—and becoming "hooked" in a very real physiological sense.

Marihuana is still in general circulation among musicians, but the comparatively high use of addicting drugs (notably heroin) in the "modern" period, is a more disturbing fact. The majority of musicians would not dream of going near the "hard stuff," but the number of those who have, and do, is too high. Heroin, in particular, is the sinister specter behind the untimely deaths and shattered careers of several contemporary "greats." Because it takes only a short period of use to become addicted to heroin, and for it to begin taking its toll of the body and mind, its danger cannot be overestimated.

Winick believes that there is more than a coincidence in the fact that the music played by the "modern" jazz-men is often described by them as "way out"—the same expression they use to describe the effect of heroin.[13] The complexities and emotional flatness of the "cool" school of jazz mirror the passivity and detachment of the heroin addict, he feels. That these same musicians often call each other "cats" is also interesting, since cats are symbols of passivity. Winick insists that here, again, the extreme degree of social alienation felt for so many years by a large number of "modern" musicians was operative in their tendency to drug use. To be led to take something as dangerous as heroin is an index of the gravity of their sense of social isolation. Falling in line with this is the affinity for "cool" jazz and drugs of the "beatniks," another startling antisocial product of our times.

The outer social pressures on the jazz musician, from the beginning of the forties on, have been extreme. First, there was the war itself, with its horrors, tensions and uncertainties. For the Negro, it was a particular-ly critical period: he found himself involved in a major population shift, with all its attendant upheaval in values and new aspirations; he suffered augmented racial perse-cution and was the object of several bloody riots; as a soldier, he had to live with the irony of fighting a war for "freedom" even though his own experience of freedom at home was severely circumscribed. Heightened racial awareness was an important development out of the stresses and strains of the war years, and it played an increasingly important role in the thinking of the indi-vidual Negro musician.

On a musical plane, a revolution was brewing, too, finally taking shape in the bop movement. Bop's initial problem was not to find an audience, but to achieve some kind of status and recognition amongst the jazz musicians themselves. In a few exciting years, in the jamming seminars in out-of-the-way clubs in Harlem and the Village, bop developed a group of brilliant in-strumentalists, whose talents and ideas simply could not

[13] Winick, *op. cit. supra* note 11, at pp. 15, 21.

be laughed away. Baffled as many of the older musicians were by the new "sounds," bop clearly had a "message" for a new era setting in. The audience materialized, too: the young people, who in those years were always thought of by their elders as confused, rootless and amoral, and to whom bop must have seemed the embodiment of all that and more.

For a time in the mid-forties, it seemed that bop was not merely a fad, it became practically a whole way of life. We all remember the bop talk and the bop jokes. In our mind's eye, we can still see the enthusiasts in berets, gold-and-black horn-rimmed glasses, leopard-skin vests, and goatees. It had all the characteristics of a miniature society that might have been created (and dressed) by the *Madwoman of Chaillot*.

Granted, this caricature was the public image of the bopster—and underneath it was serious music-making of a value that perhaps is being fully appreciated only now. It is symptomatic of a deep personality fault, however, when music that is at heart aggressively self-conscious, uncertain, defensive and inferiority-complex-ridden (as bop was) is presented in a jocular manner. Underneath all the hilarity of bop lay a poorly concealed hostility to society. The very word *bop,* as Ralph Ellison has pointed out, suggests a kind of schizophrenia: "a word which throws up its hands in clownish self-depreciation before all the complexity of sound and rhythm and self-assertive passion which it pretends to name; a mask-word for the charged ambiguities of the new sound, hiding the serious face of art."[14]

It is against this broad background of outer and inner pressures that we have to try to understand the *hipness* of drug use in bop's heyday. It was so smart that some clubs all but advertised publicly that addict-musicians made their place their headquarters. There were individual musicians, too, in those days, who dramatized their "habit," sometimes in rather bizarre ways. One musician, for instance, would come to the stand for a new set with a white towel wrapped around his arm, suggesting that he had just had an injection. It was a joke on his part, since he was a nonuser, but it illustrates

[14] Ralph Ellison, "The Golden Age/Time Past"; Manners and Morals at Minton's, 1941: the setting for a revolution, *Esquire,* January 1959, p. 108.

the kind of "way out" thinking that one encountered.

Some of this exhibitionism is, of course, in the best show-business tradition. We don't want to go to the movies, after a hard day at the office, to see something that reminds us of our own humdrum reality. What is wanted is something glamorous, exotic, weird or sensational. Those are familiar entertainment values, and many people must have gone to the jazz spots in those days *hoping* to see a reefer-smoking musician or someone with puncture scars on his arm (in the same way that in an earlier day people paid admission to see the screaming "loonies" in an insane asylum).

It is a little sacrilegious to suggest that the bop years were something less than the "good old days," but the high frequency of drug use in that period would in itself suggest that there were unpleasant features to the bop movement which we tend to forget now. The surface-level gaiety and insouciance of the boppers and their casual, hip use of drugs represent only one side of the coin; fanaticism, malice,[15] deep-seated anxiety, expressions of inadequacy and a wish for withdrawal from "reality" were a part of bop, too.

The *raison d'être* of the clubs, to some extent, seemed to lie in this situation. Ellison speaks of Minton's, for example, "Most of them, black and white alike, were hardly aware of where they were or what time it was; nor did they wish to be. They thought of Minton's as a sanctuary, where in an atmosphere blended of nostalgia and a music-and-drink-lulled suspension of time they could retreat from the wartime tensions of the town. The meaning of time-present was not their concern."[16]

In June 1950, Dizzy Gillespie, breaking up his big band, cried, "Bop is at the end of the road. Now everybody wants dance music." Bop *was* dead, and it had been pretty sick for a few years before Dizzy's announcement. The late forties offered shrinking opportunities for employment, and by 1950 practically none (except of the "commercial" type). More than ever before, drug

[15] Louis Armstrong used the word "malice" in connection with bop musicians in a memorable article (*Down Beat,* April 7, 1948, p. 2). What he had to say about the music-making of the bop musicians wasn't entirely justified, but he certainly struck home with his expression, "that modern malice."

[16] Ellison, *op. cit. supra* note 14, at p. 107.

177

use played an important role in jazz circles in the following lean years. It is true that from 1948 on, a general increase in drug use was noted all over the country. Whatever the reasons for this for the rest of the population, it isn't hard to see why musicians at that time felt a strong need, both to withdraw from an unappreciative world and at the same time to show hostility to it.

In intramural jazz circles, one particularly bitter argument in those years concerned allegations by Negro musicians that the few jobs that were available were going to white musicians. The resentment was all the deeper for their feeling that the Negro musician had pioneered the "modern" movement, and therefore if anyone worked, *he* should. This was not the usual kind of "sour grapes." Several of the most important Negro musicians went through personal crises of an extreme kind in the 1947-1950 period, and in each case feelings of racial persecution, on both the personal and the artistic level, played a critical part in their breakdowns. Not unexpectedly, each of these individuals had tried to alleviate his troubles by drug use.

With only weak public support, the jazz musicians, in the post-bop years, were forced into a highly introverted world. Many stuck to their convictions about the worth of the music they had been playing and starved rather than "go commercial." They played for each other and forgot everything else. Their open disinterest and all but neurotic anxiety to show contempt for their audience were their ways of attacking the "world" (although what it really consisted of was their last, few diehard friends). *Coolness* came to describe not only a way of playing, but the glacial stage mannerisms, the lack of body movement, the unresponsiveness to audience reaction that the younger musicians refined little by little to a sadistic nicety. More than one writer has noted that the cool musicians acted as if they wanted to convey the *impression* that they were addicts in a trance.

To what a catastrophic end all this might have come is hard to say. Fortunately, the entire situation has been tremendously improved by the revival of jazz on a very big scale in the past five years. The proliferation of jazz festivals about the country, the unprecedentedly high sales volume of jazz recordings, the popularity of jazz in movies and TV, are just a few of the signs that a new era has dawned for jazz—and the jazz musician. Jazz, happily, is again becoming the property of the many, rather than the few, and this has been a healthy tonic all the way round.

The jazzman today faces a great opportunity. Not only can he expect to be relieved of many of his old financial anxieties, the potential is here for him to achieve status on a professional and social level to a degree that was never possible before. There are many indications, too, that the racial issue, on a strictly musical plane at least, is disappearing. All these developments are essential first steps to removing the conditions that have given narcotics the particular place they have had in jazz in the past.

By no means have we reached the millennium, however. Just as the music we are hearing today is simply a further development of what was being played in the bop and "cool" periods, and has survived attacks and neglect— so have some of the attitudes and mannerisms of a decade ago remained alive and been carried over into the present. The music industry can do much to prevent drug use from having the place in jazz in the future that it had in the past by taking some constructive action— and taking it now.

Nothing can be done on this one plane, however, unless a more enlightened approach to the whole problem of narcotics addiction is taken on the national, state and community levels as well. The press continually agitates against pushers and "dope fiends." Congressional committees can always spare time and appropriate money to "investigate" the problem—so long as this is public and productive of headlines. The more tedious job of revising outdated laws and educating the public to the real nature of drug addiction, making them aware of the urgent need of much greater appropriations for more specialized hospitals and research, seems to be too great a self-sacrifice to expect from these crusaders. It is on the local level that one hears most noise and sees least constructive action. State and city governments have long been content to throw their narcotics problems into the lap of the Federal Government. A city like New York in these last years has had only one hospital offering special facilities for treating and rehabilitating addicts—this was limited to addicts under twenty-

179

one years of age—and this is scheduled to be closed down at the end of 1959.

To merely get addicts into hospitals and give them the "cure" is only the first step in their eventual rehabilitation. They will fall back on narcotics on their return home, if the social, economic and personal problems that induced them to take drugs in the first place still seem insoluble. Addicts can be completely cured, but they need strong motivation to keep from returning to the drug. The artist's feeling of self-respect and pride in his work can be used as an important tool in keeping the jazzman "straight."

THE NEW YORK "POLICE CARD" PROBLEM

A jazz musician who has once been convicted on a narcotics charge faces one particularly difficult hurdle in achieving rehabilitation. In addition to having to overcome the reluctance of the night-club owner to hire someone known to have been an addict (since the employer will always have lingering doubts as to whether the ex-addict will stay "cured"), the musician is confronted in New York (and Miami) with the necessity of having his cabaret employee's identification card reissued by the police department. This was taken from him at the time of arrest, and without it he cannot work in any establishment that sells liquor.

For many jazz musicians, it is absolutely essential to be able to play in New York clubs—and therefore it is tragic that some of them, on leaving prison or the Federal hospital at Lexington, Kentucky, are cut off from their livelihood at a time when they need it most, for financial, therapeutic and psychic reasons. Ordinarily, the card, which is referred to by musicians as "the police card," will be withheld by the police for a lengthy, indeterminate period of time. One jazz musician, whose records have been best sellers for years, has not had a chance to work in a New York club in eight years. Another world-famous "great" who was one of the founding fathers of modern jazz has been denied his card for thirteen years. The tragic plight of Billie Holiday in this matter has been well publicized. Apart from these stars, who could work in other cities if they wished and do pretty well financially, there are any number of less well-

180

known musicians on whom this ban has worked to a more devastating degree.

Theoretically, after "keeping clean" for a long time, the ex-addict may re-apply for his "police card." The burden of proof is on him to show that he has "kicked the habit." He also must prove that he has been on good behavior ("reformed," so to speak), by presenting affidavits to that effect from citizens of unquestioned integrity. After a hearing (which, incidentally, is held before a police officer, and not a competent civil authority) and investigations, the card may be restored—usually, a "temporary" or "restrictive" card.

Many protests have been made against this system. It seems unjust that an addict—in contrast to persons convicted of other crimes—does not pay his "debt to society" merely by serving his allotted time in prison. He goes on paying, by being deprived of a basic right—the right to work—for as long as a decade later under this system. It is to the lasting credit of the jazz magazines, *Down Beat* and *Metronome,* that for years they have courageously and consistently attacked the barbarism of this ordinance.

The crusading New York attorney, Maxwell T. Cohen, who has defended a number of musicians who have had narcotics problems, questioned the constitutionality of this law in *Rubenstein et al.* v. *Kennedy, McElroy et al.* Cohen's crucial point is that no statutory authority exists now (nor has it ever existed) that requires a person to have a card issued by the police department to obtain gainful employment—nor does such authority exist to deprive people of work, should they have no such card. Although cards were issued to the successful plaintiffs in the *Rubenstein* case, for technical reasons, the Constitutional question raised here was not adjudicated. In some future test case, it will be, and there is reasonable hope that this will knock out the props from under this "police card" system. If the music industry had had the courage to defend the rights of musicians in this matter, this inequitable system would have been abolished long ago. The unwillingness of the record companies, booking agencies, and especially the executive board of Local 802 of the musicians' union, to antagonize the police department has led them to pursue a "do nothing" attitude.

181

The New York Police Department, at least in recent years, cannot be said to have pursued a policy of persecution aimed at musician groups specifically. Significantly, in a recent random roundup of "pushers" and addicts in New York, 127 persons were arrested; not one was a musician or cabaret employee. Other large cities —like Philadelphia and Los Angeles—that do not have the "police card" system, employ other methods of harassment and legal persecution of musicians that are equally unjust and perhaps have an even more damaging effect on a musician's employment possibilities in those particular cities.

THE PRESSING NEED FOR RESEARCH

Along with improved legislation and more adequate hospital facilities for treatment, the most important need in this whole area is greatly expanded *research*. Our ignorance of the general nature of drug addiction is profound, and as for the special problem of jazz, the jazz musician and drug use, our ignorance is virtually complete. There is not one scientific paper that deals with the latter subject exclusively and in detail. The subject, as a matter of fact, never got the benefit of a single, serious public discussion until the Newport Jazz Festival of 1957. One morning, during the Festival that year, a panel of musicians and outside experts discussed the problem, but only after considerable protest and controversy within jazz ranks.

That panel discussion at Newport led to some constructive action.[17] At the urging of John Hammond, Louis Lorillard and other Festival officials decided to set aside $5,000 from the receipts of the Festival to study the role of narcotics in jazz. As a consequence of this grant, the Musicians' Clinic was set up in New York, with Charles Winick as its executive director. The Clinic is not a medical facility, but a research organization whose central purpose is to study the dynamics of drug use by

[17] There is also some indication that another positive result of the Newport panel discussion in 1957 has been improved press relations for jazz on the narcotics problem. Maxwell T. Cohen documented some of the biased reporting and out-and-out smears that jazz musicians are plagued with when they get involved with narcotics. The many reporters in the audience took to heart his criticism of their stereotyped link of drug use and jazz—and their tendency to sensationalize jazz-drug "incidents."

182

musicians. Another important function of the Clinic is to assist musicians to obtain medical help, legal assistance and psychiatric treatment they may need. Dr. Winick and his group have already had detailed interviews with several hundred musicians who are or have been addicts. This has already brought up extremely important information about the backgrounds of musician addicts, its effect on their playing, their attitudes to drugs, the effectiveness of treatment, and so on.

The Musicans' Clinic and the work it is doing represent the first constructive step taken to get at the root of the narcotics problem as it specifically affects the musician. The work of this organization has so far been made possible through the contributions of private individuals, and the voluntary offer of services by doctors, psychiatrists, lawyers, social workers, and other individuals conscientiously concerned about the narcotics problem as it affects jazz. On an official level, the music industry has done nothing to support the Musicians' Clinic (though several record-company officials have been generous contributors), nor have the unions who collect dues from many musicians who could benefit from the Clinic's work.

We hear much these days about the new maturity of jazz. Writers on jazz speak as if it were an accomplished fact that jazz has attained the status of older art forms. If jazz has come that far, then it ought to be possible to identify oneself with jazz in all its ramifications with the same confidence and pride as with classical music or the plastic arts. Only when it is completely clear to the general public that jazz is not the sinister Muse of a deviant culture can it achieve its legitimate place in American life.

8. NEW YORK: It's a Soul Town

THE OPENER

IN THE JAZZ world as in nearly every world, New York is where the action is. Anyone who wants to *make* it must sooner or later come to New York.

Burt Korall's panoramic view of New York sets the stage for Jon Hendricks' swinging poem and George Russell's incisive music in the album, New York, N.Y. *Hendricks' poem and Russell's music sing a jazz symphony of the city, and this prose-poem is the perfect overture.*

(*New York, N.Y.,* Decca DL 9216. Portion of liner notes reprinted by permission.)

NEW YORK, N. Y....
The Most Fascinating Address
by Burt Korall

NEW YORK, N.Y. is a world unto itself, a world of tumult and silence, love and hate, towering buildings and tenements, big people and small . . . and the gradations between.

New York, N.Y. is a look up and live town, or a sigh, cry, die town; the big juicy apple that tempts and magnetizes, nourishes or consumes, but is never forgotten.

New York, N.Y. has a face of concrete that menaces those who have not found the key to her heart. And she *is* a woman—fickle, sometimes cold, warm to those who know her ways. It takes time to know and love her. She is not easy.

New York, N.Y.. is always on the move; motion is native to her torso, and whether good or bad, profitable or not, it's there, day and night, like the beat of a tom-tom or a heart—faster by day, slower by night; pushing, easing time along.

New York, N.Y. has many moods. She broods and all her glitter is but a well-spring for sadness. She is just as frequently happy, even frivolous, fresh and new, depending on your view.

New York, N.Y. is a blues/dues town. She can take and forsake . . . and without conscience. In no time, her beauty can become unforgivable to those to whom she yields nothing.

New York, N.Y., a compound of all those that live within her arms, is liberal and bigoted, probing and

184

disinterested. She is affected, phony, and unstintingly real. All these things and more . . .

She is rich and poor—Sutton Place and Harlem, Madison Avenue and "The Village," Park Avenue and "Hell's Kitchen"; Brooklyn, the Bronx and Staten Island, too; all the boroughs and sections, streets and avenues, in sum, are New York, N.Y. . . . and contribute to her heart, body and soul.

In essence, New York, N.Y. is people; each one important, each one in need of the other.

New York, N.Y. is filled with the sounds of jazz.

Jazz musicians come pouring into New York, N.Y. "Let's go to *the Apple,* man, that's where it is," they cry, not realizing that the taste of it is reserved for only the equipped. Many return to their home hamlets disappointed; some, more than a little changed for being here.

New York, N.Y. is a cruel mistress. Bring her something new and she is torn between a desire to understand and an inclination to resist change. "Prove it!" she tauntingly says to those who come to her bearing the future in their hands.

Jon Hendricks is the poet laureate of jazz. Middleman in the fabulous trio of Lambert, Hendricks and Ross, he is also one of the top improvisers in jazz; his horn is his voice. Jon has a way with words; those of others, and especially his own. Although originally written to be recited over the music of George Russell's score for New York, N.Y.,* Hendricks' verse deserves wider recognition. It swings, captures the beat of the city, and acidly etches some of the town's sore spots. But most of all, it swings.

* New York, N.Y., Decca Records DL 9216. *Transcribed by the editors and reprinted by permission of the author and Decca Records.*

NEW YORK, N. Y.

by Jon Hendricks

Think you can lick it?
Get to the wicket.
Buy you a ticket.
Go!

Go by bus, by plane, by car, by train . . .
New York, New York
What they call a somethin' else town.
A city of more than eight million people,
with a million people passing through every day.
Some come just to visit,
and some come to stay.
If you scuffle hard enough and you ain't no dunce,
You can always get by in New York City I heard
    somebody say once.
Yeah . . . if you can't make it in New York City,
    man,
You can't make it nowhere.
So where do people come to scuffle?
Right here.
Think you can lick it?
Get to the wicket.
Buy you a ticket,
Go!

186

New York, N.Y.,
A city so nice
They had to name it twice.
It may seem like a cold town,
But, man, lemme tell ya,
It's a soul town.
It ain't a bit hard to find someone who's lone-
        some or forlorn here . . .
But it's like finding a needle in a haystack to find
        somebody who was born here.
New York, N.Y.,
A somethin' else town, all right!
East side, west side,
Uptown, downtown,
There's one thing all New York City has,
And that's jazz.
A while ago there were cats readin' while cats
        played jazz behind 'em,
But wasn't nothing happening, so the musicians
    cooked right on like they didn't even mind 'em.
I wrote the shortest jazz poem ever heard.
Nothing about lovin' 'n' kissin' . . .
One word . . .
Listen!

Big City Blues

Yes. . . .
If you pay New York dues, you get New York
        blues.
There's a lot of givin' and takin' while you're
        tryin' to get by,
And the buildings got somethin' in common with
        the cost of livin' . . .
They're both sky high.
New Yorkers brag about their buildings bein'
        tall . . .
Hah! As narrow as Manhattan Island is,
You go up or nowhere at all.
And on one thing you can rely:
We got New York's finest.
The finest money can buy.
Some give a little, now, and some lean hard.
But they're all right in general. . . .
As long as you ain't the wrong cat,

187

Tryin' to get a cabaret card.
So cats keep on strugglin' to say their say.
But between them and their audience,
There sits the D.J.
And I'm hip lack of acceptance is a drag . . .
People not diggin' the only thing that's their
own . . .
Man, that's really in another bag.
But lack of acceptance is less like somethin' to
hide from
And more like somethin' Bird died from.

MANHATTA-RICO

Ninety-five dollars to get to heaven!
That's what it costs to fly from San Juan, Puerto
Rico, to New York City.
And, if you're down in your native land
And you're not standin' out on no moonlit veranda
in a full dress suit
With a long, cool drink in your hand,
And you want to get where it's nice . . .
That's the price.

Ninety-five dollars to get to heaven!
And here comes another kinda soul:
To find that in the hottest part of summer it can
still get very cold.
A quick look around'll tell you what's goin' on . . .
You dig who's livin' high on the hog,
And who's the underdog.
You dig what shape the underdog was in
'Cause you're livin' where he just been.
So, you dig him and you dig your host . . .
And you dig who it is you resemble the most.
Right on down to the rhythm that moves you.
There may be some slight difference in the way
you say the word,
But Machito didn't have no trouble cuttin' some
sides with Bird.
They probably had trouble pronouncin' each other's
name,
But they showed how two things could sound al-
together different, and yet have a familiar ring,
Because they're the same thing.

188

THE EAST SIDE

Well . . . another side to New York City
Where everybody is very seditty
And much too discreet
to even to be seen too often out in the street.
Nobody would ever think of it as the beauty and
the beast side. . . .
Not the East Side!

A HELLUVA TOWN

Think you can lick it?
Get to the wicket.
Buy you a ticket.
Go!

By bus, by plane, by car, by train.
New York, N.Y.
What they call a somethin' else town!
A city of more than eight million people
With a million people passin' through every day.

Some come just to visit, and some come to stay.
Think you can lick it?
Get to the wicket.
Buy you a ticket.
Go!

The words of an elder statesman should be listened to and respected. In this case, the elder statesman is Coleman Hawkins, who has actively contributed to jazz for nearly four decades. The jazz story is best told by the men who create it. The Hawk's observations* on the effect of New York on jazzmen, and vice versa, are especially cogent. The interviewer's question appears in italics.

* Coleman Hawkins: A Documentary *(RLP 12-117/8)*. *Transcribed by the editors and reprinted by permission of Orrin Keepnews, Riverside Records.*

THE HAWK TALKS

by Coleman Hawkins

Do you remember any kind of group that had a New York sound or that thought of themselves as having a New York sound? Do you think there is any such thing as a New York sound?

I NEVER heard of any such thing as a "New York sound." It's a funny thing . . . they have always kept any originality in jazz away from New York City . . . I don't know why, either. This places makes *all* musicians sound kind of funny when they come around. When they first come here, I don't care what they were in their home towns, when they come *here,* they get cut. They get cut every time. They have to come here and learn all over again, practically. Then when they come back they are all right. Or, if they stay around they can develop to be all right. I don't know, they sound fine out West. You go out to some of those small towns and you hear the band and you say "Man, you guys sound good," you know. That's why I'm always skeptical. I have never brought any of the western bands I had or any of the other bands I worked with . . . into New York. I never will, either. Do you remember when Basie came in? The band Basie first brought here nobody has seen since. It disappeared. . . . Remember up at the Savoy . . . when John Hammond was fooling around with him. Why, he was hiring and firing so fast . . . before you knew it he had Dickie Wells in the band and all those other Eastern boys. I said to Basie, "Whatever became of all those Kansas City people? Ain't nobody here but *you*!" Basie said, "We came in . . . we opened at the Savoy and man, we were *nothing*! People would come in, stop to listen and say, *'Ugh, that,'* turn around and walk out. I'd have given up, but John Hammond talked to us. We would go out and come back and make some changes." I said, "Why did you ever bring the band *in*?" He said, "Well, John came out and heard us and thought we were the greatest thing in the world. I believed it."

That's the thing I was talking about . . . *New York*.

. . . I can give you a good example right now of something that happened in the past year to a certain boy and you know him . . . Cannonball. I heard Cannonball a little better than two years ago when I was at the Miami *Birdland*. Cannonball use to come in and play and Cannonball sounded g-o-o-d . . . he was *blowin*! "Why don't you go up to New York instead of wasting your time with that much hard blowing down here?" He came up last summer [1955, Ed.]. I don't know whether you heard him or not, but he was down the Bohemia—and all the boys went in and listened to him. "Is *that* Cannonball? *That's* the way he plays? *Let me go get my horn.*" The boys were going out and getting their horns and coming back and blowing and they were talking . . . "Too bad, his brother's not bad . . . his brother plays a nice trumpet, but man, he's *nothing*! I don't hear nothing. Anybody can do that." Well, Cannonball left—he came back . . . he can play now . . . he's blowin' now, really . . . New York . . . I have never seen it fail.

9. CRITICS: The Sound and the Furious

THE OPENER

IN NO OTHER art form has the role of the critic been assumed by so many persons of varied background and experience. And in no other art form has the critic

191

been subjected to such universal damning, largely because of his qualifications or lack of them.

For in jazz, the range of writing and opinion is wide. Because the music itself is so alive and dynamic, virtually every writer has an opinion wholly at odds with the opinions of his colleagues. These divergences of thought often manifest themselves in colorful writing which, somehow, gets off the subject of jazz pretty quickly and onto the subject of so-and-so's opinion.

Just as jazz itself is a music without literal definition and with very few ground rules, so is the field of jazz criticism.

The importance of critics has been variously underrated and overrated. But it is generally conceded that the critical function includes that of "discovering" new talents, attempting to chart a course in the stormy waters of the music, and seeking to bring a greater public awareness of jazz to the world.

Who are the critics?

Well, they are musicians, professional writers, interested college boys, radio broadcasters, night-club owners, record producers, and many, many more. In jazz, a critic with a depth of musical background and experience often becomes a participant in the idiom, either as a performer or a record producer or a promoter of artists.

For *The Jazz Word,* the leading critics of the world were set to a difficult task . . . the selection of what they considered *the three most indispensable records ever issued.*

They searched their jazz souls and, after untold torment at choosing this artist while leaving out that favorite, came through grudgingly with a selection of three— often four, six . . . even 12—and in most cases, added comments covering other "desert island" wants. Some critics found the task impossible.

Oddly enough, the European critics, for the most part, buckled down to the task without caviling. Their choices were sure and immediate.

It is interesting to note that the critics singled out Duke Ellington, Louis Armstrong, and Charlie Parker as the three outstanding jazz figures of our time by the number of votes and mentions made of them. Two albums emerged as being of world-wide significance: Duke Elling-

ton's *At His Very Best.* (RCA Victor) and Miles Davis'
Birth Of The Cool (Capitol).
The survey follows.

WILDER HOBSON

(Saturday Review)

1. Louis Armstrong's *Hot Five* (Columbia)
2. Jelly Roll Morton's *Vocal Blues* (Commodore)
3. Louis Armstrong's *Hot Seven* (Columbia)
   No comments.

RUSS WILSON

(Oakland, California *Tribune*)

No Choices.

Comment: Believe it or not, I devoted several upsetting hours to attempting to fulfill your request for three
"indispensable records"; then gave up on it. I think a
man's a fool to try it. Why? To begin with, anyone who is
at all serious about jazz must include something of Louis'.
Coleman Hawkins cannot be passed by, nor Pres. Then
there's Bird, Diz, Miles, Brubeck, and the MJQ, Basie,
Ellington, Herman, Kenton, Getz, Tatum, Hines, Monk—
and we haven't even touched on the vocalists! Anyone
who would pick three, or five, "indispensable" albums
is a braver—or more foolhardy—man than I.

RALPH J. GLEASON

(The Rhythm Section, Syndicated column)

1. *Black, Brown & Beige,* Ellington Orchestra
   with Mahalia Jackson (Columbia)
2. *Milestones,* Miles Davis (Columbia)
3. Any Dizzy Gillespie LP

Comments: Also *The Three Herds,* Woody Herman
(Columbia); *Blues,* Count Basie (Columbia). Gentlemen:
I have hesitated to answer (and still do) your query.
It is, as we all know, an impossible question. I wish that
you could append to my arbitrary answer that statement.
There are thousands of indispensable LPs, and millions of
combinations of three that would make it more com-

fortable on a desert isle. But what we all really want—
and for which no LP is ever a substitute—is the real
jazz. Say, Miss Monroe, or some such.

JOSEPH BALCERAK
(Editor, *Jazz,* Polish Weekly)

1. *Basie* (Roulette)
2. *Concert By The Sea,* Erroll Garner (Columbia)
3. *Armstrong Plays W.C. Handy* (Columbia)

Comments: As you know, friends, we have not large
record collections (about 40 LPs); therefore my choices
may be untypical . . . sorry.

HARRY M. NICOLAUSSON
(Editor, *Orkester Journalen, Sweden*)

1. *Ellington Jazz Party* (Columbia)
2. *Red Norvo Plays The Blues* (RCA Victor)
3. *John Lewis Piano* (Atlantic)

No comments.

ALLAN MORRISON
(Entertainment Editor, *Ebony* Magazine)

1. *Jo Jones Special* (Vanguard)
2. *Lester Young Memorial Album* (Epic)
3. *Ellington Jazz Party* (Columbia)

No comments.

ANDRE HODEIR
(Author and Critic, France)

1. *Bags' Groove*, Miles Davis and Thelonious Monk
   (Prestige)
2. *Koko* (1940 version), Duke Ellington (RCA
   Victor)
3. *Embraceable You,* Charlie Parker (Dial)

Also, *I Can't Give You Anything But Love* (1938
version), Louis Armstrong (Decca).

194

JOHN S. WILSON
(Jazz Critic, *New York Times*)

1. *At His Very Best,* Duke Ellington (RCA Victor)
2. *King Of New Orleans Jazz,* Jelly Roll Morton (RCA Victor)
3. *Louis Armstrong Story,* Vol. 3 (Columbia)

No comments.

BILL SIMON
(Jazz Writer)

1. *At His Very Best,* Duke Ellington (RCA Victor)
2. *Birth Of The Cool,* Miles Davis (Capitol)
3. *Louis Armstrong Story,* Vol. 1 (Columbia)

Also, *Way Out West,* Sonny Rollins (Contemporary); *Tony Scott In Hi-Fi* (Brunswick); *Count Basie And The Band That Swings The Blues* (ARS).

MAX HARRISON
(Jazz Monthly, England)

1. *Louis Armstrong Story,* Vol. 3 (Columbia)
2. *Such Sweet Thunder,* Duke Ellington (Columbia)
3. *Charlie Parker,* Vol. 5 (Savoy)

Comments: With only three records to choose, one must confine oneself to the giants, and for me, Armstrong, Ellington, and Parker represent, in their very different ways, the best the music has to offer.

ARRIGO POLILLO
(Critic, Italy)

1. *Louis Armstrong Story,* Vol. 3 (Columbia)
2. *In A Mellotone,* Duke Ellington (RCA Victor)
3. *Charlie Parker Memorial,* Vol. 2 (Savoy)

Comments: I can't see any jazz musician comparable to

Louis, Duke, and Bird. That's why I have chosen their records. These are the ones that show them at their very best, in my opinion, at least.

NAT SHAPIRO
(Jazz Writer)

1. *Louis Armstrong Story,* Vol. 2 (Columbia)
2. *Count Basie* (Brunswick)
3. *Duke Ellington Plays the Music of Duke Ellington* (Columbia)

No comments.

BILL COSS
(Editor, *Metronome-Music USA*)

1. *Good Queen Bess* by Johnny Hodges (Bluebird)
2. *Just Friends,* Charlie Parker (Verve)
3. *Yesterdays,* Billie Holiday (Commodore)

Comments: Indispensable is not the word, but these are certainly among the records which have given me immense satisfaction.

GEORGE HOEFER
(New York Editor, *Downbeat*)

1. *Satchmo—A Musical Autobiography* (Decca)
2. *Greatest Recording Session,* Charlie Parker (Savoy)
3. *At His Very Best,* Duke Ellington (RCA Victor)

Comments: Also, *Basie* (Roulette); *Lady Sings The Blues,* Billie Holiday (Clef). This gives me as complete a library of American jazz as can be capsuled into so few records.

LEONARD FEATHER
(Author and Critic)

No choices.

Comments: It would be impossible to single out, from among the countless thousands of LPs now available, such a limited number of items. My feeling is that a vote on this basis would be an implied insult to the countless artists whose LPs would have to be omitted and I would be grateful if you could publish my opinion to this effect.

STANLEY DANCE
(Author and Critic, England)

1. *In A Mellotone*, Duke Ellington (RCA Victor)
2. *Solo,* Earl Hines (Fantasy)
3. *Bones For The King,* Dicky Wells (Felsted)

Comments: Far more than three records seem indispensable to me, and the top three will vary somewhat according to mood. Fortunately, "indispensable" is not synonymous with "best," so I don't have to apologize for the absence of items by Coleman Hawkins, Count Basie, Louis Armstrong, Johnny Hodges, and Buck Clayton, which are next on my list.

IRA GITLER
(Writer and Critic)

1. *The Jazz Scene* (Chef)
2. *Lester Young Memorial* (Epic)
3. *The Immortal Charlie Parker* (Savoy)

Comments: Also, *The Genius of Bud Powell* (Verve); *Brilliant Corners,* Thelonious Monk (Riverside); *Milestones,* Miles Davis (Columbia); *The Brothers* (Prestige). These aren't necessarily the records I'd take to a desert island, but they are vital to me. If I had the choice of one I'd probably take *The Jazz Scene,* because it has Bird, Pres, Bud, Duke and Hawk on one LP (how's that for name-dropping?). Also there is some beautiful, swinging tenor by Herbie Steward. I think that Norman Granz really put something down for posterity when he conceived this album.

NAT HENTOFF
(Author and Critic)

1. *The Louis Armstrong Story,* Vols. 1-4 (Columbia)

197

2. *Lester Young Memorial Album* (Epic)
3. *Lady Day,* Billie Holiday (Columbia)
Also, *Charlie Parker Memorial Series* (Savoy); *Walkin',*
Miles Davis (Prestige); *The Bessie Smith Story,* Vols.
1-4 (Columbia).

TOM SCANLAN
(Jazz Writer, *Army Times*)

Comments: I have no "indispensable" LPs, although I
could list more than 100 that I enjoy very much. The
records I value the most and have received most pleasure
from are 78s, not LPs. I am thinking of the Teddy Wilson pick-up groups with Billie Holiday vocals on Brunswick, Columbia, Okeh; the Goodman Trio and Quartet
on Victor; the Goodman Sextet on Columbia; the old
Basie band on Decca and Basie combos on other labels;
the Ellington Victors. A good many of these records have
been issued on LP, but the original sound has almost always been butchered for some reason plain to engineers
and A&R men, perhaps, but not to me.

CHARLES EDWARD SMITH
(Author and Critic)

1. *The Louis Armstrong Story,* Vol. 2 (Columbia)
2. *The Bix Beiderbecke Story,* Vol. 2 (Columbia)
3. *Lester Young Memorial Album* (Epic)
Comments: Also, *Swedish Schnapps,* Charlie Parker
(Verve); *Miles Davis,* Vol. 1 (Blue Note); *Brilliant Corners,* Thelonious Monk (Riverside). If I had my choice
of one indispensable disc, I think I'd choose one including *Potato Head Blues.* That is why I lead off with an
album of the old Hot Five and Hot Seven, and with some
Hines' tracks that suggest his then developing style that
was the gateway to linear improvisation. I include the
Bix-Tram set because the influence of both is only now
beginning to be appreciated. To these, subsequent sets
including Lester Young, Charlie Parker, Miles Davis, Thelonious Monk and J. J. Johnson are related in approaches
to improvisation, in treatment of the beat, affinity to the
blues. In fact, something of the scope of jazz is indicated, and though another six records might serve the

purpose, these records should give any listener an idea of the depth and dignity of jazz, as well as its high entertainment value.

WHITNEY BALLIETT
(Author and Critic, *The New Yorker*)

No choices.

Comments: I don't think I can be much help in the essential LP category . . . In shuffling through my mind, I find so many indispensable isolated numbers that are either not on LP at all or that are scattered over dozens of LPs that I'd just as soon leave the whole thing alone.

REV. NORMAN O'CONNOR
(Jazz Writer, *The Boston Globe*)

1. Louis Armstrong, any one of the *Golden Era* series on Columbia.
2. Duke Ellington, *Great Jazz Composers Series* on Columbia.
3. Charlie Parker, any of the early recordings on various labels . . . Savoy, Dial, Comet, etc.

Comments: Also, Art Tatum, any of the recordings previous to the sets he did for Norman Granz; Miles Davis, the sides on Capitol made in 1949. These are five LP recordings that I would like to have around. I shy away from the indispensable category since I believe that there are few things in that category. These records I keep around for listening and learning pleasure.

JOHN TYNAN
(West Coast Editor, *Downbeat*)

1. *Miles Ahead,* Miles Davis and Gil Evans (Columbia)
2. *Louis Armstrong Plays W.C. Handy* (Columbia)
3. *Black, Brown and Beige,* Duke Ellington (Columbia)

Comments: There is so much Charlie Parker available I couldn't even begin to make a selection (LP, that is) of his work. But any good Bird and Diz or Bird and Miles would certainly rank as indispensable.

199

SINCLAIR TRAILL
(Director, *Jazz Journal,* England)

1. *Louis Armstrong Story,* Vol. 3 (Columbia)
2. *Duke Ellington At The Cotton Club* (RCA Camden)
3. *The Jazz Odyssey of James Rushing Esq.* (Columbia)

Comments: The Armstrong record contains some of his most imaginative work, made in company with the greatest jazz piano innovator, Earl Hines—both are indispensable. The Ellington record is by no means his latest, but when has any band played more exciting music than such tracks as *Stevedore Stomp, Ring Dem Bells,* etc. The music contained on these two records has given pleasure for over three decades, there is no reason it should not continue to do so. The Jimmy Rushing for a vocal (the most difficult instrument in jazz) because I think he is the best jazz singer today, and because of the superb accompaniment by such great mainstream warriors as Buck Clayton, Vic Dickenson, Buddy Tate, Hilton Jefferson, Jo Jones, etc.

MARTIN T. WILLIAMS
(Critic, Co-Editor, *The Jazz Review*)

1. *King Creole Jazz Band* (Riverside)
2. *Red Hot Peppers,* Jelly Roll Morton (RCA Victor)
3. *The Louis Armstrong Story,* Vol. 2 (Columbia)

Comments: Also, *At His Very Best,* Duke Ellington (RCA Victor); Count Basie and Lester Young (Epic); Dizzy and Bird (Savoy); Thelonious Monk (Blue Note); *Birth Of The Cool,* Miles Davis (Capitol); *Saxophone Colossus* (Prestige); *Bessie Smith Story,* Vol. 3 (Columbia); Billie Holiday (Commodore); *Modern Jazz Quartet* (Atlantic).

I wish there were a Mahalia Jackson LP I rate as high as I rate her. Closest may be Newport '58 thing. Several made tough choices. The Victor Morton set used some inferior takes of some superior compositions, for some reason. The Louis set is arbitrary as hell—a selection from several Columbia sets and Decca DL 8327 would have been far better. The ideal Ellington set would be drawn from this and Victor LPM 1364. I hated to leave out Pres on Commodore 30,013 and with Billie on Columbia CL 626, as well as some of the Basie Deccas. The best Monk set would be drawn from Blue Note 1509 and 1510. The same is true of Bessie; I'd like some from both 855 and 857. A really good MJQ set would have to draw on almost everything they've released on LP. This seems to be a minimal list of living art, not a "jazz history." Lots of bad art can have "historical importance."

ALBERT J. McCARTHY

(Editor, *Jazz Monthly,* England)

1. *Blues,* Ma Rainey (Riverside)
2. *Piano Jazz, Barrelhouse and Boogie Woogie* (Brunswick)
3. *Classic Folk Blues,* Blind Lemon Jefferson (Riverside)

Comments: Few aspects of jazz have received such lip service as the blues, but the early blues singers and pianists still remain relatively unknown to many jazz followers. Ma Rainey, along with Bessie Smith, is the greatest of the "classic" blues singers, while Jefferson is the finest of the rougher country artists. The piano LP has wonderful work by some of the little-known pioneers like Montana Taylor and Romeo Nelson. All three are indispensable to a balanced collection.

CARLOS DE RADZITZKY

(Vice-President, Hot Club of Belgium)

1. One with Louis Armstrong (1926-27)
2. One with Duke Ellington (1940)
3. One with Charlie Parker

Comments: It is impossible to give a reasonable answer to such a question—in fact, the choice of an LP is the choice of a musician! Dozens of LPs (or musicians) are "indispensable" for dozens of good reasons. Any choice is a bet!

BARRY ULANOV

(Author and Critic)

1. *At His Very Best,* Duke Ellington (RCA Victor)
2. *The Genius of Charlie Parker* (Savoy)
3. *Lennie Tristano* (Atlantic)

Comments: This is an absurd idea, as foolish as trying to reduce English or French literature to three works. I have simply chosen three of the several dozen collections I consider indispensable, three that demonstrate as well as any other three what jazz is about. But to leave out Basie and Louis Armstrong, Bix and Benny Goodman, Billie Holiday and Bessie Smith and Earl Hines, Christian and Mingus and Dizzy, Lester Young and Roy Eldridge, Peiffer and Mary Lou Williams, Ella and Woody Herman, is as ridiculous as a similar distillation of poetry that skipped John Donne and George Herbert and Henry Vaughan and William Wordsworth and Gerard Manley Hopkins. What a thing to do to me on a hot day in Vermont!

STEVE RACE

(Columnist, *The Melody Maker,* England)

1. *Basie* (Roulette)
2. *Jazz Impressions of Eurasia,* Dave Brubeck (Columbia)
3. *At His Very Best,* Duke Ellington (RCA Victor)

Comments: The task is, of course, impossible. Certainly these are among the first twenty records I would reach for if my house caught fire. Only later—maybe at the fire station—would I wish I'd stayed long enough to pick up some examples of Diz, Louis, Ella, or the cool genius of Bix Beiderbecke. Come to think of it, for Bix I might even go back into the flames; and if one of Ella's records happened to be on, I'd stay there.

ERIK WIEDEMANN

(Critic and Author, Denmark)

1. *Louis Armstrong Story*, Vol. 3 (Columbia)
2. *In a Mellotone*, Duke Ellington (RCA Victor)

3. *All Star Sextet* (And Quintet!), Charlie Parker (Roost)

Comments: With such a limited number of choices, I have to select the best of the current collections by each of the three greatest figures of jazz. However, I very much regret that there is no space for at least Count Basie, Miles Davis and Thelonious Monk.

ALUN MORGAN
(Writer and Critic, England)

1. *Birth Of The Cool,* Miles Davis (Capitol)
2. *Charlie Parker Memorial Album* (British Vogue, from Dial)
3. *In A Mellotone,* Duke Ellington (RCA Victor)

Comments: Naturally, I regret the omission of Louis' Hot Fives and Sevens, to say nothing of Lester, Hawk, Hines, etc., but the pruned list is an honest reflection of my personal taste. Parker remains, to my mind, the greatest soloist jazz has ever known; Ellington is the orchestral master with a unique conception of melody, harmony, voicings and all the indefinable qualities which have set his music so far ahead. *In A Mellotone* contains examples by what is, I think, his greatest band. The Miles Davis LP still represents the high-water mark so far as arranged modern jazz is concerned.

DON GOLD
(Jazz Writer)

1. *Birth Of The Cool,* Miles Davis (Capitol)
2. *The Louis Armstrong Story,* Vol. 1 (Columbia)
3. *An Image,* Lee Konitz (with Bill Russo arrangements) (Verve)

Comments: These LPs, of course, are just three of many I feel to be significant and indispensable. *The Birth Of The Cool* LP is probably the most often played in my collection. The early Armstrong is of great documentary, historic significance. The recent Konitz with strings LP is a milestone, I feel, for its indication of Konitz' ability, Russo's strength as a transitional (between jazz and classical music) figure, and for pure beauty of the works.

203

CHARLES DELAUNAY
(Critic and Writer, France)

1. *Wild Cat,* Clarence Williams Blue Five with Sidney Bechet (Okeh)
2. *Tight Like This,* Louis Armstrong (Okeh)
3. *Body and Soul,* Coleman Hawkins (Bluebird)

Comments: Also, *Hot House,* Dizzy Gillespie, Charlie Parker. These items are selected not only because I think these are among the best renditions and feature some of the most important creative soloists of their times, but because these records are major steps in the evolution of jazz.

JOACHIM E. BERENDT
(Author and Critic, Germany)

1. *Birth Of The Cool,* Miles Davis (Capitol)
2. *Freedom Suite,* Sonny Rollins (Riverside)
3. *In A Mellotone,* Duke Ellington (RCA Victor)

Comments: I hate this question. It simplifies. *My* indespensable jazz records change quite often. Jazz lives, and I live with jazz. So they *must* change. The only one I have kept since many years is Miles' *Capitol Orchestra.* But I would have liked to include a newer Miles LP, since the trumpet player Miles Davis is better now than he was in 1949. The Rollins LP was chosen because it represents many aspects: (a) Modern bop being the music where jazz is most lively right now; (b) "integration" and compositional viewpoints; (c) three wonderful musicians in lots of freedom; (d)-(z) freedom.

CLAES DAHLGREN
(Critic and Writer, *Expressen, Orkester Journalen,* Sweden. Also Jazz Disc Jockey for Swedish Broadcasting Corp.)

1. *At His Very Best,* Duke Ellington (RCA Victor)
2. *Charlie Parker Story* (Savoy)
3. *Relaxin',* Miles Davis (Prestige)

Comments: Also, the Dizzy Gillespie Musicraft big

band sides; Count Basie's Brunswick LP; *Basie* on Roulette; a sampling of Lester Young, preferably the sides cut with Basie that were recently re-released by Epic; and *Miles Ahead,* Miles Davis and Gil Evans, Columbia. Selecting three LPs is a challenging yet uncomfortable task. It's like having a big family on a sinking ship and being asked to select three or four among all you love and treasure to be put in the last lifeboat.

BURT KORALL

(Co-editor, *The Jazz Word*)

1. *Lester Young Memorial* (Epic)
2. *Birth Of The Cool,* Miles Davis (Capitol)
3. *At His Very Best,* Duke Ellington (RCA Victor)

Comments: Bird's records for Dial and Savoy and the Louis Armstrong four-volume set on Columbia should be included to create some sort of jazz perspective. If pressed, however, the three above would be most missed if they weren't in my collection.

DOM CERULLI

(Co-editor, *The Jazz Word*)

1. *Louis Armstrong Plays W.C. Handy* (Columbia)
2. *The Jazz Odyssey Of James Rushing, Esq.* (Columbia)
3. *At His Very Best,* Duke Ellington (RCA Victor)

MORT L. NASATIR

(Co-editor, *The Jazz Word*)

1. *Ella Sings Rodgers and Hart* (Verve)
2. *Lennie Tristano* (Atlantic)
3. *Satchmo* (Decca)

Comments: A record that would place two or three on my list isn't out as of this writing. It's *New York, N.Y.,* by George Russell (Decca).

10. DIRECTIONS: Routes and Detours

THE OPENER

THE DIRECTION of jazz is determined by three things: the men, their instruments, and the times. Jazz is so flexible a medium that *one man* may emerge, and by pioneering new forms and methods or by extending the technical and emotional range of his instrument, may alter the movement of jazz. A jazzman is, of course, subject to the vicissitudes of his time and fellow musicians; he may not emerge at once as an explosive force, but ultimately his catalytic influence must be felt throughout all of jazz. Louis Armstrong, Lester Young, and Charlie Parker were such men.

Like any other alive, vital, self-discriminating art, jazz contains within its often vague boundaries constant cycles of growth and change. Sometimes, the changes are valid and lasting; sometimes, they are abortive and ephemeral. But with every passing of a fad or fancy, the best of the movement is absorbed into the mainstream of jazz.

Where has jazz been? What is it doing? Where is it going?

These questions are most obviously answered by the jazzmen themselves, through their playing and their composing. It remains for the jazz historians, critics, and students to place in proper perspective both the routes and the detours. There are almost as many directions in jazz thought as there are jazzmen, for it is in the nature of the music at all times to be highly personal and deeply expressive.

What are the blues? Paul Ackerman, Music Editor of The Billboard *and an expert on the music form, attempted this description: "Many blues are sad, for they originally came from backgrounds of slavery and repression. However, with the passing of years the story content of the blues has become very broad, so that there are also happy blues and uptempo blues, which make the listener want to jump and shout; satiric blues, comedy blues, and didactic blues which give advice, generally to simple men who have been put upon by sharp women. Blues is The Mother," concludes Ackerman.*

Nat Hentoff has emerged as one of the most read writers in the jazz idiom. Co-editor of The Jazz Review, *jazz critic for* Esquire *and* Hi-Fi Review, *author of several jazz books, he is also a frequent contributor to* The New Yorker, The Reporter, Saturday Review, *and other publications. His discussion of the blues, originally written as a liner note, is authoritative and pointedly documented.*

From The Blues Is Everybody's Business *(Coral 59101), reprinted by permission.*

THE BLUES
by Nat Hentoff

BILLIE Holiday recently summarized what the title of this album means: "The blues to me is like being very sad, very sick, going to church, being very happy. The blues is sort of a mixed-up thing. You just have to feel it. You sing the blues when you're sad, but you can also sing blues very well when you're feeling good, because you can tell another kind of story about the blues then. There's happy blues and there's sad blues."

Or as Leadbelly once sang:

"When I got up this mornin', Blues walkin' round my bed.
When I got up this mornin', Blues walkin' round my bed.

I went up to eat my breakfast, Blues was all in
my bread. . .

"Good mornin' Blues, Blues how do you do?
Good mornin' Blues, Blues how do you do?
'I'm doin' all right, good mornin', how are you?' "

The blues, then, are more than a song of despair, of
renunciation, of a twilight with not even darkness to
come. The blues can and do express all the emotions we
experience. There's no one who hasn't known the blues
intimately, and the blues singer or player talks not only
to us but through us. In fact, he talks to his subject as
well. "You gotta talk to the blues," said Leadbelly. "They
wanna talk to you. You gotta tell 'em something."

In other words, no blues singer or player worth hearing just moans or pities himself to a beat. He has to
contribute to the blues—irony, imagery, his own musical
conception. He has to contribute anything and everything
that makes clear that the blues hasn't swallowed him,
that he still can express *himself* and recoup his strength
and pride that way.

The blues goes back to the beginning of Afro-American
musical experiences in this country, and that means to at
least the seventeenth century. It wasn't until after
the Civil War that classic blues began to be heard and
transcribed, but the roots of the blues in form and content were planted long before. The voice was the first—
and for more than two hundred years the primary—
musical instrument of the Negro slave. He wasn't allowed
other instruments, but he had to express his despair,
rage, hope, and swift joys in some way that transcended
just talk, and so he made his voice an instrument.

There were wordless cries, field hollers, cries that, as
Professor Willis James notes in *The Romance of the Negro
Folk Cry in America,* could be "the source for a series
of startling variations, done in the freest manner imagina-
ble—depending, of course, upon the gifts of the crier."
Then there were field calls. As Harold Courlander explains in the invaluable Folkways series, *Negro Folk
Music of Alabama:* "During slavery days in the South
the plantation laborers were not permitted to mingle at
will with friends on nearby plantations. Men and women
working together over a wide stretch of fields maintained

social contact throughout the workday by calling back and forth and singing songs together. On occasion the songs were of the type we have come to know as 'work songs.' . . . But there was also the 'call' or 'sign.' The field call served primarily as communication. It might be a message, or a familiar signal. Sometimes the call contained information. . . . The tradition continued on after the Civil War, disappearing slowly as the conditions of life changed. But the calls are still to be heard in many rural parts of the South."

And just as in jazz "everybody had his own style," so in these very early pre-jazz days, nearly everybody had his own cry. You could identify a man by the way he used his voice. Musical self-expression had begun. In time, a complex, emotionally volcanic body of Afro-American material had been built. There were work songs out of the cries; children's ring games; spirituals; dances; lullabies. All these and more were the roots from which jazz was to emerge.

After the Civil War, when Negroes finally were able to travel, to exchange their stories and their way of telling their lives in music, the blues began to be formed as we know it now. It came especially from the wanderers. As Abbe Niles describes the carriers of the blues in the late nineteenth century, they were "barroom pianists, careless nomadic laborers, watchers of incoming trains and steamboats, street-corner guitar players, strumpets and outcasts." At the beginning of wandering, classic blues, the blues was usually "a one-man affair, originating typically as the expression of the singer's feelings, and complete in a single verse. It might start as little more than an interjection, a single line; sung, because singing was as natural a method of expression as speaking."

In time, a basic structure of the blues became recognizable, although always subject to variations. Explained in its simplest form, twelve bars in length, in the key of B flat, Leonard Feather notes of the basic blues in his *Encyclopedia of Jazz*: "The first four bars of the blues are based on the chord of the tonic, or first note of the scale. The next four are based on the subdominant, or fourth note of the scale. The last four begin with the dominant, or fifth note of the scale. Thus the blues in its

209

earliest . . . form might be based on the chords of B flat, E Flat and F."

For each of these three four-bar sections, the blues singer strung a line. The first was usually repeated, and the third made the barbed point:

"Sittin' in the house with everythin' on my mind,
Sittin' in the house with everythin' on my mind,
Lookin' at the clock an' can't even tell the time."

But the singer usually used up only about half of each four-bar line. This waiting area, as Abbe Niles indicated in his 1926 preface to *The Blues* by W. C. Handy: "affords the improviser, for one thing, a space in which his next idea may go through its period of gestation . . . but . . . assuming he isn't compelled to concentrate on what is to follow, he can utilize this space, not as a hold, but as a *play-ground* in which his voice or instrument may be allowed to wander in such fantastic musical paths as he pleases, returning (not necessarily, but usually) to the key-note, third, or fifth, yet again before vacation is over." And if it's a singer backed by an instrumentalist, the result, as Leonard Bernstein pointed out in his *Omnibus* lecture on jazz, is a "break" in which the open area is filled by an instrument. "And here we have," added Bernstein, "the . . . instrument imitating the voice, the very soil in which jazz grows. Louis Armstrong improvising the breaks in a blues song by Bessie Smith is the essential sound in jazz, from which all instrumental improvisation has since developed."

And Niles makes a further perceptive analysis: "The melody would consist of three brief phrases, favoring a syncopated jugglery of a very few notes—often, though not necessarily, those of the pentatonic scale. . . . The frequent return to the keynote gave an almost hypnotic effect, and the only equally favored note was the tonic third; a fact of the first importance to the blues because of a tendency of the untrained Negro voice when singing the latter tone at an important point, to *worry* it, slurring or wavering between flat and natural." [A "blue" note, in short, Ed.] And there was also a "characteristic fondness for the flatted *seventh*—and a feeling for the key of the subdominant, of which the tonic third itself *is* the seventh. . . ."

210

It is oversimplified, however, to talk of the third and seventh degrees of the scale as being the only "blue" notes, although they were the primary ones. In the work of an untrained blues singer or player, we would normally, as Sidney Finkelstein described the process in *Jazz: A People's Music:* "instead of hearing intervals such as we might play on a piano, hear intervals dangling between a major second and a minor third, or between a minor third and a major third, or between a fourth and a diminished fifth. These deviations from the pitch familiar to concert music are not, of course, the result of an inability to sing or play in tune. They mean that the blues are a non-diatonic music. . . . This description of the blues melody is put down with the full knowledge that it differs from those found in many books on jazz. These studies generally describe the blues as a sequence of chords, such as the tonic, subdominant and dominant seventh. Such a definition, however, is like putting the cart before the horse. There are definite patterns of chords which have been evolved to support the blues, but these do not define the blues, and the blues can exist as a melody perfectly recognizable as the blues, without them. Neither are the blues simply a use of the major scale with the 'third' and 'seventh' slightly blue or flattened. The fact is that both this explanation, and the chord explanation, are attempts to explain one musical system in terms of another; to describe a non-diatonic music in diatonic terms."

I have quoted from Finkelstein to underline the fact that the blues is protean; it is not restricted to any one essential sequence of chords. The authentic "blues" feeling is just that—a feeling—and it has come to pervade a large part of jazz, including songs and performances that are not overtly considered "blues" in the narrow classic definition of the term. Nor are there only twelve-bar blues; and while it's true that the blues, as Finkelstein comments, "have a regular, recurrent beat . . . it is elastic and fluent. It may be stretched or contracted." And as Duke Ellington, Jimmy Giuffre and others have proved, the beat of the blues may be implicit as well as definitely, explicitly stated.

As flexible as is the musical form of the blues, so its content, as noted previously, is infinitely varied, although it's quite true that the most powerful blues have

211

usually been those sung in protest, in bitterness and in determination to be free. "Oh I feel like hollering," Big Bill Broonzy began one of his songs, "but the town is too small." Even the most bitter blues, however, have almost always had an intermixture of mordant wit, of a knowledge of mortality and the unpredictable war between flesh and spirit at the mysterious center of all of us:

"I'm gonna lay my head on the railroad track.
Yes, gonna lay my head on the railroad track.
And when the train comes, gonna yank it back."

"You so beautiful but you gotta die some day.
You so beautiful but you gotta die some day.
All I want's a little lovin' before you pass away."

The blues, which began as vocal music (like the rest of the pre-jazz Afro-American material), turned instrumental as soon as the post-Civil War Negroes were able to buy or invent instruments. The instrumental music, however, was vocalized—these were "singing horns." "The relation between voice and instrument," to return to Finkelstein, "takes place on a higher level than that of mere imitation. Rather, the horn becomes an extension of the human voice, and translates the accents of speech, the staccato consonants and long drawn vowels, into the particular timbre of the horn. These timbres are expansions of possibilities within the horn itself. And so jazz, rather than limiting the instrument to vocal imitation, has enormously expanded the technical and expressive possibilities of the instruments."

And as jazz gradually and inexorably began to utilize more complex and challenging harmonies, rhythms and melodic patterns, the blues nonetheless remained an essential element of jazz improvisation, of jazz feeling. "The blues," says Pee Wee Russell, "are a beautiful thing. They're not something to be thrown away, like 'What'll we play; let's play the blues.' After all, so much of what we all play is based on the blues."

"Anytime," says Jimmy Rushing, "a person can play the blues, he has a soul and that gives him a sort of lift to play anything else he wants to play. The blues are sort of a base, like a foundation to a building, because

212

any time you get into trouble playing a number, you curve the blues down and get out of it."

"The blues," summarized Art Blakey, "are the beginning of jazz. That's where it comes from. The last thing Charlie Parker said to me was he wondered when the young people would come back to playing the blues. I tell you, if you can learn how to play the blues, you can play anything."

The young have come back to the blues. Without exception, every major individualist in jazz today is a superior sayer of the blues—Sonny Rollins, John Coltrane, Miles Davis, Thelonious Monk, Dizzy Gillespie, John Lewis, and the more creative writers like George Russell, Charles Mingus and Manny Albam. All the current terms of approbation among jazzmen—"soul," "funk," "down home"—all mean basically that if a man can play the blues from inside himself without straining to play a part, he's a legitimate jazzman. *The blues is everybody's business,* whether they have consciously been aware of ever hearing the blues or not. In jazz, the blues besides is everybody's vocation, everybody's calling—and answering.

In the late forties, the time was ripe for change; the impact of Charlie Parker was being felt, and musicians were encouraged to look for ways and means to better express themselves in orchestral as well as virtuoso terms. Actually, the former grew from the latter, and one of the greater translators of jazz into orchestral terms, Gil Evans, felt Parker, sought to understand him and the implications growing from his work, and in the process took the music one step further—to a discipline it did not know in its other guise. He orchestrated as the soloist would play, and put additional flesh on an already imposing body of material. In doing so, he was instrumental in helping to create the so-called "cool school" of modern jazz, which started as a trend and never reached complete fulfillment. Nat Hentoff's interview in depth with Gil Evans stands out as one of his pieces of lasting value.

(Birth of the Cool, *Parts 1 & 2*, Down Beat, *May 2 and 16, 1957; reprinted by permission of Maher Publications, Inc.)*

THE BIRTH OF THE COOL
by Nat Hentoff

I

AMONG jazzmen, particularly player-writers, Gil Evans is uniquely admired.

"For my taste," Miles Davis says, "he's the best. I haven't heard anything that knocks me out as consistently as he does since I first heard Charlie Parker."

Coincident with Miles' recent tribute, Capitol released a few weeks ago the first complete collection of those 1949-50 Davis combo sides which were to influence deeply one important direction of modern chamber jazz (*Birth of the Cool,* Capitol 12-inch LP T762).

Evans was perhaps the primary background factor in making these sessions happen, and he wrote the arrangements for *Moon Dreams* and *Boplicity.*

Boplicity is listed as the work of "Cleo Henry," a nom-de-date for Davis, who wrote the melody, after which Evans scored the written ensembles. *"Boplicity,"* declares Andre Hodeir in *Jazz: Its Evolution and Essence,* "is enough to make Gil Evans qualify as one of jazz's greatest arranger-composers."

Despite these and other endorsements from impressive jazz figures, Evans is just a name to most jazz listeners. In the last few years, he has written comparatively little in the jazz field as such; but his influence on modern jazz writing through the effect of his work for the Claude Thornhill band of the forties and the Davis sides has remained persistent.

"Not many people really heard Gil," Gerry Mulligan explains. "Those who did, those who came up through the Thornhill band, were tremendously affected, and they in turn affected others."

He was born Ian Gilmore Green in Toronto, Canada, on May 13, 1912, and took his stepfather's name. Gil is self-taught and says, "I've always learned through practical work. I didn't learn any theory except through the practical use of it; and in fact, I started in music with a little band that could play the music as soon as I'd write it."

Evans first learned about music through jazz and popular records and radio broadcasts of bands. Since he had no traditional European background either in studying or listening, he built his style entirely on his pragmatic approach to jazz and pop material.

Sound itself was his first motivation. "Before I ever attached sound to notes in my mind, sound attracted me," he says. "When I was a kid, I could tell what kind of car was coming with my back turned."

Later, "it was the *sound* of Louis' horn, the people in Red Nichols' units like Jack Teagarden and Benny Goodman, Dukes's band, the McKinney Cotton Pickers, Don Redman. Redman's Brunswick records ought to be reissued. The band swung, but the voicings also gave the band a compact sound. I also was interested in popular bands. Like the Casa Loma approach to ballads. Gene Gifford broke up the instrumentation more imaginatively than was usual at the time."

Gil led his own band in Stockton, California, from 1933 to 1938, playing accompaniment-rhythm piano and scoring a book of pop songs and some jazz tunes.

215

When the band was taken over by Skinnay Ennis, Gil remained as arranger until 1941.

"I was also beginning to get an introduction to show music and the entertainment end of the business," Evans recalls. "We used to play for acts on Sunday nights at Victor Hugo's in Beverly Hills, and the chance to write for vaudeville routines gave me another look at the whole picture."

Thornhill had also joined the Ennis arranging staff, and the two wrote for the Bob Hope radio show while the Ennis band was on the series. The radio assignments gave Evans more pragmatic experience in yet another medium.

"Even then," Evans remembers, "Claude had a unique way with a dance band. He'd use the trombones, for example, with the woodwinds in a way that gave them a horn sound."

In 1939, Claude decided to form his own band. Evans recommended the band for a summer job at Balboa, and he notes that Claude was then developing his sound, a sound based on the horns playing without vibrato except for specific places where Thornhill would indicate vibrato was to be used for expressive purposes.

"I think," Gil adds, "he was the first among the pop or jazz bands to evolve that sound. Someone once said, by the way, that Claude was the only man who could play the piano without vibrato.

"Claude's band," continues Evans, "was always very popular with players. The Benny Goodman band style was beginning to pall and he had gotten to be commercial. I enjoyed it all, as did the men.

"The sound of the band didn't necessarily restrict the soloists," Gil points out. "Most of his soloists had an individual style. The sound of the band may have calmed down the over-all mood, but that made everyone feel very relaxed."

Evans went on to examine the Thornhill sound more specifically: "Even before Claude added French horns, the band began to sound like a French horn band. The trombones and trumpets began to take on that character, began to play in derby hats without a vibrato.

"Claude added the French horns in 1941. He had written an obbligato for them to a Fazola solo to surprise Fats. Fazola got up to play; Claude signaled the French horns at the other end of the room to come up to the bandstand; and that was the first time Fazola knew they were to be added to the band.

"Claude was the first leader to use French horns as a functioning part of a dance band. That distant, haunting, no-vibrato sound came to be blended with the reed and brass sections in various combinations.

"When I first heard the Thornhill band," Gil continues, "it sounded, with regard to the registers in which the sections played, a little like Glenn Miller, but it soon became evident that Claude's use of no-vibrato demanded that the registers be lowered. Actually, the natural range of the French horn helped cause the lowering of the registers. In addition, I was constantly experimenting with varying combinations and intensities of instruments that were in the same register.

"A characteristic voicing for the Thornhill band was what often happened on ballads. There was a French horn lead, one and sometimes two French horns playing in unison or a duet depending on the character of the melody. The clarinet doubled the melody, also playing lead. Below were two altos, a tenor, and a baritone, or two altos and two tenors. The bottom was normally a double on the melody by the baritone or tenor. The reed section sometimes went very low with the saxes being forced to play in a sub-tone and very soft.

"What made for further variations in sound was the personal element; a man might have a personal sound in playing—let's say, his bottom part—that differed from the sound someone else might get."

Evans is concerned with making clear that "Claude deserves credit for the sound. My influence, such as it has been, was really through him. His orchestra served as my instrument to work with. That's where my influence and his join, so to speak."

"In essence," Evans clarifies, "at first, the sound of the band was almost a reduction to an inactivity of music, to a stillness. Everything—melody, harmony, rhythm—was moving at a minimum speed. The melody was very slow, static; the rhythm was nothing much faster than quarter notes and a minimum of syncopation. Everything was lowered to create a sound, and nothing was to be used to distract from that sound. The sound hung like a cloud.

"But once this stationary effect, this sound, was created, it was ready to have other things added to it. The sound itself can only hold interest for a certain length of time. Then you have to make certain changes within that sound; you have to make personal use of harmonies rather than work with the traditional ones; there has to be more movement in the melody; more dynamics; more syncopation; speeding up of the rhythms.

"For me, I had to make those changes, those additions, to sustain *my* interest in the band, and I started to as soon as I joined. I began to add from my background in jazz, and that's where the jazz influence began to be intensified."

The next addition Thornhill made in modern band instrumentation was the tuba.

"In the old days," Gil explains, "the tuba had been used mainly as a rhythm instrument. The new concept with Thornhill started when Bill Barber joined the band, around the middle of 1947 or in 1948. Claude deserves credit, too, for the character of the sound with tuba added.

"But as I said, things had to be added to the sound. Claude gave me a fairly free hand, and our association was a good one until he began to feel there were elements being left out of his music that he wanted in there and that elements were being added that he didn't want in there.

"I had been with him from 1941 to 42. Then came the war, and when he reorganized, I was with him again from 1946 to 48. My final leaving was friendly. The sound had become a little too somber for my taste, generally speaking, a little too bleak in character. It began to have a hypnotic effect at times. The band could put you to sleep.

"An example of the variation in our thinking was the tuba. He liked the static sound of the tuba on chords. I wanted the tuba to play flexible, moving jazz passages. He liked a stationary effect so much in fact, that if he could have had his way, I think he would have had the band hold a chord for one hundred bars with him compensating ably for the static effect with the activity of his piano. You see, the static sound of the orchestra put the demand for activity on him."

Gil returned to the jazz aspects of his work with Thornhill, saying, "I wrote arrangements of three of Bird's

218

originals, *Anthropology, Yardbird Suite,* and *Donna Lee.*
And I also got to know Charlie well. We were personal
friends, and were roommates for a year or so. Months
after we had become friends and roommates, he had
never heard my music, and it was a long time before he
did."

(Gerry Mulligan explains: "What attracted Bird to Gil
was Gil's musical *attitude.* How would I describe that attitude? 'Probing' is the most accurate word I can think
of.")

"When Bird did hear my music," Gil continues, "he
liked it very much. Unfortunately, by the time he was
ready to use me, I wasn't ready to write for him. I was
going through another period of learning by then.

"As it turned out, Miles, who was playing with Bird
then, was attracted to me and my music. He did what
Charlie might have done if at that time Charlie had been
ready to use himself as a voice, as part of an over-all
picture, instead of a straight soloist."

Gil's influence worked in other ways as a corollary to
the Davis Capitol sessions and to his writing for Thornhill. "I was always interested in other musicians. I was
hungry for musical companionship, because I hadn't had
much of it before. Like bull sessions in musical theory.
Since I hadn't gone to school, I hadn't had that before.

"I got to know a lot of the writers, and I used to rec-
ommend my musical friends to Claude as arrangers—men
like Gerry Mulligan, Johnny Carisi, Gene Roland and Tom
Merriman."

It was during this 1946-48 period, incidentally, that
among Thornhill's sidemen were Lee Konitz, Red Rodney,
Rusty Dedrick, Roland, Louis Mucci, and Jake Koven,
whom Evans describes as "a very good trumpet player in
the Louis Armstrong tradition with his own voice—there
aren't many of those left."

Evans was asked what he thought his influence had
been on the development of Mulligan.

"I don't really know," Gil replied. "We got together
often; we were musically attracted to each other. Gerry,
John Brooks, John Carisi, and George Russell, and I.
The way we influenced each other was not of much importance. I feel we kept our own individuality through
having each other as musical colleagues, rather than by
having a common platform or working alone.

"As for the influence of Claude's band, its sound and writers, I would say that the sound was made ready to be used by other forces in music. I did not create the sound; Claude did. I did more or less match up with the sound the different movements by people like Lester, Charlie, and Dizzy in which I was interested. It was their rhythmic and harmonic revolutions that had influenced me. I liked both aspects and put them together. Of course, I'm not the only one who has done that. Those elements were around, looking for each other.

"Jazz musicians had arrived at a time when they needed a sound vehicle for ensembles, for working with larger bands, in addition to the unison playing between solo work to which they were accustomed.

"The point was," Evans goes on, "that an interdependence of modern thought and its expression was needed. If you express new thoughts and ideas in old ways, you take the vigor and excitement out of the new thoughts.

"For example, Miles couldn't play like Louis because the sound would interfere with his thoughts. Miles had to start almost with no sound and then develop one as he went along, a sound suitable for the ideas he wanted to express. He couldn't afford to trust those thoughts to an old means of expression. If you remember, his sound now is much more highly developed than it was at first.

"The idea of Miles' little band for the Capitol session came, I think, from Claude's band in the sound sense. Miles had liked some of what Gerry and I had written for Claude. The instrumentation for the Miles session was caused by the fact that this was the smallest number of instruments that could get the sound and still express all the harmonies the Thornhill band used. Miles wanted to play his idiom with that kind of sound.

"Miles, by the way, was the complete leader for those Capitol sides. He organized the band, sold it for the record contract, and for the Royal Roost where we played.

"I remember," Gil says grinning, "that original Miles band during the two weeks we played at the Royal Roost. There was a sign outside—'Arrangements by Gerry Mulligan, Gil Evans, and John Lewis.' Miles had it put in front; no one before had ever done that, given credit that way to arrangers.

"Those records by Miles indicate," Gil says, "what voicing can do, how it can give intensity and relaxation.

Consider the six horns Miles had in a nine-piece band. When they played together, they could be a single voice playing a single line. One-part writing, in a way. But that sound could be altered and modified in many ways by the various juxtapositions of instruments. If the trombone played a high second part to the trumpet, for instance, there would be more intensity because he'd find it harder to play the notes. But you have to work these things out. I never know until I can hear it.

"After those records, what we had done seemed to appeal to other arrangers. There was, for one thing, a lot of tuba-type bands. I'm glad for Barber's sake, but I think it was overdone. It was done sometimes without any definite meaning except to be 'traditional.' It got to be traditional awfully fast to do a date with French horn and tuba."

II

After Thornhill, Evans continued his own way, the way that made it impossible for him to be part of a movement for any length of time, or for that matter, to be full-time in jazz. He had to follow his curiosity into other phases of music.

"My interest in jazz, pop, and sound in various combinations has dictated what I would do at various times," he explains. "At different times, one of the three has been the stronger.

"Since 1948, I've been having a lot of additional experiences in music—act music, vaudeville, night clubs. I learned to cross voices so that an arrangement that was good in Erie, Pennsylvania, for five voices could be used for twenty musicians on TV. I learned about the pacing of singers' songs. My pacing up until then had been orchestral, not vocal.

"I also did some radio work and some TV orchestrating. As for jazz dates, one reason I didn't do much was that nobody asked me. About seven or eight years ago, I did some writing for Billy Butterfield on London. And then Helen Merrill called me recently and asked me to write her EmArcy album (EmArcy 12-inch LP MG 36078). I was glad she did.

"I also did some writing for Lucy Reed on Fantasy and Marcy Lutes on Decca, and I did one arrangement for the Teddy Charles tentet album on Atlantic. I have a couple coming out on a Hal McKusick Victor album.

"I've also been trying to fill in gaps in my musical development in the past year. I've been reading music history, biographies of composers, articles on criticism, and listening to records from the library. And I'm working as much as I can.

"There are other reasons for my not having done too much jazz writing in the last few years. As I said, I have a kind of direction of my own that seems to cross three things—pop, jazz, and sound. Now I feel ready to do more jazz.

"An additional reason is that I won't write underscale. There's a lot of underscale writing in the business, package deals whereby an arranger does a certain amount of scores for so much money. A lot of a&r men work that way, and there are enough good craftsmen and some creative writers who go along. I'm enough of a union member to refuse. It makes me too mad.

"I feel a lot of victories were won in the union movement by men who had to sacrifice a lot, and it's a shame to have it thrown down the drain by the next generation.

"A friend of mine, a young writer just getting started, was told by an a&r man at a relatively new major label that if he insisted on charging scale, he'd never be used there again.

"You have to decide what kind of a writer you're going to be. You've got to have enough confidence in your own ability to stick up for scale."

Gil was asked about a reputation he has among part of the trade of being a slow writer, and he said:

"I have more craft and speed than I sometimes want to admit. I want to avoid getting into a rut. I can't keep doing the same thing over and over. I'm not a craftsman in the same sense as a lot of writers I hear who do commercial and jazz work too. They have a wonderful ability with the details of their craft. The details are all authentic, but when it's over, you realize that the whole is less than the sum of the parts."

Another facet of the way Evans works is that he has to rehearse his arrangements personally. "They're very personal, and they're not so highly stylized that it's easy to catch on to what I have in mind right away. My arrangements don't sound right unless they're played by a certain group of players, and unless I've rehearsed them."

("Gil," says Mulligan, "is the one arranger I've ever played who can really notate a thing the way the soloist would blow it. He can notate things the way they really sound. For example, the down beats don't always fall on the down beats in a solo, and he makes note of that. It makes for a complicated notation, but because what he writes is melodic and makes sense, it's not hard to play. The notation makes the parts look harder than they are, but Gil can work with a band, can sing to them what he wants, and he gets it out of them.")

"Up to now," Evans summarizes his present attitude, "there were some sections on records I'd done that I liked, but I didn't like any as entities. I'm still developing my own personal sense of form, which comes out of all this background I've told you about. Until recently I hadn't done much composing of originals because the path I follow hadn't led toward it.

"Now my interests and need for further self-expression are developed to a point where I am concerned with original composition. I've been more of a sentence composer up to now. I was interested in the language. I did good bits of work. Maybe sixteen bars in a pop song. I'd take my own chorus, so to speak. And I would always stay pretty close to the melodic line.

"Economics has also convinced me not to give all my attention to arranging any more. I used to do my composition inside standards, other people's songs. But that's been a dead end for me. Once I'm paid for the arrangement, I'm done. With originals, it's different.

"I've never really been too concerned with the importance of what I was doing. I was more interested in learning and the practical way. I didn't look back until recently when I started to be mentioned in books and articles.

"This being mentioned is a disadvantage as well as an advantage. It kind of establishes one as an elder statesman before one feels like one. I don't enjoy being called a granddaddy when I'm still active, still learning, still writing, and will always be writing.

"Being an elder statesman may be all right for someone who doesn't want to establish new landmarks. But it's not my groove."

223

Until recently, Gunther Schuller was perhaps best known as first horn of the Metropolitan Opera Orchestra. However, since his participation in some of the now historic Capitol Birth Of The Cool *Miles Davis sides, he has become more widely known for his compositions, which bridge the gap between jazz and what is known as "serious" or classical music. This piece perhaps best embodies the application of research and scholarship in an area of tremendous importance in modern music.*

(From Musical America, *Feb. 1959, reprinted by permission.)*

IS JAZZ COMING OF AGE?

by Gunther Schuller

IN 1954 a significant event took place in the little German town of Donaueschingen in the Black Forest. For the first time, jazz was considered substantial enough to be included in a festival devoted exclusively to contemporary music. Two and a half years later an American university subsidized a festival concert with commissioned works by both jazz and classical composers, played side by side by jazz and classical* musicians—works ranging from all-out freewheeling improvisation to tightly organized pieces using serial techniques. And early last year a quintet of jazz musicians performed as soloists with the New York Philharmonic in regular subscription concerts in Carnegie Hall.

All three events—and one could name others—are symbolic of an ever-widening process of cross-fertilization on a compositional as well as a performer level between the worlds of classical music and jazz. The growing interest in this interrelationship, and the increasing number of students graduating from music schools and universities who are not only aware of both kinds of music but are able to perform them authentically, are a clear indication that we are no longer dealing with iso-

---

* The term "classical" is used throughout in its broadest sense, for our purposes equivalent to "non-jazz."

lated phenomena but are in the midst of a fairly broad and well-founded trend.

Of course, this trend is not entirely new. As a matter of fact, its history goes back some forty-odd years and divides itself into two rather distinct phases, in the second of which we find ourselves at the present time. These two phases differ in certain fundamental respects. In the first period, falling roughly in the 1920's, interaction of the two idioms remained strictly one-directional (i.e., classical music borrowed from jazz) and, at that, largely superficial. In the present phase, on the other hand, interest and influence work in both directions. Moreover, since musicians on both sides are finally coming to grips with the knotty problem of improvisation—an element the earlier generation seemed to be mostly unaware of— the present phase is characterized by a much more realistic, more authentic approach than ever before. This raises the possibility (and hope) that a new and vital kind of music may result from this partnership, a music that may actually turn out to be specifically American. By that I do *not* mean American in the sense of a special, regional "Americana" style, but American in a more general universal way—in the sense with which one speaks of the universality of jazz itself, for instance; that is, a music that is unquestionably American, but whose appeal transcends all nationalities and races, as attested to by recent Asiatic and Oriental tours of American jazz ensembles.

Before evaluating the present state of this fusion and interrelationship between jazz and classical music, it might be appropriate to cast a quick glance at the history of its development and the achievements (if any) of the above-mentioned earlier generation. This generation consisted of some of the most famous young composers of the time. First to be attracted to jazz was Stravinsky, and in due time others followed, among them Satie, Auric, and Milhaud, in France; Casella, in Italy; Hindemith and, later, Krenek, in Germany; John Alden Carpenter and Copland, in our country; and finally in the late twenties, Ravel and innumerable others. With the advantage of a thirty- to forty-year perspective, we know today that almost none of the jazz-influenced works of that period were masterpieces or works of real, lasting value. Indeed, many of them were far from it. The relationship all

225

these composers had to jazz was of a superficial and in some cases even patronizing nature, and the result of this preoccupation with jazz as an *exotic style* led to a situation analogous to the famous "Alla Turca" movement of the end of the eighteenth and beginning of the nineteenth century, when public and composers alike—even Beethoven and Mozart—were caught up in a craze of fascination for Turkish marches.

This first wave of fascination with the jazz idiom did, however, produce one first-rate work, Milhaud's *La Creation du Monde* (1923). It had been preceded by a number of varyingly successful experiments, including: (1917) Stravinsky's *Ragtime for 11 Instruments* (which for some reason included a Hungarian fold instrument, the cimbalom); (1918) the *Ragtime* from Stravinsky's *Histoire du Soldat;* (1919) Satie's *Ragtime* from the ballet *Parade;* Stravinsky's *Piano Rag Music;* Auric's *Adieu, New York;* (1920) Milhaud's shimmy, *Caramel Mou,* and a movement from Casella's String Quartet; (1921) Hindemith's *Kammermusik* (last movement), and (1922) his *Ragtime and Shimmy* from a piano suite; and (1923) William Walton's *Cakewalk* from the *Façade Suite.*

Of these nine works, as the titles already indicate, almost all were directly influenced by ragtime or derivations thereof. Jazz in its full-fledged form did not reach Europe until 1919 and the earliest 1920's (and even then in moderate amounts), whereas ragtime, which was only one of the many tributary sources of jazz as it became crystallized during World War I, had traveled across the Atlantic around 1907-08. Ragtime was a well-established musical style (even in Europe) by the time Stravinsky wrote his first ragtime piece in 1917. It must be remembered that the word jazz itself did not come into general use to designate the new music from America until that same year (1917), when the first "jazz" recordings were made by the Original Dixieland Jazz Band. It was this group also that, in 1919-20 toured Europe, and only then did jazz reach Europe in its fully-developed form (a music compounded not only of ragtime but also of the brass-band tradition of the Midwest and the field hollers and country blues of the entire South).

As a matter of fact, we have it on Stravinsky's own testimony that he wrote his 1917 ragtime *after* (to quote him from his *Chroniques de ma vie*) at his request he

226

"had been sent a whole pile of this music." So far as I can establish, of these composers the only one who heard authentic jazz, and more important, the only one who heard Negro jazz, was Milhaud, on his trip to America in 1922. This is significant, I think, because it accounts to some extent for the fact that Milhaud's *Creation* is the only enduring work of all those that concerned themselves with jazz.

Lately it has become fashionable on the part of critics and musicians (jazz and classical alike) to deprecate the above compositions, including the *Creation,* citing them as hopelessly inferior works within the mainstream of contemporary music, and accusing them in some cases of not being real jazz—something, it should hardly be necessary to point out, these composers never set out to do in the first place. (One does not expect a *menuetto* movement in a Mozart symphony to be an authentic, danceable minuet.) At any rate, Milhaud, by virtue of the fact that he *was* more acquainted with authentic jazz, in his *Creation* came much closer to capturing the sound, atmosphere and specific techniques of jazz as played in the early twenties.

With the benefit of some thirty years of hindsight, it is, of course, easy to see the shortcomings of these jazz-influenced works. But it should be remembered that for the European composers (and, as the record shows, also for the Americans) there were obstacles to an appreciation of the essence of pure jazz. To the average European, jazz was represented by the big (mostly white) orchestras of Paul Whiteman, Art Hickman and Billy Arnold. It is true that Milhaud at first also succumbed to the slickness and mechanical precision of these bands. But it is significant to note that, though his fascination with jazz prompted him to write a big "jazz piece" as early as 1919, he did not actually do so until he had heard Negro jazz with its basically different and—to him —more profound feeling. He was so impressed by this music (which he describes at some length in his book of essays, *Etudes*), that he resolved upon his return to France to "use jazz in a chamber-music work."

Although the influence of groups like the Original Dixieland Jazz Band is still discernible in Milhaud's *Creation,* it reflects their music at its best, tastefully avoiding the corny barnyard effects which most people took for jazz in the earliest twenties, and beyond that achieves (if only fleetingly) the kind of abandon and spontaneity the best early jazz had already developed. He achieved this by rather direct and simple means. The musical material of *Creation* divides itself into roughly two categories: a stylized emulation of blues (or bluesish elements) and the contrapuntal, simultaneous improvisations of the smaller Negro combos.

Harmonically and melodically the language is that of his then blossoming polytonality mixed with elements of the blues scale. He also used such jazz devices as the "break" (usually a two- or four-bar solo bridging one chorus to another), and was not above borrowing some of the then current jazz clichés. But above all he recognized that the element of simultaneous improvisation by three to six instruments led to an (at times) highly complex contrapuntal structure, where only the fact that, at any given point, each musician was playing on the same chord insured any organization at all. It resulted in a sort of organized chaos. Milhaud was fascinated by this and wanted to incorporate it in his piece.

To him, the most effective and direct way was to write (in the second movement) a fugue. This would guarantee the linear development he had heard in Harlem jazz and the simultaneous superimposition of five or six contrapuntal lines would give him the desired complexity, while, at the same time, cleverly basing the whole section on one of the most respected classical forms. In the final movement he goes one step further by combining elements of this same fugue with a section featuring the clarinet and (later) saxophone in solo breaks, first separately, then simultaneously superimposing both sections.

If I have stressed the relative value of Milhaud's *Creation,* it is to indicate some of the problems and possible solutions already encountered in this fusing process, and to set a perspective (and perhaps a level) against which more recent developments can be appraised more realistically.

By the mid-twenties, the borrowing of jazz devices had grown into a widespread movement without, however, adding basically to what Milhaud had already achieved. Nevertheless, mention should be made of John Alden Carpenter's *Skyscrapers* (1924); Ravel's foxtrot in *L'Enfant et les Sortilèges* (1925); Krenek's sensational but hopelessly dated jazz opera, *Jonny spielt auf* (1926); Aaron Copland's *Music for the Theatre* (1925) and, a year later, his touching *Piano Blues,* which, with its juxtaposition of typical stride piano and a short bluesish refrain, is an interesting epigrammatic distillation of jazz materials of the time; Ravel's *Violin Sonata* (1927); and in the same year Milhaud's *Piano Rags,* weak pieces in which he simply used some left-over material from *Creation* and in general borrowed from his earlier opus; and Kurt Weill's 1928 social commentary, *Die Dreigroschenoper,* which made use of jazz elements in a consciously limited and stylized manner.

So far, little has been said about improvisations, the element that seems most distinctly to separate jazz from contemporary classical performance; also the element that many believe is an absolute prerequisite for a true fusion of jazz and classical music. But the composers so far discussed were primarily working from a model (ragtime) which was essentially nonimprovised. Furthermore, they were writing for classically trained musicians, and the art of improvisation, once the backbone of all musicmaking, had died out in the early part of the nineteenth century. This had turned the instrumentalist into a *re*-creative rather than a creative musician. Except among a handful of organists, it was not until jazz arrived that improvisation once again became a part of the musician's *métier.* But since jazz musicians were, at best, very limited in their ability to read music, the gap between them and classical musicians who could read but not improvise could not be bridged; and thus improvisation never figured in the works of the twenties and thirties that were concerned with the amalgamation of classical music.

Today, thirty years later, we are much closer to the solution of this knotty problem. Although *the* jazz symphony (as envisioned, for example, by Bix Beiderbecke) still has to be composed, works written by musicians on both sides of the fence have come a lot closer to eliminating the gap left by the missing link of improvisation. The determining ingredient, however, as I have already indicated, was supplied not so much by the composers as the players. The jazz musician has learned to read, and the classical musician is becoming increasingly interested in improvisation.

The slow and arduous process of cross-fertilization

229

that brought us to the second phase has not been shaped by theoretical or intellectual considerations. It developed largely intuitively out of the practical needs of the idioms involved, which is as it should be. A cursory glance at some of the prominent landmarks along this road shows that after the twenties classical composers lost interest in jazz, and until quite recently any innovations in this area occurred almost entirely on the jazz side.

Duke Ellington, for example, among many other achievements, created an imposing array of jazz *compositions,* pieces that were more than mere arrangements, yet always took into account improvisation. He was also an innovator in form in the jazz field, experimenting with larger forms—*Creole Rhapsody* (1931), *Reminiscin' in Tempo* (1935), *Black, Brown and Beige* (1944), etc.— and in a number of recordings achieving a remarkable formal clarity and perfection, as in *Ko-Ko,* for example, recorded in 1940. Although Ellington may not have thought of it in this specific way, *Ko-Ko,* with its seven chaconne-like variations on a minor blues progression, in a very simple direct way shows an instinctive concern for compositional unity that had until then been virtually unknown in jazz except for some of the work of Jelly Roll Morton.

Ellington's successor in this area has been John Lewis, whose leadership of the Modern Jazz Quartet and whose composing founded on the most thorough knowledge of both jazz and classical music have brought a refreshing clarity, directness and artistic simplicity to modern jazz.

Ellington was also an innovator in the realm of harmony and melody. To some extent influenced by impressionist composers, but relying in the main on his own highly original approach to harmony and voice leading, he had developed a highly personal, at times bitonal language by 1940. Subsequently, other composers, players and arrangers ventured further into the outer extensions of tonality (Lennie Tristano's work of the mid- and late forties gave a momentary glimpse of possibilities in this direction), culminating today in the work of pianists like Cecil Taylor and Bill Evans, composers like George Russell and Charles Mingus, who have in distinctly separate ways arrived at individual styles that point to the same common future.

Others experimented with introducing instruments and

230

sounds new to jazz, just as earlier classical composers had borrowed jazz sounds and instruments (various mutes for brass instruments, etc.). To date, one of the most successful exercises in this direction was carried out by the now famous though short-lived Miles Davis Nonet of 1949-50. Arranger Gil Evans gave a new dimension to jazz instrumentation and color when he introduced the French horn and tuba into the small combo.

On a performer level a giant step forward in closing the aforementioned gap was made when the "King of Swing," Benny Goodman, took to playing classical music with such illustrious institutions as the New York Philharmonic and with musicians like Joseph Szigeti. While Goodman left something to be desired as a classical clarinettist, he did immeasurable good by indicating to a wide public that it *was* possible to perform authoritatively in both fields. He did a lot to eliminate prejudices of various kinds on both sides. More recently, audience reaction and behavior have undergone further modification, notably through the dedicated efforts and well-bred deportment of groups like the Modern Jazz Quartet, which have won a new respect for jazz players as individuals.

Other experiments have recently been undertaken in respect to rhythm. Musicians like Sonny Rollins, Randy Weston and Dave Brubeck have attempted jazz in meters other than 4/4, and Jimmy Giuffre has been trying (as yet not conclusively) to replace the *explicit* rhythm of bass and drums by an *implied* beat. Still others have felt the need for more thematic continuity in jazz, notably Thelonious Monk and Sonny Rollins in improvisation, and John Lewis and Andre Hodeir (in France) with the aid of compositional means.

Experiments such as these—and I could cite still others—have, while retaining the element of improvisation, widened the scope of jazz considerably. Indeed, the borderline between jazz and classical music recently has been at times barely discernible. This is not necessarily a virtue but perhaps a necessary transitional symptom.

On the classical side, as I already noted, young players are becoming increasingly interested in improvisation, and composers have begun to incorporate improvisational or quasi-improvisational procedures in their works. This most recent development is, however, only in its infancy, and some time must pass before the efforts of composers such as Stockhausen (in Germany), Boulez (in France), John Cage and this writer in America can be fully assimilated. As limited as these attempts may be, they are bringing the player into a more positive (or at least more than passive) relationship with the music he is performing. By his intuitive reactions and his thinking, he can thus contribute personally to the actual ultimate creation of a work.

In closing, one general point must be emphasized. The music and musicians I have discussed constitute just one specific area in the development of twentieth-century music. On either side of it there are two healthy mainstreams, one in jazz and one in classical music, unconcerned with any process of fusion. Two small offshoots of these mainstreams have been veering toward each other for some forty years, and have, in recent years, become tangent.

Whether this confluence of two idioms can broaden into a self-sufficient third stream remains to be seen. Some predict that jazz like other fold-derived idioms (the troubadour music of the early Middle Ages, for example, or all manner of folk dances of later centuries) will one day be absorbed by the mainstream of classical music. Others maintain that jazz has shown too much individual strength and character, as well as a sophistication all its own, to be so readily absorbed.

To the purists (in both the classical and jazz fields) such talk is heresy, of course. And this despite the fact that the history of music has seen century after century of a similar broadening and absorbing process, much like a great river fed by countless lesser tributaries. But whatever the future may ultimately bring, at mid-century the reciprocal impact of classical music and jazz upon each other has already made an irreversible impression on twentieth-century music.

Today composer George Russell is beginning to gain long-merited recognition. He is our choice for prognosticator of the jazz of the future because his music already embodies daring concepts of harmony, rhythm and tonality. George's philosophy of tomorrow's jazz is perhaps more brilliantly expressed in his jazz compositions, for he is a writer of music, not words. However, he agreed to participate in a taped discussion of jazz present and future. The authorized transcript presented here contains the essence of his point of view.

WHERE DO WE GO FROM HERE?

George Russell

IN CONTEMPORARY jazz, I think up to now it has been a sort of reciprocal thing between the contributions of the composer and the improvisor. Certainly the most significant contributions have come from organizations which had very good improvisers. Ellington had good improvisers, and so did Basie. I would leave Lunceford out because he had some very good men, no doubt about it, but not of the caliber of either Basie or Ellington. I don't mean that they weren't of good solo caliber, but the band wasn't really going that way, and the music—the composer framework—wasn't as lasting or as durable as the Basie framework or the Ellington framework.

I think up to Bird's time it would be very debatable as to who had made the greater contribution, the composer or the improviser. Preceding Bird's era there were ten years that might be called "the big-band era," a very important period. Big bands needed composer music, so the composer had a great deal to do with the forward motion of music at that time, and the soloists—like Lester (Young)—had a great deal to do; but it was an integrated thing. It would be very hard to separate the contributions up to that point.

Now, when Bird came with the small group—once again the small group was the laboratory and Bird started off with the small group—the contribution of the improviser became much stronger than the composed things;

233

despite the fact that the things Bird composed were gems. This was probably because they were so much like his own solo work.

So, we moved into an era when the improviser became the dominant force. This was largely because there wasn't a compositional technique to really match the improvisation. I think we are beginning to move out of this era.

Most of the people who really made a contribution to music have been both instrumentalists and composers. It's hard to separate their written work from their solos, because the most successful of them wrote like they played. They *translated* their playing ideas, so in a purely physical sense this concept is right—a man has to play an idea and hear it before he is able to write it down.

But I don't think this is necessarily going to be true for all time. A composer might have to *hear* his idea, but he may also write an idea that will sound so *improvised* it might influence improvisers to play something that they have never played before.

Everyone wants to preserve the intuitive nature of jazz, even the composer. He wants his written lines to sound as intuitive as possible, no matter how much organization there is behind them. I think the point is that music should always sound intuitive, as though it is being improvised. It might even sound more intuitive than a purely improvised solo. It might sound more fresh and alive therefore, and might influence more people than any improviser on the scene.

I think Monk's current popularity is an indication that the composer is a good deal more influential today. I should say because of Monk's popularity and acceptance *by* the improviser. You see, the composer has to prove himself to the improviser. That's sort of the test of the jazz composer. When the improviser puts his stamp of approval on a jazz composer, then a jazz composer is *made*. And the improviser today is certainly, for the first time in many years, really putting his stamp of approval on Monk.

The improviser is playing Monk's lines. Monk is influencing the improviser. And I can add that Benny Golson is another case of a composer influencing the thinking —in this case the *harmonic* thinking and the over-all thinking—of the improviser. Benny's a wonderful song

234

writer, and has written some very good songs. Songs are frames for improvisation; he has set up some very good frames for improvising, much as Mulligan has done. Now, Monk is also setting up good frames, but I think—and I hope—that there will be composers coming along who will not merely create frames for improvisers, but will actually influence all their musical thinking.

How much further Monk and Golson and Mulligan can influence the jazz improviser, I don't know. But I do believe it is possible for a composer to influence an improviser even more. For instance, if a composer writes a line that is so intuitive . . . one containing a feeling of improvisation so strong and so new . . . then I think the jazz improviser will turn to that composer to see what can be learned from that line.

The improviser has always pioneered in the technology. Ellington is another thing entirely, because he has always been far ahead of any improviser in his band. There is nobody in the band that has ever reached out as Duke's music reaches out. Now, in the Basie band, you have just the opposite thing. You have Pres reaching out, while the arrangements are just frames. You have Lester spearheading and pioneering.

I think the whole core of the problem is just simply this: there have been too many writers without enough melodic equipment to influence the improviser. After all, the improviser deals with melody. This is why the writer hasn't influenced the improviser. There have been hardly any writers with enough melodic equipment to be able to take hold of the improviser and have the improviser investigate the writer for what he is doing; so that the improviser can emerge with that new thing that the writer has.

This hasn't happened yet. It hasn't even happened with Duke.

In my album [*New York, N.Y.*—Decca] for instance, what I have tried to do is to force the soloist into polymodality. I gave him symbols, which, when superimposed upon the music that's happening under it, create a pan-tonal sort of effect. So I speak to the soloist in terms of his familiar symbols, but, as I like to say—you have to fool the soloist into playing *out*.

The chief problem today is rehearsing; there is the problem of musicians, too. The writer in New York today has to really depend on the nucleus of good musicians around who are, unfortunately, making a living. I should say *fortunately,* from an economic standpoint, and unfortunately from an artistic one. They're making a living playing jingles, doing studio work, and doing mostly commercial work. The writer, due to union regulations, finds it impossible to rehearse because you have to, I believe, pay them the same amount to rehearse that you do for a date, so it's practically impossible to rehearse. And, of course, the larger the band, the bigger this problem becomes. So you have to go into a studio and cut the music cold turkey (and that really is the biggest problem), with men who are probably fresh out of a Coca-Cola jingle session.

So that's the one and only pressure that I feel is on a jazz composer, except, also, that I think we're underpaid. I guess the record companies don't make enough money on the jazz albums or something. That's definitely a problem. I wouldn't want to be a young jazz composer coming to New York trying to make it, because it would be very difficult.

What outlets does a jazz composer have? There are no other outlets unless he is a working member of a jazz group; then, of course, he can write for that particular group. But a jazz composer who has to stay in New York and make it just from composing jazz has a tough economic and a tough aesthetic problem, because there are no outlets. There are no workshops, and the only good thing about the economic problem is that it forces the jazz composer to write for a small group. This is a very good thing because, as we've pointed out, the best jazz—big-band jazz—is really an enlargement of some experiment that has been worked out with a small group.

I really didn't know, until I met this kid from North Texas State who studied with me recently, but there are some very good musicians throughout the country. And he expressed the opinion that there would be fewer and fewer major musicians actually *living* in New York—and not only New York, but big cities in general. Big-city jazz is on the wane, and he thinks that jazz will be propagated through various spots throughout the country —for instance, Denton, Texas, where they have this very jazz-conscious college, North Texas State. That's where they have this wonderful band with a brass section that . . . well, it sounds like Ernie Royal and the pros.

But jazz in college is definitely . . . well, I was going to say that it's chic to have jazz in colleges, but no matter what the motive is, the fact is that jazz is being promoted in colleges. The University of Michigan is starting a jazz course. Northwestern is starting a jazz course. All over the country, jazz is really beginning to infiltrate the colleges. This, of course, means that there will be a jazz technology, of which there is precious little now.

I heard about something else that musicians are doing now to prove this, too. Big-city musicians are lending themselves out to small-town groups. I know of a musician who just last week went to Minneapolis to work with a local rhythm section for a week. Al Cohn is going to some town just for a week to play with a local group there. This opens up an entirely new thing, because you can't play jazz in New York. There is no opportunity to play jazz other than in a studio, and I think that that is really forcing the music out into the other communities of this country.

There's a program . . . one of the foundations plans to have jazz musicians in *residence* at various colleges and in various cities. In other words, *name musicians* would be paid a sum to live in a city and start jazz activities.

TOMORROW:

As for the music . . . the jazz music of the future . . . the techniques are going to get more complex, and it will be a challenge for the composer to master the techniques and yet preserve his intuitive approach. And it will be a challenge for the improviser to master these techniques and also preserve the intuitive, earthy dignity of jazz.

Specifically, it's going to be a pan-rhythmic, pan-tonal age. I think jazz will by-pass atonality because jazz actually has its roots in folk music, and folk music is scale-based music; and atonality negates the scale. I think jazz will be intensely chromatic; but you can be chromatic and not be atonal.

If you're atonal, you're not tonal. You're negating scales, and jazz is a scale-based music. So I think that atonality is technically just a means of expressing the
237

chromatic scale without repeating any of the tones. It's an intellectual concept, in other words. It is terribly restricting in the sense that you must repeat, constantly, the tones of the chromatic scale, if you are a strict atonalist.

Even classical music is beginning to turn from that direction, because atonality is the extreme of tonality. It's the outer limb. It's as far as you can actually go in terms of extreme chromaticism.

But there is another realm between this and the very tonal music such as Mozart and the classicists wrote. This is called "pan-tonality," where the basic folk nature of the scales is preserved, and yet, because you can use any number of scales or you can be in any number of tonalities at once, and/or sequentially, it also creates a very chromatic kind of feeling, so that it's sort of like being atonal with a Big Bill Broonzy sound. *You can retain the funk.*

As for jazz and classical music coming together, it depends on how you define classical. If you define it as meaning music which is art, music that is intellectually developed; music that is treated intellectually and thematically—if that's the way you define classical—then I'd say that jazz will become a classical music and that there will be writers who will write in the jazz idiom, using all the dowry that jazz has to bring to this new music. And there will also be writers who will not use the jazz idiom. But the two musics will certainly be equal. Equally good or equally bad . . . that depends upon the composers.

The techniques are becoming more complex. Pan-rhythm is certainly a more complex notion than the traditional approach to jazz. In pan-tonality, you have a number of tonalities occurring vertically and sequentially; and in pan-rhythm you have a number of meters juxtaposed. Not just a composition in 3/4 or 4/4, but a composition which utilizes many different meters . . . all kinds of rhythmic feelings, with music weaving a pattern over this fabric of various meters. You're dealing with elements so complex it's absolutely necessary that the performer have tremendous technique. And pan-tonality is a concept of melody which is the same. In other words, music weaving in and out and through all sorts of tonalities, both horizontally and vertically. I

238

think, again, just as in the past, the great people who will come out of music are those who have mastered the techniques of music, mastered the mechanics, and preserved their intuitive approach.

There is no limit on human capacity for mastering mechanics, and this process goes on endlessly. No matter how complicated the techniques become, we can always master them and produce good art.

It's a precarious balance, but in that way art, I suppose, reflects life. An artist's very existence is precarious.

You can parallel it to life in this way: it reflects man's striving to overcome nature. And nature, I believe, has placed these musical elements, like rhythm and tonality, at our disposal to make beauty out of them. That's what we've been doing for centuries, trying to make beauty out of these elements—the sound system of nature—and in the meantime, we've built up some sort of musical know-how. We've always digested and produced good music, and we are still in the process of doing that now.

So, it just represents a continuance of man's struggle with nature to accept ever-more complex materials and subdue them, and build art or bridges or atomic bombs. . .

THE OUT-CHORUS

As long as jazz is played, words will be written about it.

You have just read the jazz word. Not the jazz word for all time, but for here and now. The jazz word according to the men who make the music and the men who keep their days and their nights.

"Music! What a splendid art, but what a sad profession!"

—Georges Bizet

"I want to get it over with real quick. I want to die soon. Why? I got no guy. Who the hell will care besides you? You tell me people love me but how the hell can you tell? Sure, they love my singing. But me? *I'm tired. I'm human. I want to be loved."*

—Billie Holiday, as told to William Dufty

Titles of Related Interest —

ENCYCLOPEDIA OF JAZZ
by Leonard Feather

TOWARD JAZZ
by André Hodeir

THE WORLD OF COUNT BASIE
by Stanley Dance

THE WORLD OF DUKE ELLINGTON
by Stanley Dance

THE WORLD OF EARL HINES
by Stanley Dance

THE WORLD OF SWING
by Stanley Dance

JAZZ MASTERS OF NEW ORLEANS
by Martin Williams

BLUES WHO'S WHO
by Sheldon Harris

JAZZ IN THE MOVIES: New Edition
by David Meeker

Available at bookstores or direct from

DA CAPO PRESS
233 Spring Street
New York, NY 10013
Toll-free 800-221-9369